MW00669348

Winning E-Learning Proposals

The Art of Development and Delivery

Karl M. Kapp, Ed.D.

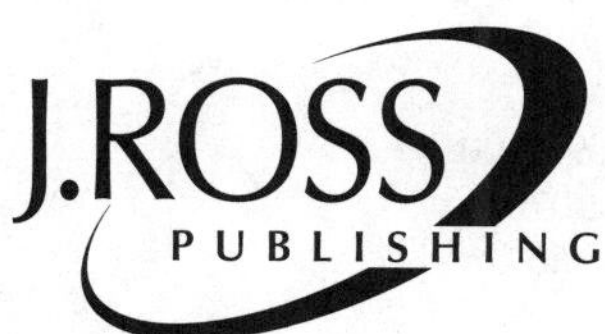

Institute for
Interactive Technologies

ISBN 1-932159-04-5

Printed and bound in the U.S.A. Printed on acid-free paper.
10 9 8 7 6 5 4 3 2 1

Library of Congress Cataloging-in-Publication Data

Kapp, Karl M., 1967-
Winning e-learning proposals : the art of development and delivery / by Karl M. Kapp.
p. cm.
Includes bibliographical references and index.
ISBN 1-932159-04-5
1. Proposal writing in business. 2. Business presentations. 3. Internet in education. 4. Computer-assisted instruction. I. Title: Winning electronic-learning proposals. II. Title.
HF5718.5.K37 2003
658.3'12404--dc21 2003000222

Direct all inquiries to J. Ross Publishing, Inc., 6501 Park of Commerce Blvd., Suite 200, Boca Raton, Florida 33487.

Phone: (561) 869-3900
Fax: (561) 892-0700
Web: www.jrosspub.com

DEDICATION

To all students of the E-learning Business Acquisition Process wherever they are and in whatever role they play.

TABLE OF CONTENTS

FOREWORD

WINGING IT

Even though it was over a decade ago, I remember the scene like it was yesterday. I had managed to secure a meeting with one of the best-known financial services companies in the country through a referral from a friend of a friend. Only a few months earlier I had started my own custom content development company out of a spare bedroom, and to date had nothing tangible to show for it other than one employee and a stack of business cards. For us, this meeting was big. While this particular project was only a two-hour CBT program, we badly needed to land our first client, not only to pay the bills, but also to get other clients.

As my entire workforce and I walked into the posh lobby of our new prospect, I realized we were pretty nervous. Although we felt confident that we could hold our own talking about the multimedia and design aspects of the proposed program, we did not really have an exact plan for winning the business from the client. We were just going to discuss how we would build the training and hoped that they liked what they heard.

These were the early days of our industry. The term "e-learning" would not be coined for several years, and there was no such thing as the World Wide Web. Therefore, the whole process of securing business, pricing, and producing work was a constant exercise in trial and error, and any knowledge of the process of securing business from clients was incredibly secretive and proprietary.

Resigned that we would just have to "wing it," we marched into the office suite and were asked by the receptionist to wait outside the cubicle of the person with whom we were meeting. Within a few seconds we realized, much to our horror, that she was having a meeting with the CEO of one of the best-known content development companies in the industry. We had seen this guy speak at industry meetings and read articles he had written. His company had an impressive client list and dozens of employees. Suddenly, our nervousness doubled.

We realized we had not formalized any strategy for winning the business, while he was clearly articulating a well-developed, well-thought-out strategy. With our meeting only minutes away, and a competitor clearly adhering to a well-developed capture strategy, we needed our own strategy and fast. We nervously glanced at each other wondering how to develop a successful strategy in less than five minutes to counter an industry leader.

However, we were about to get extremely lucky. While cubicles have their overall benefits and drawbacks, at that moment I discovered something about these cloth-walled structures that ultimately proved extremely helpful to us winning this project. Cubicles are not soundproof.

As our competitor loudly and proudly discussed the benefits of selecting his company for this project, the strengths of his organization, and the process it used to secure business, we could not help but overhear his strategy for winning the business.

My partner and I looked at each other, smiled, and quickly hatched our own strategy. We would highlight our strengths, go after our competitor's weaknesses, and focus on producing the project within the client's budgetary constraints. Although we could not be sure that our competitor would propose exactly what he had discussed that day, we were pretty sure that our hasty strategy would at least keep us in the game. We had no other basis upon which to develop a strategy. We just had to think fast and wing it, but at least we now had a semblance of a strategy.

Our "make-do" strategy worked, and a few weeks later we were awarded the business. It was that deal that helped us, over the next few years, to become one of the best-known content development companies in the industry. To this day, that financial services company remains one of our largest clients.

Now, I am not particularly proud of how we won that first deal, nor do I advocate the "winging-it" method of selling e-learning. Today I consider our practices to be the most ethical in the industry, and my sales force typically has a well-developed strategy for capturing the business long before they meet with a prospect. However, in those early days everyone was making it up as they went along. There was no clear process for fairly and objectively presenting your business case to clients. We often refer to that time as the "Wild West" because of the unstructured way that vendors and buyers consummated deals.

A STRATEGY IS NOW AVAILABLE

Clearly the e-learning industry has matured. Buyers have become more and more sophisticated in developing Requests for Information and Requests for Proposals and in their overall vendor selection process. In order to continue to win business, over the years our company and others steadily developed targeted sales practices and proposal skills to keep pace with the industry's evolution. In fact, vendors often differentiate themselves by their sales processes and proposals and consider these to be core, strategic assets.

Today, the process for acquiring business that used to be so incredibly secretive, and which takes new companies years to learn, is clearly laid out in *Winning E-Learning Proposals: The Art of Development and Delivery.* This is the first book in a co-published series between J. Ross Publishing and the Institute for Interactive Technologies at Bloomsburg University. For years the Institute has been instrumental in preparing students for careers in technology-delivered learning, and their graduates can be found in leading companies across the industry helping them to develop effective e-learning and to strategically capture business. For the first time, this wealth of experience has been captured by Karl Kapp in this comprehensive book.

This is the only book that I have come across that fully describes the entire process for securing e-learning business. Coined "E-BAP" for E-learning Business Acquisition Process, Dr. Kapp lays out easy-to-comprehend steps for vendors and buyers alike. Understanding this process will assist vendors in securing business, as well as buyers who want to communicate their needs more effectively.

This book not only contains information on how to develop a proposal, it also contains information on how to estimate a project and how to schedule resources. It can be equally useful to a salesperson trying to win business and a project manager who needs to understand how to estimate a project. This book also serves as a good review for instructional design students of all kinds in order to gain a complete understanding of how the business acquisition process works.

As the title suggests, *Winning E-Learning Proposals* contains a great deal of information on one of the most important aspects of securing e-learning business: the proposal. The tips and techniques in the book are extremely useful to novice proposal writers who want to learn how to develop winning proposals. Seasoned veterans can pick up new ideas and insights from the examples of actual proposals contained in the book. The worksheets throughout the book guide a proposal development team through the entire proposal writing process.

For salespeople, the book contains valuable information on how to position their company's offerings and effectively sell their e-learning solutions. The insights and ideas from multiple professionals in the field — from both the vendor side and the client side — give the book different perspectives on the e-learning business acquisition process. Most importantly, these ideas are helpful in setting a company's solution apart from the myriad competitors in the field.

While it is easy to wax nostalgic about "the good old days," this book erases the rudimentary sales processes of the early e-learning industry and, for the first time, makes available the strategies that leading companies are using to win and develop e-learning business. All in all, the lessons taught in this book will help e-learning professionals develop winning strategies that they can build on and evolve as their business evolves.

Whether you are a buyer or a seller, I wish you the best of luck in your e-learning endeavors. And for the vendors out there, I have one important piece of advice learned early in my career: when meeting with a prospect in a cubicle, speak softly. You never know who might overhear.

Kevin Oakes, CEO
Click2learn, Inc.

PREFACE

WHY READ THIS BOOK

The business of e-learning is competitive, cut-throat, and constantly changing. To stay ahead, you must remain current and focused on winning business through effective proposal writing and dynamite sales presentations. This holds true whether you are selling e-learning to your boss or to a potential client. You need a road map to navigate the difficult process of selling e-learning. This book helps you develop and articulate strategies for winning e-learning business that is "up for grabs" in the competitive $50 billion training industry.

WHAT IS IN THIS BOOK

Winning E-Learning Proposals: The Art of Development and Delivery meets the needs of professionals assigned the task of developing, writing, and presenting e-learning solutions. It is designed to provide step-by-step practical tips and techniques to conceptualize a winning idea, write a winning proposal, and stage a winning presentation.

While many people view the e-learning proposal and presentation process as more art than science, the fact is that winning techniques and formulas can be codified and presented in a logical and repeatable pattern — as much as 90% of the process is mechanical and rote. In this book, these mechanical elements have been turned into a science: a listing of items expected and anticipated in an e-learning proposal.

Mastering the mechanics is important, but it is the last 10% — the art — that separates the winning proposals from the losers. The last 10% is still, and always will be, pure *art*. To win e-learning proposals time and time again, you need to know the techniques of "master proposal artists."

Winning E-Learning Proposals contains over a dozen vignettes from "master proposal artists" who deal with RFPs, proposals, sales presentations, business cases, and the e-learning business acquisition process on a daily basis. These professionals are from both the vendor and the client side of the business. They are founders of e-learning companies, e-learning project managers, vice presidents, operations managers, and instructional technologists. The vendor and client perspectives provide a holistic view of winning e-learning proposals. These e-learning veterans understand how to win. The result is a book that describes a proven process that can net your organization millions of e-learning dollars, just as it has for the professionals who contributed to this work.

HOW TO READ THIS BOOK

An ideal method of reading this book is as a team. Divide your firm into teams and have each member read Chapter 1 and then each team member can read a different chapter. Each week the teams can get together and discuss the salient points. This method strengthens your firm's proposal writing and increases your proposal hit rate. It provides a common dialogue for your team and increases awareness of the issues involved with e-learning.

This book can either be read cover to cover to understand the entire process or used as a reference to pinpoint exactly the piece of advice you need to "seal your next deal." The book is organized around the E-learning Business Acquisition Process (E-BAP). The E-BAP is the method by which e-learning firms secure business. It is a predictable process with each stage carefully explained throughout the book in three distinct but interrelated parts.

Part I describes the preliminary work that must be done before e-learning firms can effectively respond to an RFP. This part contains advice and counsel on obtaining e-learning RFPs, reviewing the RFP to see if it is worth responding to, defining the problem described by the potential client, and conceptualizing a solution. It also contains instruction on good writing, team writing, and the effective use of graphics within a proposal. These foundational elements are the basis for writing an effective proposal.

Part II describes each section of an e-learning proposal and explains how to write the document and what should be contained in each section. It provides checklists and advice on crafting an e-learning proposal so that you win business. Each chapter in this part contains proposal samples based on actual proposals. These samples provide ideas and concepts for the proposal writing team to consider.

Part III focuses on the presentation portion of the E-BAP. Few books in the field of e-learning discuss effective methods for selling your solution to e-learning clients in the context of a sales presentation. This part of the book provides both novice and experienced professionals with tips and techniques for being successful.

WHO SHOULD READ THIS BOOK

This book has been written to satisfy a diversity of audiences interested in the E-BAP and how it relates to winning proposals. Each audience will approach the book from different angles and viewpoints and each will read the book with different goals in mind. The writing style of the book and its organization have been specifically designed to enable different readers to use the book in a manner most appropriate for them.

NOVICE E-LEARNING SALESPEOPLE

This book will guide the novice e-learning salesperson through the entire E-BAP. The concepts, ideas, and techniques in this book will literally take years off of the learning curve for understanding what clients want in proposals, how you should develop a solution, and how to present your solution in a sales situation. Reading Chapter 1 (The E-Learning Business Acquisition Process) will provide you with a good overview of the entire process and then you can proceed chapter by chapter to gain additional knowledge. Understanding the process will help you write your first winning proposal.

EXPERIENCED E-LEARNING SALESPEOPLE

Sometimes winning a proposal comes down to one or two details that are either overlooked or missed in the proposal process. This book reminds experienced salespeople about those details and also provides some insights into new methods of winning business.

As an experienced salesperson, you will want to turn to specific chapters of interest to gain insight or knowledge pertaining to a specific part of the process. For example, Chapter 9 covers the topic of a letter of transmittal. The chapter includes information on eight items that should be in every letter. Unfortunately, most proposal writers leave out one or two elements — potentially costing them the business. This book serves as a reminder to include all eight items and explains why those items should be included. *Winning E-Learning Proposals* is a reference book that provides checklists and worksheets to trigger the veteran to consider new ideas or concepts in his or her e-learning proposals.

ANYONE PREPARING AN E-LEARNING RFP

While it is important to write a good proposal to win e-learning business, good proposals start with good RFPs. Reading this book will help any internal person who is struggling with trying to write a good RFP. Of particular interest to this audience will be Chapter 3. This chapter describes common errors in most RFPs and provides advice from vendors on how to develop an effective RFP that allows you to make a fair and objective decision. Chapter 6 provides solid advice on writing styles and techniques that are as effective for RFPs as they are for proposals.

By reading this book as a potential customer of e-learning vendors, you will also get to look "behind the curtain" at how vendors prepare e-learning proposals and what types of issues they consider when presenting a solution. You will know what to look for in a proposal and how vendors go about pricing their products and services. You will understand the E-BAP better and be able to make more intelligent decisions regarding e-learning.

ANYONE "SELLING" E-LEARNING INTERNALLY

Not only is e-learning sold to clients but, many times, you must sell e-learning internally. This book helps managers, supervisors, and others develop a solid business case to sell e-learning to top executives and others within their organization.

One of the first steps in the process of selling e-learning is to create a business case and describe how e-learning will positively impact the organization. Chapter 15 provides the tools you need to develop an effective business case for the e-learning investment not from a cost-savings perspective but from a performance improvement perspective — a much stronger sell.

Chapter 4 provides ideas and techniques for defining your organization's e-learning needs so you can present them to internal management. Understanding the entire E-BAP will help you to describe the process to management so it understands what internal resources are needed to put e-learning in place. You can also use the information from Chapter 14 to learn about the average price for e-learning products and services.

CHIEF LEARNING OFFICERS

As a chief learning officer, you have numerous organizational responsibilities, and one of those responsibilities is to make intelligent choices regarding e-learning. Chapter 12 describes both instructional design elements and technological elements needed for an effective e-learning solution. The chapter also contains descriptions of requirements you should look for when considering an e-learning solution for your organization. This book will provide a holistic view of e-learning and insight into e-learning considerations from leading professionals working in the field.

PROJECT MANAGERS

If you are an internal or external manager for an e-learning project, this book can help. Chapter 13 describes four methods for estimating the amount of time it will take for you to complete an e-learning project. This can help you scope a project before you begin work. Chapter 8 describes what it takes for a team to learn to work together to produce desired results. The book will help you with the difficult task of using a team to develop an e-learning solution. You will also learn about the budget process as well as how to deal with some technical issues concerning e-learning.

ENTREPRENEURS

If you are just starting an e-learning business or thinking of starting one, this book describes what you need to be successful. You will want to read Chapter 2. This chapter describes how to get RFPs for e-learning and how you can ensure a steady flow of RFPs into your organization. Once you get a steady flow of RFPs, use the rest of the book to begin winning those RFPs.

CONSULTANTS

There is money to be made in helping organizations write e-learning proposals. This book provides the worksheets, tips, and examples needed for you to help a client write an e-learning proposal. If you are selling services as an e-learning strategist, this book helps you develop a strategy and a direction for your clients by providing insight into what clients want and what vendors are able to offer. Of particular interest is Chapter 5, which will help you work with the client to brainstorm ideas related to e-learning.

INSTRUCTIONAL DESIGN STUDENTS

This book is a textbook for instructional design students who want to know how the design process is applied "in the field." If you are a student learning about the business of e-learning or if you are an instructional design student, this book describes, in detail, how the E-BAP works. It is one thing to know about the theory of instructional design; it is another to learn how to *sell* it to a potential client. Students will gain a huge advantage by understanding the business side of the online learning industry. As a student, you will be able to use the knowledge gained in this book to sell yourself to a potential employer because you will know the industry lingo, the trends in the industry, and the direction in which you need to go to be successful.

EMPLOYEES IN E-LEARNING FIRMS

Ideally everyone within an e-learning firm involved with writing a proposal will own a copy of this book…from the sales force to instructional designers to graphic artists to Web designers. *Winning E-Learning Proposals: The Art of Development and Delivery* is a ready reference for answering questions, crafting responses, and helping the organization win business. It also contains information about instructional design, technological considerations, and other critical day-to-day aspects of working within an e-learning firm.

THE BOTTOM LINE

Effective proposal writing is imperative for e-learning success. *Winning E-Learning Proposals: The Art of Development and Delivery* provides you with the knowledge, advice, and insights required to win e-learning proposals.

ACKNOWLEDGMENTS

Many people helped to make this book possible. I would like to thank Karen Swartz and Karen Downs — the two Karens — for helping with proofreading. Karyn Gandenberger for her careful read of early drafts and her assistance with some of the analogies within the book as well as the contribution of a graphic. Carl Seidel for taking time out of his busy proposal writing schedule to read an initial draft of the book and for his helpful comments and for always providing an honest critique. Divjot Punia for his positive comments and contribution of a screen capture and graphic.

Special thanks to Beth Bailey, Peter You, Shannon Mausteller, Bridget Geist, and Nancy Kapp for the use of the Workforce Interactive Proposal. Even though they pulled an all-nighter in my kitchen it still turned out okay.

Thanks also to Richard Kralevich, Jennifer Neumer, James Gilliam Jr., Rosemary L. Storaska, Kristie Schaffer, Pam Berman, Curvin Huber, Carol Lopashanski, Brian Richards, Aimee Piccirilli, Beth Rogowsky, Cyle Nunemaker, David Manney, Michael Coffey, Ramon Ruiz, John Fetterman, Dennis Thomas, Lisa Verge, Rebecca Ohl, Bill Austin, Michael Smith, Summer Harling, and Joseph Wood, for ideas used in the book from their proposal writing work. Thanks also to the SoluTeach team of Becky Blue, Bridgette Collier, Jeanette Farm, Kristy Nickles, Richard Peck, and Stanley Strzempek for their ideas and concepts.

Thank you to Drew Gierman and the entire team at J. Ross Publishing who believed in this book and who helped to make it a reality. Thanks for your help. A special thanks to my editor, Susan Fox.

I would like to thank all of the contributors to this book. Without your insight, experience, and knowledge, this book would not have the value that you instilled within it. Also thanks to all my students from whom I learn a tremendous amount. Of course, a special and sincere thank you to my family, Nathan, Nick, and Nancy, who have had to endure an obsessed author for way too long.

THE AUTHOR

Karl M. Kapp, Ed.D., CFPIM, CIRM, is a scholar, consultant, and expert on the convergence of learning, technology, and business operations. His background teaching e-learning classes, knowledge of adult learning theory, and experience training CEOs and front line staff provide him with a unique perspective on organizational learning.

Karl understands how to promote effective e-learning within an organization. He received his Doctorate of Education in Instructional Design at the University of Pittsburgh in Pittsburgh, PA. The field of Instructional Design focuses on the systematic design, development, delivery, implementation, and evaluation of instruction.

As Assistant Director of Bloomsburg University's Institute for Interactive Technologies (IIT), Karl helps organizations such as Aetna, CIGNA Healthcare, the Pennsylvania Department of Public Welfare, and L'OREAL understand how e-learning technologies impact employee productivity and learning.

As Associate Professor of Instructional Technology at Bloomsburg University, Karl teaches a unique class. Students are formed into "companies," write a business plan, receive an e-learning Request for Proposal (RFP), respond with a proposal, develop a working prototype, and present their solution to representatives from various corporations. Typical corporations represented include Click2Learn, CIGNA Healthcare, Merck, Newton Gravity Shift, EduNeering, Bristol-Myers Squib, Verizon, and others. Karl was instrumental in forming Bloomsburg's online E-Learning Developer's Certificate which provides online education to traditional instructional designers who want to transition to developing online instruction.

Karl is a frequently sought expert in the e-learning field who has been interviewed by magazines such as *Software Strategies, Knowledge Management, Distance Learning,* and *Training*. In addition, he has published dozens of articles in publications such as *Performance Improvement Quarterly, APICS — The Performance Advantage,* and other industry journals. He is also the author of an informative book about using Learning Requirements Planning (LRP) to implement a large-scale technology project, titled *Integrated Learning for ERP Success: A Learning Requirements Planning Approach.*

Karl is committed to helping organizations develop a strategic, enterprisewide approach to organizational learning. He believes that effective education and training are the keys to increased productivity and profitability. Visit Karl at www.karlkapp.com.

THE CONTRIBUTORS

Clayton Ajello, Ph.D. is Founder of Accelera, a Licensee of the Johns Hopkins University — a leading provider of learning and communications solutions to the pharmaceutical, medical device, and biotechnology industries. Dr. Ajello spent 18 years in a variety of public and private institutions situated in more than 30 countries before becoming Vice President for Programming at the Johns Hopkins University. There he was co-responsible for planning and implementing expansion of the world's largest international clinical continuing education program with 1000 employees worldwide and a budget of $100 million. He was also tasked as founding director of the university's largest IT office. There he developed the first *blended* clinical learning programs and introduced these into the Johns Hopkins international clinical training programs, and organized development and testing of the university's first e-learning products. Dr. Ajello spun this group off as a for-profit company with a unique licensing agreement with Johns Hopkins: LearnWare International Corporation, predecessor of Accelera. He is a recognized authority in strengthening large-scale learning systems to nurture performance-oriented workforces. An epidemiologist by training, Dr. Ajello's interest is working to shape or improve learning systems that support the health care industry and health care professionals. Dr. Ajello is a graduate of the State University of New York, Yale University, and the Johns Hopkins Medical Institutions. Accelera is an industry partner in the Society of Pharmaceutical and Biotechnology Trainers.

Harold J. Bailey, Ph.D. is the founder of the Institute for Interactive Technologies (IIT) and implemented the Master of Science program in Instructional Technology (MSIT) in 1985 at Bloomsburg University in Bloomsburg, PA. After serving as Director of the IIT and as Coordinator of the MSIT for 12 years, Dr. Bailey retired from Bloomsburg University in 1997 with Faculty Emeritus status and received the university's prestigious Distinguished Alumni Award. Dr. Bailey founded and is President of Bailey Interactive, Inc., a company that provides technology-based solutions for education and training. He is frequently invited to speak at national and international professional conferences and has published several articles pertaining to instructional technology. Dr. Bailey's combined experience in education and business has allowed him to integrate the theoretical aspects of academia with the real-life applications of the private sector. Dr. Bailey has a Ph.D. in Curriculum and Instruction from Penn State University. He serves on the Bloomsburg University Foundation Board and is a member of the Society for Applied Learning Technology (SALT).

Ronald W. Berman, Ph.D. is Vice President of Education at Interwise, Inc. Interwise is based in Cambridge, MA, and develops and markets software that enables companies to teach live over the Internet. In just seven years, the company's customer base has grown to include Fortune 100 companies and leading academic institutions. Dr. Berman is a senior executive who enjoys adapting new technologies to practical academic and business solutions. He began his career as a programmer at IBM, where he created the company's first electronic mail system (and proved its viability). He then continued his career at SAP just prior to the company introduction of its flagship product, R/3. As Director of Education, Dr. Berman successfully led the creation of a for-profit training division that rapidly became one of America's largest and most profitable training entities. Dr. Berman has a Ph.D. in Education, an M.S. in Computer Engineering, and a B.S. in Business Administration.

Louis Biggie is Managing Director for Technology, Research and Development of Accelera, a Licensee of the Johns Hopkins University. Mr. Biggie has 20 years experience in analysis, design, and implementation of large-scale technology, research, and development efforts designed to realize practical prototype products that meet marketplace needs. Mr. Biggie draws upon a background in linguistics, interactive multimedia development processes and tools, systems level software design, graphical user interfaces, distributed learning systems, instructional systems design, and hypermedia to advance ideas to products. Mr. Biggie's career spans diverse experiences ranging from associations with the Johns Hopkins Applied Physics Laboratory, where he served as designer and lead programmer of instructional software packages and authoring systems, to co-founding LearnWare International Corporation (predecessor of Accelera), where he served as Vice President for Research and Development. He studied linguistics at the University of Lancaster, England and the University of Seville, Spain. He holds a faculty appointment at the Johns Hopkins School of Public Health and retains a long-standing interest in furthering his specialty area expertise, children with learning disabilities. He teaches a course called Multimedia Software Integration at the Johns Hopkins Whiting School of Engineering.

Robert P. Delamontagne, Ph.D. is the Chairman and Founder of EduNeering, Inc. Before founding EduNeering in 1980, Dr. Delamontagne earned a Master's in Educational Leadership and a Ph.D. in Educational Psychology and Organization Development from Georgia State University. He pioneered the field of computer-based training and produced *The CBT Report*, the first publication devoted exclusively to the field. In partnership with the Coca-Cola Corporation, he conducted the first research measuring the effectiveness of computer-based training on the economic performance of a large manufacturing operation. In partnership with Williams Energy, he produced the largest regulatory compliance training library in the energy industry. Under his leadership, EduNeering has become the leading provider of online solutions for compliance education.

Kathleen Ergott is a Team Leader for the E-Learning Development Group at Siemens Health Services. Adept at providing realistic guidelines, organizing teams, and monitoring production, she has managed projects from both a vendor and corporate perspective. Prior to entering the multimedia field over 10 years ago, Ms. Ergott founded and ran her own business, where she had primary responsibility for management, video production, cost projections, budgeting, and marketing. Ms. Ergott currently leads a team that is responsible for the development surrounding Siemens Medical Academy, a Web site offering virtual class registration, online courses, and ordering of offline course materials for Siemens employees and customers. She is responsible for overseeing team projects and for the team rollout of the company's new quality initiative. Ms. Ergott earned an M.S. degree in Instructional Technology from Bloomsburg University.

Chad Hostetler is Vice President of Operations at Get Thinking, Inc. His primary responsibilities include the development of client relationships and strategic business initiatives, project management, and overseeing courseware design and development using a number of online technologies. Under his guidance, Get Thinking has successfully designed, developed, and deployed learning solutions for some of the largest names in the restaurant, financial, and retail industries. Mr. Hostetler has an M.S. degree in Instructional Technology from Bloomsburg University.

Debra L. Newton is President of Newton Gravity Shift, a company formed in October 2002 by the merger of two well-established technology-based communications companies: Newton Interactive, which Ms. Newton founded in 1991, and Gravity Shift Solutions, founded in 1985. Ms. Newton's energy, vision, and passion for strategically linking interactive technologies with creative techniques to achieve business objectives drive Newton Gravity Shift. Newton Gravity Shift offers a suite of proprietary products and leverages its technology partnerships with leading learning and content management companies to provide powerful internal and external platforms for collaboration and information exchange. Clients have said of Ms. Newton, "She gets it. Newton Gravity Shift completely understands technology and the pharmaceutical industry." The company has successfully deployed interactive solutions for a wide variety of healthcare businesses, including AstraZeneca, Bayer, Berlex Laboratories, Bristol-Myers Squibb, CV Therapeutics, Eisai, Ortho-McNeil, Sankyo Pharma, Solvay, and Wyeth. Ms. Newton is a member of the Healthcare Businesswoman's Association (HBA), the Medical Marketing Association, the New Jersey Chamber of Commerce, and the New Jersey Technology Council, and she is an industry partner in the Society of Pharmaceutical & Biotechnology Trainers (SPBT). Ms. Newton graduated in 1988 with a B.A. in Business Administration from St. Mary's College in Moraga, CA.

Richard Peck is an instructional designer at the Institute for Interactive Technologies. He is responsible for Flash development at the IIT as well as for the development of online, interactive exercises. In addition, Mr. Peck teaches a number of authoring courses as an adjunct faculty member at Bloomsburg University. He has worked on projects for organizations such as L'OREAL and the Pennsylvania Department of Public Welfare. Mr. Peck has an M.S. degree in Instructional Technology from Bloomsburg University.

Francis J. Peters, III (Chip) is currently employed as a Senior Education Consultant with Aetna, Inc.'s Information Services function, where his responsibilities include consulting, project management, and the design, development, and implementation of enterprisewide corporate training and performance improvement initiatives. From the mid-1980s through the early 1990s, Mr. Peters held various host, segment reporting, and production positions at several commercial and public service radio stations in both the U.S. and Norway. Since 1994, Mr. Peters has held instructional design and project management positions in the health insurance and manufacturing sectors. As an adjunct professor with the Department of Communication at the University of Hartford in Connecticut, he designed and taught the course *Multimedia Communication*. He is an active member of the Department of Interactive Technology's Corporate Advisory Council at Bloomsburg University. Mr. Peters has an M.S. degree in Instructional Technology from Bloomsburg University. He has authored or co-authored numerous papers and presentations on the topic of learning technologies.

Timothy L. Phillips, Ph.D. is Director of the Institute for Interactive Technologies and coordinator of the Master of Science in Instructional Technology program at Bloomsburg University. His area of expertise is project management and Web site development. He completed his doctoral work at the Pennsylvania State University and has considerable experience in training, multimedia development, consulting, and Web site management. Dr. Phillips has been teaching instructional technology at the university level for 10 years and has presented papers and workshops at many state and national conferences. He has been involved with numerous instructional technology projects for state and university clients, including work on the Pennsylvania Department of Public Welfare and the PPL needs assessments as well as working with local organizations to develop e-learning solutions to solve their needs.

Maria Plano is Manager of E-Learning Solutions at Latitude360, a division of RWD Technologies. Her areas of focus include e-learning consulting and project management, as well as the analysis and design of engaging, interactive Web-based courseware. RWD's clients in the consumer products, sales, pharmaceutical, and financial industries have benefited from Ms. Plano's expertise in proposing and profitably managing large e-learning courseware development projects. Ms. Plano has an M.S. degree in Instructional Technology from Bloomsburg University.

Kevin Schmohl is Operations Manager with Universal Systems and Technology in Northern Virginia. Mr. Schmohl has a Master's degree in Instructional Technology as well as a Bachelor's degree in Public Relations/Advertising and a minor in Information Systems from Bloomsburg University, Bloomsburg, PA. This blended educational background between people skills and computer expertise helps Mr. Schmohl serve as a key asset in the area of instructional design from the needs analysis phase through the development and testing phases. He plays a pivotal role whether it is working with his government clients or commercial clients. He helps clients to develop a training solution that fits the learner's needs. Recently, Mr. Schmohl has been tackling e-learning issues such as Section 508 compliance and FAA 028C standards. Besides working in the government and corporate arena, Mr. Schmohl teaches part-time at local colleges. His courses range from the Internet to Multimedia Development.

Carl Seidel is a Strategic Account Manager for Newton Gravity Shift in Pennington, NJ. His areas of focus include supporting the business team with proposal development, developing and executing webinars to drive strategic business initiatives, e-learning project management, and overseeing the design and development of Assessor™, Newton Gravity Shift's online test development and administration tool. Newton Gravity Shift provides e-business applications to enhance corporate communications, improve employee performance, increase productivity, and drive revenue. Mr. Seidel has an M.S. in Instructional Technology from Bloomsburg University and a Bachelor's degree in Radio, Television and Film from Temple University.

Linda Carroll Smith, Esq. is a contract partner at Dilworth Paxson LLP and practices law in the Harrisburg, PA office. She worked for many years in state government in the areas of telecommunication and energy law prior to joining Dilworth in 1997, where she continues to practice in those areas and has expanded into the area of e-commerce. Ms. Smith also practices in the area of administrative law. She currently serves as Chair of the Web Site Committee for the Energy Bar Association based in Washington D.C., where she works extensively with the Web site host company. She has been a member of the Government Affairs Committee of the Technology Council of Central Pennsylvania for several years. Ms. Smith holds a J.D. from Dickinson School of Law, Carlisle, PA and a B.A. from Caldwell College, Caldwell, NJ.

Stacey Smith is an instructional designer for Concurrent Technologies Corporation working on the Advanced Distributed Learning (ADL) Initiative. ADL is a collaborative effort between government, industry, and academia to establish a new distributed learning environment that permits the interoperability of learning tools and course content on a global scale. Ms. Smith works closely with the SCORM™ technical team to design, develop, and test new and re-authored learning content examples that implement current versions of the SCORM. Ms. Smith also evaluates and demonstrates how various design methodologies will be implemented into the SCORM, as well as identifies gaps in the current version of the SCORM, collects lessons learned, best practices, and suggests concepts for the continuing evolution of the SCORM. Ms. Smith has an M.S. in Instructional Technology from Bloomsburg University.

Nancy Vasta is responsible for performance consulting and learning strategy for CIGNA Corporation. Her area of expertise is leveraging technology to improve employee performance and evaluating return on investment. Ms. Vasta has demonstrated practical and creative approaches to improving employee productivity in customer service, sales, and human resources. She has presented at the International Performance Conference, the E-Learning Conference & Expo, and at the Bloomsburg Corporate Advisory Council Conference. Ms. Vasta earned a Master's degree in Instructional Technology from Bloomsburg University.

Lisa Verge is a Learning Products Manager for EduNeering, Inc. in Princeton, NJ. Her primary responsibilities include project management, developing client relationships, and coordinating strategic e-learning initiatives. She assists EduNeering's clients in the pharmaceutical, healthcare, and energy industries in identifying training needs and developing training solutions to fit those needs.

Ms. Verge earned her M.S. degree in Instructional Technology from Bloomsburg University.

W. Scott Wein is Director of Learning Support for Century 21 Real Estate Corporation. Century 21 is the world's largest residential real estate brokerage with over 100,000 sales associates. Mr. Wein is responsible for the technical infrastructure of the Century 21 Learning System (CLS). This system provides both synchronous and asynchronous training to sales associates and brokers throughout the world. CLS has been named the 72nd best training program by *Training Magazine* for 2002, and has been in the Innovation 500 from *Information Week*. Mr. Wein holds an M.S. degree in Instructional Technology from Bloomsburg University. He speaks on the topics of blended learning, synchronous delivery, and the speech technique.

ABOUT THE INSTITUTE FOR INTERACTIVE TECHNOLOGIES

The Institute for Interactive Technologies (IIT) at Bloomsburg University in Bloomsburg, PA was established in 1985 as a research and development group focusing on emerging interactive learning technologies used in corporations and government agencies. It is a consortium of faculty, staff, instructional designers, and graduate students in Bloomsburg University's Department of Instructional Technology who write, research, develop, and consult within the field of instructional design.

This working consortium offers students practical hands-on experiences as they apply theoretical knowledge to real-life projects and, at the same time, fosters the development of effective and innovative instructional solutions for government, for-profit, and not-for-profit organizations.

The IIT seeks to help business and government leaders understand the impact of interactive learning technologies on their workforce, improve the performance and competitiveness of their organization, and provide a factual basis for sound instructional interventions. The IIT undertakes instructional technology projects such as: designing workshops to convert stand-up trainers to Web designers, delivering distance education courses to five sister universities, designing interactive e-learning for a large cosmetics company, developing e-learning for several large healthcare companies, conducting a needs assessment for a utility company, conducting return on investment studies, and helping the Pennsylvania Department of Public Welfare to implement e-learning for over 8000 employees.

Each of the IIT's efforts provides an opportunity to apply technical capabilities to practical business issues and provides students within the Master's of Science in Instructional Technology program an opportunity to contribute to a project that is being used in the field.

To learn more about the IIT consulting and development services or to enroll as a student in the IIT's online program or face-to-face program at Bloomsburg University, Bloomsburg, PA, visit http://iit.bloomu.edu or call (570) 389-4506.

Free value-added materials available from the Download Resource Center at www.jrosspub.com

At J. Ross Publishing we are committed to providing today's professional with practical, hands-on tools that enhance the learning experience and give readers an opportunity to apply what they have learned. That is why we offer free ancillary materials available for download on this book and all participating Web Added Value™ publications. These online resources may include interactive versions of material that appears in the book or supplemental templates, worksheets, models, plans, case studies, proposals, spreadsheets, and assessment tools, among other things. Whenever you see the WAV™ symbol in any of our publications, it means bonus materials accompany the book and are available from the Web Added Value Download Resource Center at www.jrosspub.com.

Downloads for *Winning E-Learning Proposals: The Art of Development and Delivery* consist of sample templates, worksheets, RFPs, bidder's conference questions, and proposals.

PART I: PRELIMINARY WORK

1

THE E-LEARNING BUSINESS ACQUISITION PROCESS

Education over the Internet is going to be so big
it is going to make e-mail usage look like a rounding error.
—John Chambers, President and CEO
Cisco Systems [1]

THE NEED

Our knowledge economy demands knowledgeable workers. As information doubles and triples on a yearly basis, employees need to remain up-to-date and informed. In fact, many experts believe that an organization's ability to learn faster than its competitors is the only remaining sustainable competitive advantage. Unfortunately, this competitive advantage does not come without a price.

Expenditures by organizations on formal training in the U.S. exceed $50 billion annually [2]. The costs for training employees are not only in terms of training expenses and travel dollars but, more importantly, in lost opportunity costs. Employees sitting in training classes are not out generating revenue. To keep employee training costs from spiraling out of control and to allow employees more time to contribute to the bottom line, corporate executives are demanding a better, more effective method of training. Executives are asking the question, "How do we cost effectively provide our employees with just the right training at just the right time?"

THE ANSWER

The answer is *e-learning.* E-learning is the delivery of training materials, information, and content directly to an employee's computer desktop by taking advantage of Web browser technology to purposefully change behavior or attitude. This anytime, anywhere training entices executives who see the opportunity to provide more workforce training while simultaneously increasing productivity and saving travel dollars. Today, it seems as if every executive has concluded that e-learning is a major requirement for remaining competitive.

The problem? These executives have no idea how to make e-learning happen. That is why 50% of all technology-based training programs are designed by outside vendors [2]. Corporate executives are not familiar with the technology, learner requirements, or instructional design methods needed to make e-learning a reality in their organization. Help is needed.

THE OPPORTUNITY

This cry for help has created huge financial opportunities for e-learning firms. E-learning vendors can charge a premium for helping organizations transition from an instructor-led classroom strategy to an e-learning delivery strategy. In fact, the amount of money spent on outside providers of training products and services is over $15 billion a year [2].

Today's opportunity in the e-learning market is without parallel. Organizations need to educate their employees quickly and effectively but have no idea how to develop the e-learning courses or necessary infrastructure to be successful. Companies are scrambling to convert much of their traditional instructor-led training into an online format.

For example, a large healthcare provider is attempting to flip its traditional 70/30 ratio of classroom to online instruction. The company is moving 70% of its training online while reducing stand-up delivery to 30%. Other organizations are not taking such drastic steps but are moving toward a blending of online and classroom instruction in what is known as *blended learning.*

In addition, existing software companies like Baan, SAP, and PeopleSoft have adopted e-learning for the delivery of much of their training to both customers and internal employees and are actively pursuing the development of Learning Management Systems (LMS). Even large public organizations like the Pennsylvania Department of Public Welfare are transitioning from instructor-led training to an e-learning model of training delivery. Even if an organization is not completely transitioning to e-learning, it is still adding e-learning to the mix of offerings in a blended learning approach.

These organizations cannot do it alone. They need the help of e-learning firms that understand the process and procedures of placing courses online and of setting up the technological infrastructures to support their goals. E-learning vendors that understand technology and instructional design and can write winning proposals are in an excellent position to develop a lucrative business.

THE MANY COMPETITORS

This tremendous financial opportunity has fueled the proliferation of e-learning companies competing for the limited budgets of companies with e-learning needs. E-learning companies seem to spring up overnight. ASTD, a professional training organization, estimates that more than 275 vendors are building custom and off-the-shelf content programs for delivery on corporate networks [3]. Experts who study this topic also report that "there are roughly 75 [LMS] vendors that have appeared on more than five RFPs in the United States alone" [4]. E-learning software companies like BlackBoard, Interwise, and Click2learn are all competing for a piece of the e-learning pie. E-learning is big business.

Even traditional institutions that have focused entirely on instructor-led training are reaching into the e-learning arena. Colleges such as the University of Maryland, Bloomsburg University of Pennsylvania, and the Wharton School of Business are entering the e-learning market, as are high schools such as the Florida Virtual School and Pennsylvania's Keystone National High School.

Despite the mad rush to gain access to the huge e-learning marketplace, no single company seems to have an advantage over the others. The market is wide open to all players with some type of e-learning solution. This has led to a frenzy of mergers, company closings, and acquisitions. The chaotic marketplace means corporations wanting to hire an e-learning vendor must be extremely careful in their selection process. They must develop methods to avoid low-quality, fly-by-night e-learning firms that may not be around tomorrow.

SEEKING A COMPETITIVE ADVANTAGE

One methodology for discerning the best e-learning company from hundreds of potential suitors is the E-learning Business Acquisition Process (E-BAP). The E-BAP helps clients distinguish between good, high-quality e-learning firms and the not-so-good firms through an objective screening process [5].

The E-BAP is similar to practices in other fields where work is awarded based on a written estimate of the completion of a specific project as well as a sales presentation explaining the finer points of the proposed solution. This process is not perfect but is seeing increased use within the e-learning industry.

THE REQUEST FOR PROPOSAL

The main element in the competitive E-BAP is the Request for Proposal (RFP). In its simplest form, an RFP is a description of a project a client wants completed. The RFP typically describes, in some level of detail, the needs (or perceived needs) of the client and provides a minimal description of a desired solution. The RFP usually requests a response in the form of a written proposal containing a description of the solution, a timeline, and a budget.

In addition, most RFPs contain a description of the "rules of engagement": how the proposal must be formatted, what evaluation criteria will be used, how the vendor is to respond (e-mail, fax, overnight delivery), due dates, and other elements that should be contained in the proposal (resumes of key team members, quality assurance forms, company brochures, etc.). The RFP is basically a formal problem statement sent competitively to vendors. E-learning RFPs can cover a range of topics such as:

- Converting stand-up training to Web-based training
- Developing a customized Web training solution
- Developing an online corporate university
- Recommending and implementing a Learning Content Management System (LCMS)
- Developing an interactive module for helping managers deal with remote employees
- Designing a blended learning curriculum for a sales force

While all of these topics are in the field of e-learning, each represents different projects in terms of technology, design, and development. The savvy vendor must understand the RFP, present a feasible solution, and effectively navigate the E-BAP to win the desired business.

E-LEARNING BUSINESS ACQUISITION PROCESS

The E-BAP consists of ten elements. Each of these elements contains subelements. This book examines these elements and subelements to help you gain a complete understanding of how business is acquired within the e-learning industry. Figure 1.1 provides a graphic illustration of the E-BAP.

It should be noted that not all organizations follow this process when soliciting and evaluating e-learning proposals. As with most processes, variations occur. For example, in some competitive situations, e-learning companies first present to the client their corporate capabilities and past projects and then, if they "win"

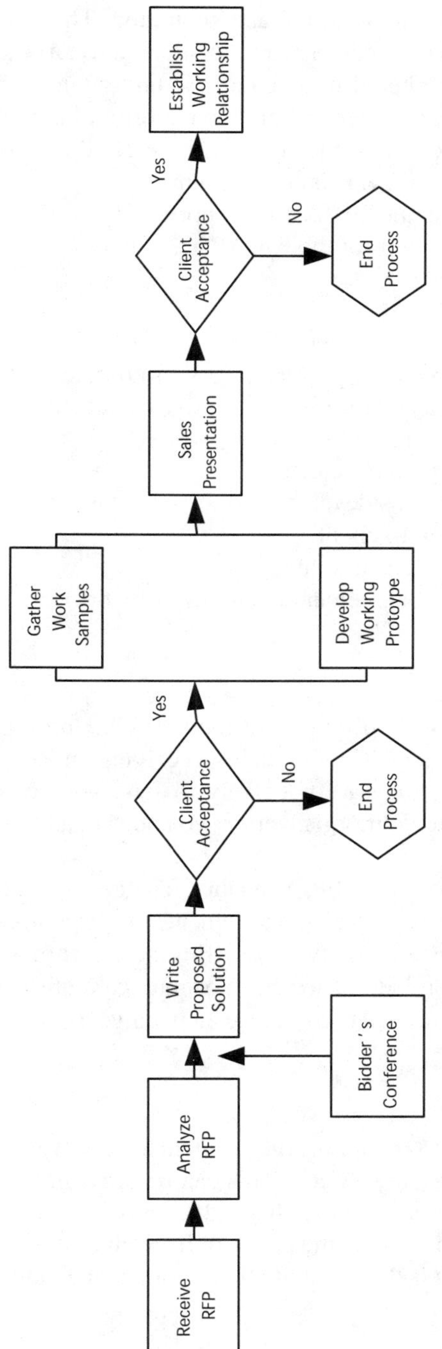

Figure 1.1 The E-Learning Business Acquisition Process (E-BAP).

the presentation, a proposal is written and submitted. The order in which these elements are presented is common in many situations and can be adapted as needed. Even if the sequence is altered or adapted, the underlying subelements do not change. The same functions occur within the majority of competitive situations. The purpose here is to describe the steps of the E-BAP and to understand how each element functions and contributes to winning.

Each of the steps in the E-BAP is important for ultimately winning the e-learning business. The steps of the E-BAP are:

1. Receive the RFP
2. Analyze the RFP
3. Ask questions to clarify problem/bidder's conference (optional)
4. Conceptualize the solution
5. Write proposed solution
6. Proposal is accepted or rejected
7. Gather work samples/develop working prototype
8. Sales presentation to client
9. Client accepts or rejects solution
10. Establish working agreement (statement of work)

RECEIVE RFP

The receipt of the RFP is the first step of the E-BAP. Unfortunately, complications can begin immediately. The first is just receiving an RFP. If clients are not familiar with your firm, they are not likely to send you an RFP. To obtain a regular flow of RFPs into your organization, you need to advertise your capabilities and services.

Another complication with RFPs is quality. The quality of RFPs ranges from well-written, clearly expressed problem statements to vague, ill-conceived descriptions of nonexistent needs. In reality, most RFPs are closer to a vague description than a clearly expressed problem statement. You must carefully read and examine an RFP to find information needed to formulate an intelligent response.

ANALYZE RFP

During this step, you must determine the problem to be solved and whether or not e-learning is the appropriate solution. This can be difficult because clients typically do not state "our problem is…" Instead, clients describe a situation and let you, the potential vendor, divine the problem from clues within the RFP. This is not done intentionally. It is the result of clients not understanding the entire scope of their learning problem.

You need to carefully review the RFP to determine the exact client requirements. You need to make sure all of the requirements outlined by the client will be addressed in the proposal. Clients tend to scatter requirements throughout the RFP. Often, you are forced to pick through the document to identify the required deliverables.

One effective method of identifying all of the requested requirements and deliverables is to create a *Requirements Matrix.* A Requirements Matrix is a list of all the requirements within the RFP identified by page and paragraph number. It is a painstaking process involving a meticulous line-by-line examination of the RFP. The value of this process is that it allows the RFP response team to identify each client requirement.

A careful analysis of the RFP and identification of all requirements is critical. Incorrect analysis of the problem or misdiagnosis of requirements can lead to *disqualification,* which means that you are no longer able to be considered for the project.

ASK QUESTIONS TO CLARIFY PROBLEM/BIDDER'S CONFERENCE (OPTIONAL)

Because most RFPs are not well written and do not explain the problem clearly, you will have many questions and desired points of clarification. However, the client representative may not be available to answer questions, or may avoid your phone calls or ignore your e-mails.

Consider it from his or her point of view: if vendors constantly contacted the client representative, the representative would spend all day answering vendor questions. Often the client would be forced to answer the same question over and over again. The representative may even give more information to one vendor than another, making the process unfair. To avoid the constant barrage of questions and to keep the process fair, the concept of a Bidder's Conference was developed.

The Bidder's Conference is a gathering (virtual or actual) of all vendors responding to an RFP. Questions are submitted via e-mail, answered, collated, and then sent back to all the vendors. The purpose of the Bidder's Conference is for the vendors to ask questions to clarify the client's needs. The conference is conducted in an open forum such as a press conference or online so all vendors can hear all questions and responses. This provides objectivity to the process and ensures that no vendor receives an unfair advantage. Everyone hears or reads the same information.

The Bidder's Conference is optional and is not held for every RFP. Often, conferences are not held and vendors are not allowed to ask any questions. In these cases, the RFP represents the sole source of knowledge about the client's problem.

CONCEPTUALIZE THE SOLUTION

One of the most important aspects of responding to an RFP is to conceptualize the solution. Proposals are won or lost on the strength of the solution. During the conceptualization phase of the E-BAP, you must determine the nature of the problem and the most feasible, cost-effective method of solving it. You must formulate an instructional strategy and technical solution that meet the client's explicit and implicit needs. The solution must be one that is comfortable for the client and congruent with the corporate culture.

To conceptualize the solution you must undertake a brainstorming session with the proposal development team to consider various solutions and their consequences. These brainstorming sessions may include developing a concept map and a fishbone diagram, as well as employing a series of thought-provoking questions to clarify the thinking of the proposal development team. The result of this effort should be a Preliminary Solutions Document, which is a one-page summary of the client's problem and your proposed solution.

You must also have a method of winning the business. This is called a *capture strategy*. A capture strategy acts as a framework into which items of the proposal such as project, instructional solution, and technical solution are placed. The idea is to focus your capture strategy on solving the needs of the client.

WRITE PROPOSED SOLUTION

One of the most critical steps in the E-BAP is the actual writing of the proposal. The proposal is the moneymaking document. A winning proposal can translate into millions of dollars of revenue. Vendors finishing second place or lower get nothing.

The proposal is the document written in response to the RFP. It usually contains the following sections:

- Introductory letter (also called transmittal or cover letter)
- Executive summary
- Description of problem/overview of solution
- Solution (technical and instructional)
- Project management and schedule (timeline, milestones, deliverables)
- Price quote/budget
- Experience/capabilities statement
- Description of key project members

Together, these sections make up the bid for the requested e-learning. The proposal explains how you plan to complete the work described in the RFP. In the proposal, you address the concerns, limitations, obstacles, deliverables, due dates, and opportunities listed in the RFP.

For example, you may be required to describe how the scores from an e-learning testing module can be downloaded into the client's existing LMS or indicate the instructional strategies used to convert stand-up instruction to e-learning.

The tricky part about writing a proposal is that if all the criteria requested in the RFP are not addressed, the requesting organization can disqualify the proposal because of noncompliance even if the solution is the "best" and most cost effective.

Therefore, writing a thoughtful, high-quality proposal that addresses all of the prospect's needs is a requirement. Unfortunately, the time frame for writing a proposal is usually short. You can receive as little as one or two days notice. In the fast-paced e-learning world, time is not a luxury. You must quickly analyze the RFP, develop a feasible solution, and write the proposal by the due date or lose the opportunity.

In addition, the proposed solution must be within a reasonable budget (which the client usually does not divulge). The proposal must be written in the prescribed format and be free from grammatical or typographical errors. Given these conditions, it is a wonder any proposals are ever written. However, if you can provide a fast turnaround and can meet the needs of the client, the relationship can be beneficial to both organizations.

For example, one vendor organization located in New Jersey provides a three-day turnaround on all proposals. The company develops e-learning for the pharmaceutical industry, which values fast turnaround. The strategy of a three-day turnaround has dramatically increased its share of the market and allows it to outmaneuver competitors. When you are responding to RFPs, be aware of what the client wants.

Because of time constraints and the nature and variety of requirements, most proposals are written by a team. A proposal development team works together to craft the proposal and to make it read as if only one person wrote it. Therefore, the team must agree on formatting conventions, tone, and style prior to each individual writing his or her piece.

Once the written proposal is completed, it is submitted to the potential client. The submission can be a hardbound copy or an e-mail attachment, depending on the client's request. The potential client then reviews all proposals received.

CLIENT ACCEPTS (OR REJECTS) PROPOSAL

Once proposals are received, they are typically judged on the quality of the writing, soundness of the instructional design, feasibility of the technical solution, timeliness of product completion, and size of the proposed budget. The client uses these criteria to accept or reject your proposed solution.

If the client does not agree with your proposed solution or does not believe the proposal is cost effective, he or she will eliminate you from consideration for this particular project. Hopefully you will be notified, but sometimes you are just ignored. Typically, the process stops if the client rejects your proposed solution [6].

If the client likes your proposed ideas and the price is reasonable, he or she will most likely ask your firm and several others to present in person at the client's site. This is sometimes called a "shootout." Vendors demonstrate their solutions, talk about their firms, and attempt to convince the client that their solution is the best.

GATHER WORK SAMPLES/DEVELOP WORKING PROTOTYPE

To win a "shootout," you have to stage an impressive presentation. This involves gathering examples or samples of previous related work or developing a working prototype to show to the client. Clients typically cannot grasp what the final e-learning solution will look like until they have an actual representation of the final product using terms and concepts familiar to them. You can help the process by displaying screen captures within the written proposal. However, clients often want to see a working prototype or demonstration.

The prototype or product demonstration provides the potential client with a visualization of the solution. If you have already developed a template or are demonstrating an existing LMS software package, place some of the client's requested information into the software and display how it functions. If software is not developed because you are bidding on a customized project, you should develop a prototype. A prototype helps the client understand how the instruction will function. If developing a prototype is not feasible, the next best thing is to show work samples from previous projects.

SALES PRESENTATION TO CLIENT

The next step in the E-BAP is presenting the proposed solution to the client. Present a prototype or your software along with information about your proposed timeline, budget, quality assurance process, and the capabilities of your development team. Presentation of the proposed solution provides an opportunity for the client to ask specific questions and to clarify items within your proposal. This process usually occurs at the client's location. A presentation should have at least the following elements:

- Benefits of proposed solution
- Overview of solution
- Previous clients
- Budget
- Timeline
- Management of the project
- Firm's capabilities

The presentation is important for a number of reasons. It establishes rapport between you and the client, it helps to clarify any additional questions the client selection team may have, and it provides a chance for you to show your firm's best work. It also allows you to convey a sense of excitement about the project.

CLIENT ACCEPTS OR REJECTS SOLUTION

This step can take a long time. Interestingly, the client is usually in a hurry to have the proposal written and returned, sometimes within days, but inevitably there are delays in awarding the contract. This can be problematic for you because, in many cases, although the award date slips the actual due date of the project remains firm.

Another frustrating aspect of the process is that occasionally the client does not award the contract to any vendor. This may be because funding for the project gets pulled, or all the proposals were too expensive, or organizational priorities shifted, or even the fact that the project champion left the company. Any of these events can lead to project cancellation.

ESTABLISH WORKING AGREEMENT

If the proposal is accepted, you and the client work out additional details required for the development of the e-learning solution. The outcome of that effort results in the final contract and the issuing of a Statement of Work (SOW).

At this stage, you and the client determine details such as the method of payment for the project, the development timeline, assignment of subject matter experts from the client organization, and other details. The SOW quantifies the solution and time frame for the project. It may indicate the precise number of screens to be developed, the exact hardware configuration, and other quantifiable elements.

A contract is also developed at this point. It covers legal arrangements between the vendor and the client and contains the SOW. The contract and SOW are the final word on what work will be completed by the vendor and what the client can expect from the project. If disputes occur, the contract is consulted. If it is well written, the dispute can be handled easily by the contract. If the contract and SOW are not well written, complications can and will arise.

SUMMARY OF E-BAP

At this point you might be saying to yourself, "Why should I care about the E-Learning Business Acquisition Process? I am a software engineer, not a salesperson!" The answer is simple. Everyone in an e-learning organization must know and understand how business is acquired.

If business is not acquired then the software engineer, graphic artist, Web designer, instructional technologist, and others will be unemployed. It behooves every individual within the company to know from where his or her paycheck comes. In addition, you never know when you will be called upon to take on a role within the E-BAP, from demonstrating software to estimating development hours.

Everyone in the company is in it together. When business is won it impacts everyone. When too many opportunities are lost it also impacts everyone. E-learning companies do not stay in business by losing proposal opportunities. There is no prize for second place.

■ ■ ■

SEEING IS BELIEVING: A CASE STUDY OF PROPOSAL WRITING AT GET THINKING, INC.

Chad Hostetler, Vice President of Operations, Get Thinking, Inc.

Client:	Footlong Industries
Industry:	Manufacturer of Building Materials
Need:	Online Orientation for New Employees
Annual Sales:	$3 billion
Employees:	16,000

Here is an example of how the E-BAP can work. Naturally, there are many variations to the process; this is just one. You will note that this example is complete with twists and turns that occur constantly in the e-learning industry and the E-BAP is not followed exactly, which is often the case. This example includes having to deal with changing budgets, working with third- party vendors, and putting together a proposal without an RFP.

Let us begin with some information about the client. Although the names are fictional, the details are all accurate. Footlong Industries is a world-class manufacturer of building materials. It is a household name in the U.S. and has more than 50 domestic and international manufacturing facilities. As with many large corporations, it has a number of subsidiaries. This is where our story begins.

About nine months prior to the case study proposal, we were awarded a project to develop an online curriculum for Spruce, one of Footlong's subsidiaries. Spruce specializes in wood products. We were developing a curriculum on its product line including installation, maintenance, and selling techniques for its wholesale and retail distributors. We won the competitive bid for many of the same reasons as the proposal in this case study. We were in the process of completing the last module. The project was going well and the client team (represented by both Spruce and Footlong) was pleased.

We were also working on a second curriculum for Footlong at the same time. The second project used the same structure and approach as the Spruce product, but focused on some flooring products for its residential channels. We were the sole bidder and about halfway through the project. Again, the project was running smoothly, which provided another strong reference within the organization.

Then one day in the last quarter of the calendar year, we received a call from someone in the human resources department of Footlong. Her supervisor, who was working with us on both of the other ongoing projects, had given her our name. She wanted to discuss a potential project.

We get a majority of our work from referrals and word of mouth. In this case, the referral was internal, which means an expanded contact base within the organization. This is an optimal situation. Ideally, and in most cases, our client partnerships go on for years. For many clients, we have completed more than a dozen projects for multiple areas of the company. Naturally, this is beneficial for both parties. We become experts in the audiences, content, approaches, and standards of our clients, which saves them time and money. We benefit by having a continued source of projects.

In the initial call, the project leader for Footlong indicated that she wanted to take their existing paper-based new hire welcome package and make it into an interactive, e-learning orientation. It would include information such as company history, benefit options information, and an introduction to the corporate campus of the headquarters. Looking over the content, Footlong's project leader estimated that the entire orientation should take an hour or less to complete, and some of the content (policies and benefits) could not be edited or modified.

We were one of several vendors invited to submit a proposal. If our proposal was accepted, we would advance to the second level of competition for the work including an on-site presentation of our proposal at Footlong's corporate headquarters.

We were immediately interested. First, we place great value in partnership. So although this project would not involve great effort, it would continue an established partnership with Footlong, a great client and a well-known name on our client list. Second, every new employee at the company would see our work. Third, we liked the content — we saw a lot of opportunities to infuse our signature creativity into the content to make a product that would really shine. Finally, it only makes sense that if your goal is to be the premiere vendor for an organization and you have the chance to impress it and keep out competition, you seize it.

As we talked through some of the details, everyone began to get excited about the possibilities. The next step was for Footlong to provide a small sample of the content so that we could begin to prepare the proposal.

A portion of the company history arrived in the next few days. Our team was already brainstorming design approaches and the ideas on the table looked good. Over the next few weeks, we exchanged a series of calls and e-mails with Footlong to gather additional details and requirements. We were even given a budget range, which is always helpful. Our proposal was well underway.

Now let us summarize what has transpired. We received a call about a potential project to gauge our interest in submitting a proposal for a competitive bid situation with two levels of elimination. We received some sample content and were already making good progress on the proposal. Anything missing? Oh yes, the RFP! This project had no RFP. In most cases, projects without RFPs are either very small, considered add-on work, or a sole-source bid. This case was an exception to that rule.

Not having an RFP is typically more work for the vendor. You need to ask or assume what information the client really needs or wants to have. Your proposal alone is responsible for clearly and accurately documenting all of the assumptions and requirements based on the information you have gathered. You also determine the formatting and sequence of the proposal, which in some cases is not such a bad thing. We have responded to some RFPs that mandate the order of the sections in ways that make the document difficult to follow.

Not having an RFP also potentially creates a situation where bidding vendors are given varying amounts of detail regarding the project. If telephone conversations are the only way information is disseminated and those phone calls are conducted individually, the opportunity for information to be missed is greater than when a single document is distributed to everyone. In addition, I believe that the client's understanding evolves and requirements may change as they are discussed.

We spend a lot of time and energy creating proposals that not only define but demonstrate the types of products we produce: clear, concise, creative, and effective. When writing our proposals, we put on our "client hat" and think about what the client really wants and needs to know, and what is the best way to communicate that information. We naturally have all of the proposal standards including an executive summary, milestones, and assumptions. We also describe our understanding of the situation and our best solution. Beyond that, we always try to include details about the features and functions and how they meet the client's needs. A key component is also a description of our process. This is not limited to what we do in our office; it includes the client's responsibilities and involvement as well. It is very important for clients to understand up front that their ongoing involvement is critical to the success of the project.

As always, we worked very hard to produce a document that concisely, but fully, presented our solution. In this case, the end result was 16 pages long, plus a completed questionnaire on general capabilities and company information. The proposal was shipped out about six weeks into the new year.

Within a week of Footlong receiving the proposal, we were invited to present our solution to the team in mid-March. There was just one catch. Some budget numbers had been revised and our bid was over the budget for the project by about 9%. Footlong asked that we provide an addendum detailing what features or services would be excluded from the original proposal to meet the new budget.

Again, another twist in the process. We reworked the solution to fit the new budget and submitted an additional document.

Throughout the proposal creation process we were already working on a prototype to include in our presentation. I think it is the most effective method we have of capturing a client's vision for what we can do as a team.

For example, when we wrote the proposal for Spruce nearly a year earlier, we included sample interactions that had animations of a manufacturing process. They clearly made a significant impression on the client. "I just could not get those animations out of my head." "Every time I pictured what the course would look like, I saw your sample." These were some of the responses we heard from the client when we were awarded the contract. The client could see, touch, and experience our solution with its content — very powerful. Whoever coined the phrase "seeing is believing" was right. Prototypes are an excellent tool in winning the proposal process.

To prepare the prototype for the new proposal, our team had a few brainstorming sessions on how to make the company history (the sample content Footlong provided) come alive. At this stage, we were working to make sure that the design supported all of the project objectives. We were wearing the "end-user hat" because they will ultimately determine the project's success. We decided to create an online version of a theme park attraction where the user would actually "ride" through the decades of the company history interacting with objects to obtain information along the way. The "*wow* factor" was huge, while the approach was totally appropriate, which is the perfect mix.

As with a large project, storyboards were created and reviewed, media produced, code developed, and much testing done. We included audio narration and the interface was full of interactive elements and animation. We find this to be key when building a prototype. If you can find a piece of content that is best presented with a design that includes all of the strengths of interactive learning and your firm's capabilities, the impression will be significant.

Naturally, this design and development effort came at our expense. We could have simply submitted our proposal and shown up with a few PowerPoint slides. But there is no doubt in my mind that the end result would have been very different.

Not only were we building an ideal presentation to showcase our skills, our team was having a ball creating it. That is when the really great ideas emerge — when everyone is into the project and contributing ideas to take it to the next level.

So, with sample and presentation in hand, we flew to the corporate headquarters of Footlong. We met in the executive boardroom, "old" stomping grounds for us as we had presented there previously for the Spruce project. There were many new faces and a few who were currently working with us. We were the first presentation of the day.

During the presentation, things went well — the pacing was right, the attention was captured, and the relationship was building. Then, we got to the prototype. As the presenter, it was a phenomenal experience to observe. I only wish I had a camera. As we progressed through the prototype, eyes widened, postures corrected, and I would even venture to say that a few jaws dropped. Some laughed with delight. It could not have gone any better. It was clear that we hit the nail squarely on the head and had set a very good pace for the other vendors to match.

Now you cannot ask for more than that in a presentation, but believe it or not, things got even better. When the question and answer session began, a question was directed to one of the other people in the room. She was not a Footlong employee, but a manager at the LMS that they were using for this and previous projects. She and I had spoken on several conference calls, but never actually met in person. The question was somewhat technical in nature, but was clearly asked to gauge her perception of our capabilities. Her response was so positive that we could not have crafted a more helpful reply. It was glowing and totally unplanned and unexpected. Now we were the ones with widened eyes and corrected postures. This goes to show just how important it is to build relationships with third-party vendors.

We left the room feeling great — not overconfident, but certain that we had achieved the impression we set out to make. As the Footlong project leader walked us out, she could not stop talking about the prototype — that was a good sign. She hoped to make a decision in the next few days and would get in touch with us.

It would actually be two weeks until we received the official word that we were awarded the project. The hard work and financial investment had paid off. But with the good news also came some bad news. The original timelines were going to be delayed for approximately six months while content was revised and some organizational changes were put into place. This is one more example of how the proposal process can be filled with delays and twists.

The sample timeline shown in Figure 1.2 shows the life cycle of this particular proposal. Again, I would classify this project as relatively small, so you can see the type of time investment that is required.

This case study shows that E-BAP is filled with uncertainty and constantly changing demands and requirements. However, if a firm follows the process and puts forth quality effort the results can be very positive. This project was won and has strengthened the relationship between Footlong and Get Thinking.

■ ■ ■

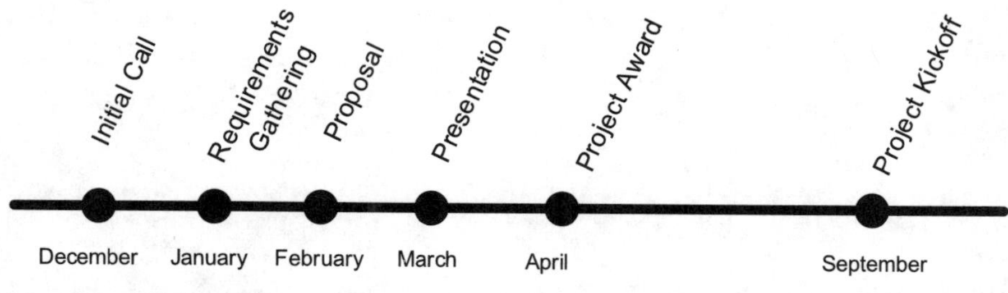

Figure 1.2 Time span from the initial call to the project kickoff for the Footlong Project.

THE BOTTOM LINE

For e-learning companies to gain access to the billions of dollars available in the online training industry, they must understand how to create a winning proposal. When an organization understands how to conceptualize, write, and present a quality proposal that meets the needs of the client, deals are done and money is made. When organizations fail to write winning proposals, firms fold and careers end.

This book has free materials available for download from the Web Added Value™ Resource Center at www.jrosspub.com.

2

RECEIVING THE RFP

INTRODUCTION

The E-BAP starts with the receipt of an RFP. Unfortunately, even this initial step is not simple or easy. Unless you are a large, well-known e-learning development or software firm, you are not likely to receive an unsolicited RFP. With over 275 companies producing some type of e-learning solution for clients, your firm must work within a highly competitive marketplace to ensure a steady flow of RFPs.

Obtaining a viable RFP can be a difficult and time-consuming process. This is especially true for new firms. Potential clients may not even be aware of your firm's existence. The job of the marketing and sales department is to obtain RFPs. The job of the production personnel is to create e-learning solutions that satisfy the clients and encourage them to return.

FINDING AN RFP

The best method of obtaining an RFP is from existing clients. They know your work and, if they are satisfied with what you have done, they are eager to work with you again. Unfortunately, there is seldom enough repeat work to keep a company growing and it is dangerous to rely on business from only one or two clients. It is imperative that companies keep a steady flow of RFPs from a variety of sources coming through the door.

Several methods exist for an e-learning company to gain access to the RFPs issued by clients. These methods should be used in combination with each other

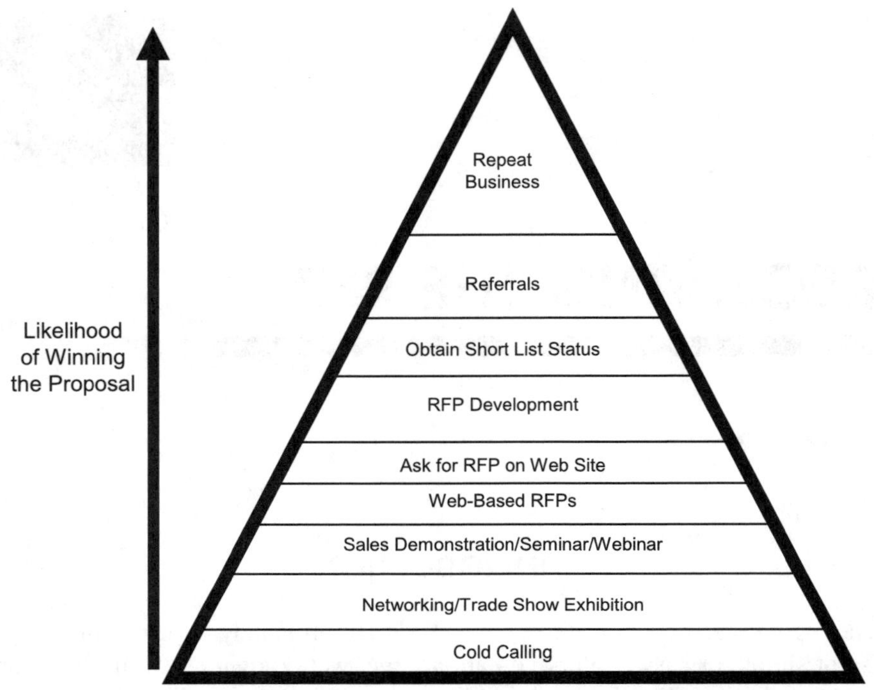

Figure 2.1 Illustration of the RFP Win Rate Pyramid. The closer to the top of the pyramid, the better the chances of winning the work.

to help you receive the highest number of RFPs possible. When large numbers of RFPs are available, you have a greater opportunity to obtain work. It is a numbers game. The more proposals you write, the more chances you have to win.

The methods of obtaining RFPs are listed in the *RFP Win Rate Pyramid.* The pyramid is organized from the bottom up to display the least effective methods of obtaining an RFP to the most effective methods. The least effective methods require the most contact and the most work by the sales force to secure the RFP. For example, when cold calling potential clients, you will have to contact many individuals to obtain an RFP — if you are able to obtain one at all. On top of the pyramid, you may need to make only one contact with your existing client to receive another RFP.

Each level in the RFP Win Rate Pyramid is described in the following. Successful e-learning firms develop an overall strategy or marketing plan to ensure a steady flow of RFPs. Figure 2.1 shows the RFP Win Rate Pyramid and the relationship between the method of obtaining the RFP and the amount of effort involved.

COLD CALLING

Using this method, a sales representative tries to generate new e-learning business and obtain RFPs by either calling clients who are not familiar with his or her organization or actually visiting the client organization without an invitation. While this method rarely results in an immediate receipt of an RFP, it can lead to a dialogue between the two companies and an opportunity for you to demonstrate e-learning capabilities or to be placed on the client's mailing list for RFPs issued in the future.

Another variation of cold calling is to call potential clients and ask to be placed on their RFP mailing list. Some clients are open to this idea. Others are not. A client who is open to the idea will request basic information about your firm and then you will be placed on the RFP mailing list. Then you, along with several dozen other e-learning firms, will receive any RFPs that are issued. This method is effective for getting RFPs but places your firm in a highly competitive situation with other vendors who are also on the client's RFP mailing list. Being one of many vendors typically does not result in a high win rate.

NETWORKING/TRADE SHOW EXHIBITION

Networking is simply meeting a number of potential clients and managing the relationship. Managing the relationship means you constantly keep in touch with the contacts in your network and assist them whenever possible. This is done in the hopes that when they need an e-learning solution they will remember you and send you an RFP. The assistance you provide is usually in the form of information or ideas that your potential client can take to his or her supervisors regarding e-learning.

Every good salesperson in an e-learning organization maintains a list of contacts interested in an e-learning solution for the short or long term. Contacts can come from business cards obtained at trade shows or from existing clients. An excellent place for meeting people to include in your network is trade shows, where the curious and serious buyers of e-learning products and services frequently visit. Another is to join local professional organizations. Networking with training professionals can help you determine if their organization is going to issue an RFP in the near future, and can get you on their list of RFP recipients.

Trade shows are important to both help a company network and to expose your firm's name and image to prospective buyers. Trade shows provide opportunities for prospects to see a large number of e-learning solutions side by side. The shows also allow you to establish brand recognition for your e-learning firm and provide a chance for networking with prospective clients.

The important part of networking is keeping in continual contact with the people in your network. While you may by constantly thinking about winning the "big one" from a prospective client at the large Fortune 50 company down the street, chances are the prospect is not constantly thinking about you or your firm. You need to periodically remind the prospect about your services and what your firm offers. Remind the prospect that when his or her company does have an e-learning need, your firm is ready to provide a quality solution. You can do this by an occasional phone call (not too many or you become a nag), finding articles on e-learning and sending them with a note, sending periodic e-mails, or inviting prospects to sales demonstrations, seminars, or webinars.

SALES DEMONSTRATIONS/SEMINARS/WEBINARS

The seminar or webinar (online seminar) focuses on educating the client rather than direct selling. The event allows you to demonstrate software and talk openly about e-learning. Often the event features a well-known figure from the training or e-learning industry to draw prospects to the seminar/webinar. The belief is that by educating the potential client, the vendor will be in a favorable position when the client decides to issue an RFP.

The seminar/webinar is usually open to a large number of potential clients who observe the software functionality. The open seminar/webinar environment allows prospects to "kick the tires" of e-learning solutions in a low-key, low-stress environment without a full-fledged sales pitch. It allows you to gauge prospects' interest and to separate serious buyers from individuals not yet prepared to issue an RFP.

The value to the potential clients is that the seminar/webinar contains educational information about e-learning that is worthwhile regardless of whether or not they intend to purchase your software or service. The event educates potential e-learning clients about the latest technology and explains to them how e-learning is being used in other companies. It allows the prospective clients to interact with others in the training industry who may be slightly ahead in the area of e-learning.

The seminar/webinar allows you to highlight your software in a comfortable environment, and provides a forum for discussion and interactions relating to e-learning. These events are a highly effective method of creating "buzz" about your e-learning company and for getting on the RFP list of potential clients.

One extremely effective method e-learning companies are using to get potential clients to events such as seminars and webinars is to partner with leading consultants and academics in the field of e-learning. The notoriety of the academic or consultant typically brings those curious about e-learning to the event. A well-known individual headlining a seminar helps the potential clients feel as if they are getting something valuable out of the seminar and not just a sales pitch.

WEB-BASED RFPS

Recently a new method of obtaining RFPs has come into its own — the use of the Internet to obtain an RFP. The process involves the client submitting an online RFP usually by answering a series of questions and adding some text to explain the needs. The next step is for the vendors (typically preregistered at the site) to be notified of the possible e-learning work. The vendor then submits a price proposal, and when a client agrees with a price quoted by the vendor, the deal is completed.

One Web site uniting clients and vendors is http://www.learn-source.com, which is an organization known as Findlearning.com. This Web site provides a method by which clients can post e-learning projects and receive responses from vendors qualified to work on the project. Findlearning.com connects companies with vendors that can fulfill their e-learning needs. It provides a service that allows companies to submit proposals to e-learning vendors for their specific learning needs and for the vendors to find the right clients for their training.

This works effectively for clearly defined and easily quantifiable projects. Projects with some ambiguity or uncertainty are not good candidates for this type of transaction. As the Internet becomes more of a medium for communication between companies, this method of obtaining RFPs will become more prevalent. This is especially true in the field of e-learning, where the Internet plays such a critical role. If training can be done over the Internet, so can the E-BAP [1].

ASK FOR RFPS ON YOUR WEB SITE

This sounds simple but is rarely done. While most e-learning companies have an elaborate and exciting Web site, they often fail to ask for RFPs on it. Web sites typically provide contact information and exciting demonstrations of work, but the site must do more. It must invite curious and serious clients to send an RFP. If potential clients take the time to visit your Web site (which is probably plastered on all of your sales literature), then you owe it to the clients to allow them to submit an RFP right then and there.

Set up an RFP drop box or an e-mail address. If you want to get a little fancier, you could have the prospects complete an online form with a few standard questions, and then have them attach the RFP and submit it. The goal is to make it easy and convenient for your prospects to send you an RFP.

A good example of a company using this technique is Accenture. Accenture is a consulting firm that provides a variety of services to clients all over the world. One of these services is assistance with e-learning. In Figure 2.2, notice the area in the bottom middle of the Web site under "Realize Your Ideas." In the list of items, the second from the bottom is "Request a Proposal for Services." Accenture

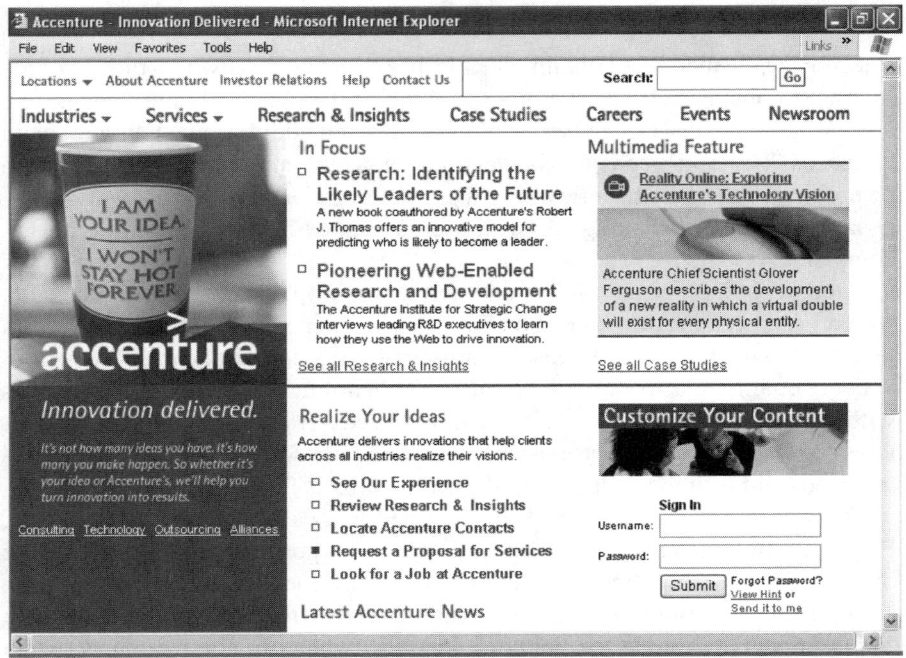

Figure 2.2 Accenture is one company that specifically asks for RFPs on its Web site. (Screen capture copyright 2002, Accenture, www.accenture.com. With permission.)

is asking for an RFP right on its Web site. This is a great way to get an RFP because when a proposal is received in this manner, there is no other competition.

RFP DEVELOPMENT

Another way to ensure that you get an e-learning project is to help the client develop the RFP. This can occur after a sales seminar or as a result of networking. In this case you can help prospective clients define their needs and a potential solution. If you are in a situation where the client needs to write an RFP and you provide insight and ideas into the document, then your organization will be in an excellent position to respond to the RFP when it is issued.

This method contains three strong warnings. The first is that the time and effort you put into preparing the RFP can be expensive. Preparing a good RFP is difficult and time consuming, and assisting a prospect in developing an RFP may not be in the best interest of your firm. In many cases, the salesperson and technical support person might better serve the e-learning firm by performing other activities.

Second, many firms and consultants position themselves as RFP writers and charge for those services. When you write an RFP for a potential client, you are "stepping on the toes" of these individuals who may, in the future, not recommend you as a vendor because you are infringing on their territory.

The third warning is the most dire. Even if you help develop the RFP, you might not win the project. You may put countless hours into developing the RFP, and when the RFP goes out for bids and your firm is the highest bid, the client's purchasing department may award the contract to some other firm. Unfortunately, this scenario happens all too often. The best advice is to charge an RFP development fee if you are going to help potential clients write an RFP. Your firm makes money and the process is more objective and fair for everyone.

OBTAIN "SHORT LIST" STATUS

A good position for an e-learning vendor is to be on the client's short list or "list of qualified vendors." A short list is simply a list of e-learning vendors that are prequalified to respond to RFPs issued by the client. The short list technique is usually associated with large companies that have the purchasing or procurement department prescreen qualified vendors, and then any department within the organization can choose from that list of vendors.

For many clients, it is difficult to constantly find vendors to whom to send RFPs. Some vendors do not respond to RFPs (too busy, too arrogant, or too crazy — can't win unless you respond), some vendors' reputations are unknown and, therefore, the risk of failure is present, some vendors are too big for some projects, and others are too small. Rather than continually searching the entire e-learning field for qualified vendors each time an e-learning project is needed, large companies create a list of qualified, competent vendors and place them on their preferred list.

When an e-learning project needs to be completed, the client sends the RFP only to those vendors on the list. This ensures two things. One is that a competitive bidding situation occurs and, two, the client receives a response from a vendor with whom he or she is familiar.

Once on the short list, a vendor is assured of receiving RFPs from the client. The difficulty is getting on the short list because many e-learning companies want to be on that list. Getting on the short list typically requires a number of presentations, samples of the vendor's work, testimonials from the vendor's clients, and proven competence in the field of e-learning.

REFERRALS

Another method for receiving RFPs is to ask existing clients for referrals. This involves asking a client to recommend other professionals who may need an e-learning vendor. Either the client can contact the person directly or the client can simply provide you with a name and contact information.

Referrals can come from another plant, department, or division within the same company or may be from outside the company. Often managers and supervisors within client companies are involved in professional organizations where they meet formally and informally to discuss their industry. These professionals often share information about good and bad experiences with vendors. If you have a good relationship with a client, ask the client to refer you to his or her colleagues. Often, a vendor will receive an RFP because a satisfied client made a favorable recommendation to a friend or colleague.

REPEAT BUSINESS

The best resource for finding RFPs is satisfied clients. They are usually eager for you to complete another project and are familiar with your work. Repeat business is inexpensive to secure and can be a great source of income.

Ask clients about possible work for your firm in other departments. A client might not even think of a fit between your firm and the needs in other departments until you ask. Get to know many people within a client organization so that if one person leaves, you still have contacts.

Repeat business from the same client can be your best source of RFPs with the least amount of competition. If a client likes your work, you may receive an RFP that is sent only to your organization. This is an ideal situation. The client simply wants you to scope out the work in a noncompetitive environment and, if the price is reasonable, you are awarded the project.

While repeat business is an effective and inexpensive method of obtaining RFPs, it is not without its problems and should not be your only source of RFPs. When dealing only with one large company, you have to be careful not to put all of your eggs in one basket. If the client chooses another vendor or if your organization falls out of favor, the flow of RFPs dries up. If this is the case, it can be difficult to find diverse sources for RFPs when you have become so dependent on one client.

BRING IT ALL TOGETHER

As you can see, to receive an RFP you must constantly be marketing your services, asking current clients for referrals, and demonstrating your corporate capabilities. Positioning your firm to receive RFPs requires basic knowledge of sales and marketing techniques common in a variety of industries.

One of the important elements to remember when soliciting RFPs is that the e-learning business is focused on solving problems; you must position your firm as one that can solve the problems and needs of the client quickly, efficiently, and at a reasonable price.

The first step in effectively marketing your firm is to have a "story to tell." Telling a story about how your firm started, its goals, and what makes your firm unique positions the firm to receive RFPs from companies that can identify with your story and have similar values. Developing this story is usually done with the creation and implementation of a marketing strategy.

A marketing strategy is the skillful planning and management of events, sales techniques, pricing plans, and promotional channels for the advancement of a particular e-learning firm. The strategy determines the mix of approaches used from the RFP Win Rate Pyramid. The marketing strategy is composed of a series of sales tactics that are used to help make your firm visible to the thousands of potential e-learning clients who need your services.

The strategy is the overarching theme or concept you use to discuss, promote, and establish your company. Do you sell solutions or do you sell training? Do you focus on innovation or 99.999% uptime? Do you position yourself as the top vendor in the field or are you positioned as a low-cost provider of quality services?

Your marketing strategy is the framework in which your RFP-seeking activities take place. The strategy includes how you position your product. Is it an off-the-shelf product, a standard product that is customizable, a completely custom-designed e-learning program, or a combination of approaches?

Strategy also determines how you price your e-learning solution. Is it the top of the market, middle-of-the-road, or bargain basement? Is it for mass consumption and, therefore, priced as a commodity or for a select group only and available at a premium?

A marketing strategy outlines how you are going to promote your e-learning solutions. Are you going to position your firm as innovative geniuses always working on the bleeding edge of technology, or are you going to be the tried-and-true vendor with a proven track record? Are you going to be a generic solution to general problems such as "leadership" or are you going to work in a specific industry like pharmaceuticals? Your marketing strategy helps you "tell a story" about your company and attracts potential clients.

While you need a strong marketing strategy, strategy alone is not enough. Clients will not be knocking down your door unless they know you are available to receive RFPs. You need to find a method of letting potential clients know you are in the e-learning business and eager to do work. There are several methods you can use to help your firm find RFPs.

One tool that is helpful for tracking and monitoring RFP sources is the *RFP Obtainment Methods Worksheet* shown in Worksheet 2.1. The worksheet provides a structured format for tracking the methods discussed in this chapter. This worksheet allows you to track the methods that are yielding the most success.

RFP Obtainment Methods Worksheet

Use this worksheet to help determine the mix of methods you will use to obtain RFPs. The worksheet provides space to indicate what percent of your total effort will be dedicated to each method (they need to equal 100%). Notes can be added for any special technique or tactics used. The results section allows you to see how successful a particular effort has been. This is important for future determination of the right mix to use when obtaining RFPs.

% of Overall Effort	Method	Notes	Results
Example: 10%	*Referral*	*This will be achieved by giving referral cards to satisfied clients*	*10 RFPs*
	Repeat Business		
	Referrals		
	Obtain Short List Status		
	RFP Development		
	Ask for RFP on Web Site		
	Web-Based RFPs		
	Sales Demonstration/Seminar		
	Networking/Trade Show Exhibition		
	Cold Calling		

Worksheet 2.1 This worksheet can help you track how you receive your RFPs and which sources are the best for obtaining RFPs.

Once you begin to track your RFP obtainment successes and failures, you may want to put more resources into the more productive methods and less effort into the others.

THE BOTTOM LINE

RFPs do not just drop from the sky or magically appear on your desk. It takes a tremendous amount of time and energy to obtain an RFP. A strategy must be put into place to ensure that your firm receives a steady flow of RFPs. Using the right mix of RFP obtainment methods and marketing strategies will add visibility and credibility to your firm. When e-learning firms are visible and highly respected, they receive many RFPs, which leads to many business opportunities.

This book has free materials available for download from the Web Added Value™ Resource Center at www.jrosspub.com.

3

REVIEWING THE RFP

INTRODUCTION

Once you have obtained an RFP, it must be reviewed so you can make a number of critical decisions, the first of which is "Do we respond?" This may seem like a silly question — of course we respond! However, it is not that simple.

First you must verify that the document is actually an RFP and not some other type of request. Second, you need to determine what the client is actually requesting. This can be more difficult than you think. Third, determine all of the requirements listed in the RFP. This is done with a Requirements Matrix. Then you need to determine the technical and instructional design requirements of the project. Once all of those determinations are made, then decide if your firm has the available resources to pursue the project and complete the work if you win the proposal (or decide to hurry up and hire people if you win). The hard part in all of this is that you usually have about a week to make all of those decisions and write the proposal.

TYPES OF REQUESTS

All documents received from potential clients are not RFPs. Two other, similar, types of requests will sometimes be circulated to e-learning companies. You should be somewhat wary of these types of requests because they do not typically result in business or income for you, even though they require resources and energy to respond. Understanding what other types of requests are available will help you distinguish an actual RFP from other, less productive, requests. This section describes the two types of requests that are not RFPs, the RFI and the RFQ, as well as a brief definition of an RFP.

RFI

The Request for Information (RFI) is a tactic used by an organization to learn as much as possible about e-learning solutions without paying for the consultation or information. The requesting organization may simply send out a document describing its current situation and ask vendors to outline a solution with no intention of actually implementing the solution in the near future. The requesting organization is simply "fact finding." While this endeavor may be of value to the organization issuing the RFI, it is of questionable value to the responding vendors.

The main reason is because the RFI rarely results in direct obtainment of an e-learning contract. In addition, many e-learning companies can actually generate revenue by conducting an analysis of an organization's e-learning needs and recommending a solution. When a vendor writes a response to an RFI, it is providing "free" consulting to the requesting organization, which is not the best use of time for the vendor organization and, as everyone knows, "you get what you pay for."

RFQ

The Request for a Quotation (RFQ) has a slightly higher chance than an RFI of resulting in business for the e-learning vendor. Typically when an organization issues an RFQ, it already has a vendor in mind and is just "shopping around" or, worse, attempting to bring the current vendor's price down.

The responding companies are usually not given the same level of detail about the problem as the "preferred" vendor, and do not have the informal or even formal relationships needed to secure the business. However, the requesting client may be required to receive a minimum of three bids to award the contract and therefore sends out the RFQs in hopes of getting either a lower price for the same work or satisfying internal procurement requirements. In either case, the chances of an RFQ resulting in a business opportunity are slim.

Sometimes RFQs are issued to determine the ballpark price range for an upcoming project. The responses to the RFQ may be providing a basis for a future funding request.

In rare cases, the RFQ may also be used when clients have a specific need and understand exactly what they want (i.e., a fully functional LCMS system to run on the Linux platform). In these cases, the client has scoped out the needs and is simply putting the requirement out for a bid.

RFP

The type of request you want to receive is the RFP. The RFP provides you with the highest chance of winning an actual contract. The RFP usually requests information concerning a project timeline, budget for the project, and the methodology for completing the tasks described in the RFP. Some RFPs are extremely detailed in terms of how the proposal should be structured. Some even specify the font and margin sizes, while others are vague and confusing. Still others ask for a project so far-fetched that the desired solution is not actually possible.

TYPICAL RFP FORMAT

RFPs vary in the quality and completeness of information. Some are well written and easy to follow and others are more like an unedited "mind dump." Regardless of the quality of the RFP, most contain four types of information:

1. Project information
2. Administrative information
3. Legal information
4. Appendix

Project information is what you need to know about the client, the project, and the learning environment. This section typically contains a brief background of the client and project, an audience description, delivery environment explanation, and a description of the technology infrastructure.

Administrative information describes the submission process, selection criteria, and required format as well as the due date for submission.

Legal information includes the copyright, licensing, confidentiality statements, and any other legal boilerplate information required by the client's procurement office.

The appendix may contain course samples, outlines, descriptions, and other information that may help the vendor make a more accurate bid on the project.

STATE OF MOST RFPS

Even though many RFPs contain much of the information listed above, many do not. A large number of RFPs are poorly written, unorganized, and contain a conglomeration of disjointed ideas. RFPs typically contain illogical statements, contradictory requirements, and even blatant mistakes. It is the task of the vendor to wade through the document and discern the wants and desires of the client from the actual needs. After the vendor interprets and understands the RFP, the job is to develop a response that satisfies the client within a reasonable time frame and budget.

Many times, business managers write RFPs with little understanding of the instructional design process, emerging technologies, or the underlying causes of performance problems. All the manager knows is that a problem must be solved and he or she assumes e-learning is the answer. From that point, the manager writes a problem statement and then tries to find a vendor who can help solve the problem.

Other times a committee is appointed to write a proposal. The committee is typically composed of a business manager, a person from the training department, and one or two people from the IT department who understand servers and networks. These individuals then compose portions of the RFP and send it to vendors. It is usually disjointed with no overarching theme or strategy holding the document together. There is no common agreement on what problem is actually being solved or what type of solution is needed.

These methods inevitably lead to confusion and frustration on the part of the vendor. If the client does not understand the problem or cannot articulate it appropriately, how can the vendor possibly expect to have a chance at writing a winning proposal? Yet, that is exactly the situation in which you will find yourself. You must wade through the information within the RFP and determine the appropriate response based on the document and any knowledge you may have about the client company or industry.

To respond appropriately, you must carefully analyze the RFP and address any mistakes and problems prior to attempting an answer. Commonly encountered RFP mistakes can be classified into several categories. Most likely, an RFP will suffer from multiple ailments, including:

- Poorly written
- Illogical
- Too little detail
- Unimaginative
- Poorly scoped
- Does not address a business need

An example of an RFP suffering from many aliments is shown in Example 3.1. This RFP was written for a needs assessment to determine the state of e-learning within the organization. As you can see, the vendors bidding on this RFP have their work cut out for them.

POORLY WRITTEN

RFPs are notorious for being poorly written. Often the client does not really understand what is being requested. This unclear understanding is reflected in the writing. Other times, the client is busy and does not have time to devote to a well-crafted document.

You must be prepared to read and reread the proposal many times, working through the poor writing. Since the RFP writing process is usually not a priority

Scope is very large.

Poor grammar.

These people are busy.

Should that be "instructor-led" delivery?

Long development cycle for their courses.

Could be an internal conflict between training department and management.

Involves needs analysis, Web-based instruction, personnel development. These guys want a little of everything.

What OSHA topics?

Is this timeline for real?

Request for Proposal

Scope—The current processes and practices used by the Client Training Group

Background

The Client Training Group is an organization within a larger company that is dedicated to improving performance by facilitating the development of individual skills and knowledge. Our internal clients are people in department's responsible for the interface with clients and the maintenance of client accounts. We provide training in call management, client contact software, client service, and compliant resolution. Approximately 90% of the training we deliver are classroom/lab lecture and hands-on practice. The remaining 10% is through independent learning and web-based training.

We have one full-time instructor and a consultant (approximately 1200 hours/year) dedicated to WBT, video tape development, and graphics support. Within the past week we added a Training Developer/Analyst to the staff whose responsibilities are divided 50% to gathering and reporting on training performance data and 50% to WBT after he learns the software required to develop WBT.

The Client Training Group has worked with WBT for approximately four years producing 2 model courses in call management in the first year and within the past 2 years developed modules to train client service representatives in complaint resolution. These modules are designed for instructor-lead delivery. We have received a commitment from our Client Service Group to develop approximately 50 more WBT modules. We also have approximately 20 OSHA safety topics we'd like to place into WBT for the technical folks at our company.

The 2 people currently working on the WBT development are self-taught. They purchase software and learn how to use it by reading the manufacturers manual. The new Developer/Analyst has a background in using EXCEL, ACCESS and MS WORD but must learn software associated with WBT development. Hardware used by the 2 experienced developers is MacIntosh. The Company uses PC hardware.

Deliverables

1. A report on the current status of The Client Training Group's WBT processes, procedures, hardware, standards, software, and staffing with recommendations on changes required meeting industry standards for the development of WBT.

2. Instruct 1 person on the use of software that should be used to develop effective WBT.

3. Develop two WBT modules on OSHA safety topics and placed on the company's Intranet for access by intended users.

Project Timeline

Project should begin no later than one month from date of contract award. All deliverables are to be completed on or before three months from the award of the contract

Private and Confidential 1 of 1

Example 3.1 A poorly written RFP.

of the client, not much time is spent on writing or editing the RFP. This means the RFP will most likely contain typographical errors, wrong word usage, and incorrect grammar.

In spite of the mistakes, this is not the time to edit the document and assign a failing grade. You must work with the poor state of the document. You must remember that poor writing does not mean the client is "stupid," "uniformed," or "uncaring" about the problem. Do not let the first impression of the RFP create a lasting impression of the client. Often the RFP response team will "demonize" the client because of the poorly written RFP. This attitude will appear unconsciously in the finished proposal as a condescending, didactic tone or a style that is too simplistic and unsophisticated.

Realize that poor writing is an element of RFPs that cannot be avoided. Overlook the poor writing and focus on the meaning. Focusing on the meaning instead of the words will keep the response team focused on a solution to the problem instead of wanting to tear up the RFP and throw it away.

ILLOGICAL

Not only does poor writing make it hard to focus on the needs of the client, but illogical statements and assumptions make interpretation of the RFP difficult as well. Clients do not really know what they need. If they did, they would not issue an RFP; they would issue a detailed RFQ.

Illogical RFPs result from the fact that many clients are not familiar with the nuances of e-learning. The clients have heard about e-learning and think they know what is needed, but they do not have a clear picture of how everything fits together. Since the picture is not clear, critical elements in the explanation of what they want are sometimes omitted or poorly articulated. Other times, clients misunderstand the elements of an e-learning solution and make requests based on that misunderstanding.

For example, the client may describe an LMS but use the term "Knowledge Management System (KMS)" throughout the document. Or the RFP may begin with an emphatic statement that an LCMS is absolutely required to solve the client's learning management issues, while further reading of the document indicates there is no real need for content management within the organization. You may learn that the only information that needs to be tracked is employee registration for online classes. In that case, a full-blown LCMS may not be the solution.

Clients also make assumptions about e-learning that are not written in the RFP. These assumptions result in seemingly illogical requests. As an example, the client may assume that it is easy to insert a course that you write into the proprietary, nonstandard LMS that the client's firm already owns. The client may not even realize the difficulties inherent in attempting to get the propriety LMS to exchange data with a course you develop.

In addition, the client may assume that the potential vendors are experts in e-learning and, therefore, do not need a detailed description of the problem. This leads to large information gaps throughout the document and confusion about the exact nature of the problem described in the RFP.

All of these factors contribute to illogical RFPs. The reactions of reading an illogical RFP run from "why would they want to do that" to "they want everything and the kitchen sink." Even though the request may not make much sense, it probably does have logical underpinnings somewhere. The goal of the RFP response team is to carefully read the document to understand what seems, on the surface, illogical.

While reading the RFP, make note of any items that seem illogical or that contradict one another. Seeking further explanation of these items from the client provides you with the opportunity to speak to the client and to better understand the problem. Sometimes you can resolve these items with a phone call, and other times you will have to submit the questions in writing and wait for a written response. Other times you will have to wait until the bidder's conference. Often the client does not realize the illogical assumptions in the document, and will be glad to clarify them. Other times, the client will not see the illogical nature of the request and will not be able to add any insight to the problem.

You must be careful in your response to illogical requests when you write your proposal. Address the stated need of the client but lead the client in a more appropriate direction. You may want to indicate that your experience in the field of e-learning is leading you to suggest a more effective alternative. If you can do it persuasively and with some tact, you can usually convince the client that the initial request was, indeed, illogical.

PROVIDING TOO LITTLE DETAIL

Vague, unclear RFPs are rampant within the e-learning industry because the writers of RFPs do not understand what it takes to develop e-learning. For example, many clients think that converting an instructor-led course with electronic slides is simply a matter of saving the material in HTML and adding a few interactive questions. Many clients do not grasp the complex nature of instructional design. They do not understand how using instructional strategies makes e-learning more effective. This lack of understanding leads to gaps and vagueness in the RFP.

Other times, the training department is writing the request and does not have any knowledge of information systems requirements. Sometimes the client feels that revealing too much information would cause a competitive disadvantage and therefore information is purposely withheld.

Whatever the reason, few RFPs contain an adequate level of detail. When reading the RFP, make note of the areas that lack detail, are too vague, or require more explanation. Once these areas are noted, you can address them in the bidder's conference or through some other means. Gently making a client aware of a lack of details helps the client to see your firm as experienced and knowledgeable in the field of e-learning.

UNIMAGINATIVE

Clients do not purposely request boring or unimaginative approaches to their e-learning needs; they simply do not know what is possible. For example, a client may not understand the power of dynamic Web pages for instruction and, therefore, request static Web pages. In these cases, you need to educate the client.

In other cases, an unimaginative approach may be just what is needed. Just because an approach does not involve a great deal of creativity or flashy animation does not mean the approach is bad. Too often, e-learning vendors get caught up in the flash and technology of their solutions and fail to realize that good e-learning does not require pizzazz.

In addition, an RFP that is unimaginative to you might be highly imaginative to the client. It may even be innovative and a bit "far out" for that client. Because it may be hard to tell if the RFP is imaginative or conservative from the client's perspective, be careful how you address the client's request.

The danger with RFPs that seem unimaginative is that you may unconsciously convey the fact that you think the RFP and resulting solution are boring and unexciting. If this "attitude" appears in the written proposal through the use of language, tone, or style, the client will approach the proposal from the standpoint that it is unimaginative and may reject it.

No matter how boring the RFP may seem, the resulting proposal must be enthusiastic and energetic. Clients want to feel that their solution is special. The RFP response team must take extra care to write a solid, exciting proposal when the RFP seems boring.

The flip side of this problem is that the client may get too imaginative and ask for a solution that cannot be accomplished, is too expensive, or will not run over the 56K modems its sales force has in the field. One client wanted full motion video to run over the company's intranet but did not have the internal bandwidth to run the video-based training and mission critical business applications at the same time. In these types of cases, the vendor must take great care to explain why some portions of the requested solution are not possible or not feasible given the current situation.

POORLY SCOPED

A poorly scoped RFP is one in which the actual need of the client is larger or smaller than what is being suggested in the RFP. For example, the client "needs" an LCMS but is describing the need for an intranet with a couple of e-learning courses. Or the client needs asynchronous e-learning courses but is describing synchronous courses. Or the client thinks it will take only two months to convert 800 hours of classroom instruction into a Web-based, fully interactive, simulation-based curriculum.

Since most clients have not previously undertaken an e-learning design and development project, they are unaware of the scope of the project. They do not have a good idea of the amount of time it takes or the amount of resources they will be required to marshal for the project. Clients may indicate assumptions within the RFP that may be incorrect or grossly underestimated. As the vendor, you must see through those assumptions and not become tied to unrealistic demands. One of the biggest areas in which this occurs is the project timeline.

Clients want an elaborate, extensive e-learning management system complete with 50 courses designed, developed, and delivered within one month. Here is an example of an actual client conversation with an e-learning vendor.

> **Client:** *So how long will it take to get this curriculum online? I want it 100% online.*
>
> **Vendor:** *This is a radical change and you need to think about the audiences' needs/profiles to see if this is the best method for them. Are you asking that the entire curriculum be converted to WBT?*
>
> **Client:** *Yes. I want it all online. How long will that take?*
>
> **Vendor:** *Well, if this is the approach you want to pursue, we need to redesign the materials completely and add additional instructional strategies. The ratio is about 100 hours to 1 hour of delivery. You've got 24 hours of delivery. It will take a few months.*
>
> **Client:** *What? Can't you just scan it all in? I thought you could just scan it into the computer. That shouldn't take too long.*

Clients do not always understand the effort needed to develop e-learning solutions. As the vendor, you must determine if the client has a realistic expectation, and you must see if the expectation matches the actual scope described in the RFP.

The first step is to determine from the RFP if the scope is large, medium, or small. Unfortunately, even determining the scope of the project is not always easy. The RFP may contain various paragraphs or sentences in different parts of the document that suggest drastically different project scopes.

Once the project scope is determined, the next step is to ascertain the client's perception of the project. How big does the client think the project is? Is the client's perception correct? Does the client perceive this small project as having a large scope? Or does the client see the large project as having a small scope (more likely)? Is this project one of several projects occurring simultaneously for the client? Is this one of many future projects? Are you requested to build an e-learning framework or just one or two courses? How stable is the content to be placed online?

Once you determine the actual scope of the project and the client's perception of the scope, you can make a better judgment of how to respond to the RFP. You can decide to stay within the client's perceived scope, or you can attempt to help the client understand that the scope of the project is larger or smaller than what was requested. The important aspect is that you, the vendor, understand the scope of the project and the client's scope perception prior to writing the proposal.

DOES NOT ADDRESS A BUSINESS NEED

This is a dangerous type of a mistake in the RFP. In fact, everything else could be perfect in the RFP (well written, logical descriptions, proper amount of detail, imaginative, proper scope), but if the underlying need for the project is not tied to the business needs driving the company, problems can arise. Funding may be discontinued, resources may be reallocated, and Subject Matter Experts (SMEs) may not be given enough time to assist with the development process. If you win this proposal and begin work, there is no assurance that the client will fund it to the end, or that the project will even get started once a vendor is chosen or that it will be used once it is delivered to the client.

You need to carefully read the RFP to see if the business need can be determined. Sometimes the need is obvious and is stated by the client. Other times the need is more obscure and harder to ascertain. Business needs usually revolve around saving money or time. You need to look through the RFP to find the business need.

If one of these needs can be located within the RFP, an actual business need is being addressed. If a need cannot be located, you should take measures to determine the need. You can either enter into conversations with the client or ask questions during the Bidder's Conference.

One note of caution: just because a business need is not obvious does not mean one does not exist. You must not assume you know everything about the client's business or industry. Also do not assume that all proposals are written to address a specific need. Some RFPs are written to see if a particular approach is feasible, and the client wants you, the vendor, to do the research to determine if a specific product should be launched or developed.

Sometimes a vendor will think a certain RFP does not make sense or will lose money from the client's business perspective. The decision to pursue the business must then be made. However, you must consider the fact that if you do not pursue the work, some other e-learning vendor will. You must balance the decision to write a proposal based on the potential success of the project, the business need driving the project, and how much your company needs or wants this work.

■ ■ ■

CREATING AND RESPONDING TO THE ACTIVE RFP

Clayton Ajello, Founder, and Louis Biggie, Managing Director for Technology, Research and Development and Co-founder, Accelera

The traditional view of learning has been that it is an expense that companies and organizations must bear as part of the cost of doing business. Forward-thinking executives are beginning to understand that this industrial age thinking is inappropriate in the knowledge economy, in which learning is perceived not as an expense, but as an investment, in the same way as the captains of the industrial age procured new machines to improve productivity and profitability. For this reason, more and more companies are employing a chief learning officer at an executive level. This individual is accountable in the boardroom, and success of the learning system he or she deploys depends not on the volume of enrollment, but on improved organizational performance that can be demonstrated in measurable terms. Simply stated, a positive return on learning investment spells success, and a negative return indicates failure.

The chief learning officer generally oversees design, development, and implementation of the corporate learning system, including specific e-learning initiatives, and is the one ultimately held accountable for its success. Whether specific e-learning resources are developed in-house or procured through outsourcing, a thorough analysis, particularly of the business objectives leading to improved organizational performance, has to be accomplished. If an identified e-learning project is outsourced, this analysis becomes the basis for the RFP. If the analysis is absent, the chances of a successful project are greatly diminished.

In a corresponding manner, just as the successful e-learning project is dependent upon a thorough analysis (the findings of which are reflected in the specifications for the subsequent e-learning resources), the successful proposal is dependent upon the vendor taking the time to evaluate the RFP before responding. Critical review of the RFP by a vendor will help the vendor gauge when it has all information needed to respond immediately, when it needs to discover more about the client's needs and business objectives, or when it may be prudent not to respond at all. Without this assessment, projects are doomed to be unmanageable from the beginning and will ultimately lose money for the vendor and will fail to accomplish the business objectives of the client.

To illustrate this point, most readers will have attended technical conferences that range from excellent to abysmal. The difference between the best and the worst is usually rooted in how the conference was organized. A conference that begins with a vague call for papers with little or no direction usually becomes "shapeless." Presentations are repetitive, contradictory, and vary in quality, and the conference does not seem to focus its attendees on the important issues. By contrast, the memorable conference begins with a proactive effort to create conference themes. The organizers then ask specific thought leaders to respond to those themes. The result is an experience in which attendees perceive that the conference is focused around specific and important issues, and that they have had an opportunity to shape current thinking in that area. The same kind of proactive series of activities is needed to create the RFP: the effort and thought that go into a winning proposal can only be as successful as the catalyst, the RFP. This success chain culminates in winning projects that further the business objectives of the client and the profitability of the successful bidder. Furthermore, superior RFPs attract the attention of the best vendors, which in turn increases the chances of success of the project.

The active RFP guides the procurement process, whereas the passive RFP forces vendors to define the learning experience (or guess at it). Passive RFPs create a reactive situation where the procurer of e-learning has to choose among the proverbial apples and oranges. Vendors are ill-positioned to respond to business objectives if they have never been articulated. At best, the client is forced to choose the vendor that has made the best guess regarding client needs. At worst, the selection is based on arbitrary issues that have nothing to do with the original purpose of the learning initiative.

Thorough thinking and precise definition of goals and objectives are at the heart of the active RFP. Although proprietary issues may preclude a client from communicating every detail of the business objectives, if these decisions have not been made, the client lacks a valid framework to evaluate proposals when they arrive. Effective corporate leadership involves defining and setting goals and objectives, creating "buy in," and communicating these goals and objectives to those responsible for their execution. Employees who do not understand the goals and objectives of management often under-perform at best, and at worst operate in a way that is actually contrary to the interests of the company and its employees. The effects of not communicating to a vendor can be just as devastating. Accordingly, the business objectives of any organization must be expressed in broad terms in an RFP.

At this stage, it is useful to reexamine the notion of analysis, to distinguish between two types of analysis, and to identify those parts of analysis that are best performed by the client before the RFP is written. The ADDIE (Analysis, Design, Development, Implementation, and Evaluation) model is accepted as a successful process model for e-learning. An essential ingredient of the active RFP involves performing a thorough analysis that goes beyond the traditional view of analysis that is usually understood to be part of the ADDIE model. Typically, analysis is considered in terms of learner-centered characteristics, including audience analysis (who, what, when, where). The active RFP is founded upon analysis of business and organizational performance. For the purposes of abbreviation, the former will be called the hows and the latter the whys. If analysis of business objectives is not thoroughly performed, success or failure of the project becomes purely subjective, and a positive return on investment (ROI) is impossible to measure and very difficult to achieve.

Although most vendors view the analysis as part of the job of creating a successful e-learning project, the active RFP transfers much of this task from the vendor to the client before the RFP is ever written. In addition, the scope of the analysis is much broader than most vendors can reasonably be expected to perform. The chief learning officer of a company typically has responsibility not simply for the hows of e-learning but also for the whys. A vendor, particularly one submitting a proposal to an organization for the first time, simply does not have enough information to understand, formulate, and articulate the whys. Furthermore, in many cases the client is better equipped to define many of the hows, and these need to be in the RFP. The whys describe the business case; the hows describe how to accomplish that business through e-learning. The why issues must be defined by the client and included in the RFP to the extent that this does not disclose proprietary information. The how issues may be performed either by the vendor as part of the project or by the client before the RFP is released, but often it is simply more efficient for the client to perform this analysis and present it as part of the RFP.

The following issues can serve as a checklist to help a vendor analyze an RFP before preparing a response. Presented in order of high level to low level (moving from the whys to the hows), they better enable a vendor to ascertain the nature and scope of the task. If these issues are not reflected in the RFP, all is not lost because frequently they can be resolved through further discovery (and relationship building) with the client. Often, a Bidder's Conference or a defined question period provides a useful opportunity to gain this information. Vendors should be aware, however, that information gained through these opportunities is usually shared with all competing vendors.

- Analysis of general business objectives
  - ☐ What is the nature of the company?
  - ☐ What are the broad aims, goals, and objectives of the company?
  - ☐ What is the business model?
- Analysis of the purpose of the learning program
  - ☐ How does the learning initiative relate to the business model?
  - ☐ What problem does the learning initiative aim to solve?
  - ☐ Can the problem be solved through learning?

- ☐ Is the goal to communicate information or improve skills?
- ☐ Will the program impact organizational performance?
- ☐ Are there regulatory, legal, or compliance considerations?
- ☐ Have attempts to solve the problem already been made? (What happened?)
- ☐ Is the organization seriously committed to this initiative?

- ROI issues
  - ☐ What would be the consequences of not executing the learning initiative?
  - ☐ What are the expected benefits of executing the learning initiative?
  - ☐ Is the purpose of the learning initiative to save money or otherwise improve performance?
  - ☐ How will the ROI be measured?

- Analysis of project risk
  - ☐ What is the scope of the project?
  - ☐ Are the expectations of the client clearly defined?
  - ☐ Has the client articulated desired product complexity with respect to levels of interactivity, multimedia, and graphic intensity?
  - ☐ What is the client's experience with e-learning?
  - ☐ Is the e-learning platform or environment established and tested?
  - ☐ What mechanisms are in place to manage project risk?
  - ☐ What processes can be accommodated if the scope changes?

- Approach to learning
  - ☐ What is the desired approach to learning?
  - ☐ How will this program be used (alone or as part of a blended solution)?
  - ☐ How will mastery be measured?
  - ☐ How will knowledge and skills be maintained?

- Learning environment
  - ☐ What is the delivery format (Web, CD-ROM, DVD, etc.)?
  - ☐ What connectivity is available to end users?
  - ☐ Will an LMS/LCMS be used?
  - ☐ Is the desired technology compatible with in-house IT standards and rules?
  - ☐ What student records need to be kept?
  - ☐ Will student records be audited?
  - ☐ What is the nature of the client's technology infrastructure?
  - ☐ Will the learning system be hosted on in-house or outsourced servers?
  - ☐ What firewall issues must be considered to ensure smooth running of the program?

- □ What are the specifications of computers to be used to access the learning program?

- ■ Standards
  - □ What standards need to be employed for compatibility with the LMS/LCMS (SCORM™/AICC)?
  - □ Does the program need to serve the needs of users with disabilities (Section 508)?
- ■ Audience analysis
  - □ What is the relevance of the required learning to the employee's position?
  - □ How is learning currently achieved for the knowledge, skills, and behavior changes sought?
  - □ What is the general profile of the intended audience?
    - ■ Age
    - ■ Sex
    - ■ Educational level
    - ■ Reading level
    - ■ Ethnic background
    - ■ Interests
    - ■ Learning styles
    - ■ Language spoken
    - ■ Comfort using computers
    - ■ Experience and acceptance of e-learning
- ■ Content analysis
  - □ What needs to be taught to achieve the overall objectives of the program?
  - □ Will the vendor supply an SME for the project?
  - □ Who will provide final content approval?
  - □ What is the format of the content?
  - □ How will the content be delivered to the vendor?
  - □ How mature is the content?
  - □ Is the content subject to frequent change?
- ■ Media analysis
  - □ What materials exist to support the learning program?
  - □ What is the format of these existing materials?
  - □ What media are desired in the learning program (3D graphics, 2D graphics, animations, sound effects, voice, etc.)?
- ■ Aesthetic analysis
  - □ What are the expectations surrounding "look and feel"?

- □ What are the issues surrounding branding (logos, colors, fonts, etc.)?
- □ Are there other materials or publications that will influence the aesthetics of the learning program (brochures, Web sites, etc.)?
- □ What kind of styles appeal to the audience?

Another important element of the well-reasoned RFP is a statement regarding desired format, length, outline, and content of the proposal. This allows clients to ascertain a vendor's responsiveness and ensures that proposals are easy to compare. Finally, a scoring scheme can provide an additional level of objectivity, but is not always communicated to vendors that may be tempted to provide only superficial coverage to an element that is "only worth five points." Where a scoring system is provided, it can be a valuable guide to the vendor to explain the ordering of the magnitude of importance of each proposal element within a larger framework.

Thinking out all of these issues benefits both clients and vendors. Clients benefit because it streamlines the procurement process. Vendors benefit because it enables them to understand the needs of their clients more precisely. Active RFPs that define all of these needs and constraints result in better proposals and projects that systematically respond to real business objectives.

■ ■ ■

TAKING ADVANTAGE OF THE MISTAKES

RFPs are typically not well-written masterpieces clearly articulating a pressing business need. They usually contain inconsistencies, vague desires, and unclear statements of direction. Overworked, highly stressed individuals looking for a quick, easy, inexpensive solution write them. Some RFPs are more like a "stream of consciousness" essay than business writing. However, as a vendor you are responsible for deciphering the RFP and developing a well-written proposal. In fact, hurried business managers and executives appreciate vendor firms that can decipher their e-learning musings and deliver clear, effective proposals.

While RFPs often have many structural and clarification issues, these should not be viewed as problems, but as opportunities. Every unclear or vague item in the RFP allows you an opportunity to enter into an additional dialogue with the client. Do not belittle a client for a poor RFP; instead, look at it as an opportunity to help someone who desperately needs assistance.

A free and open exchange of information with the potential client provides you with the best opportunity for better understanding the client's needs. It also allows the client to gain an appreciation of your attention to detail and your willingness to understand the client's specific needs.

The more you understand and can address the needs of the client, the higher your probability of winning the work. Remember that the client is not an "idiot" or an "ignorant fool" just because the RFP is not perfect. If the client knew everything about e-learning and e-learning projects, he or she would not be asking for assistance.

WHAT TO DO WITH THE RFP

You have looked through the RFP, you think you understand what is being requested, and you have decided to respond. Now what? Now you must glean key information and begin to formulate your solution and written proposal. The first step in this process is to locate and identify critical information within the RFP. This information will be used to determine your proposal development time frame and your strategy for formulating a response. It will also alert you to areas of the proposal that need clarification through the Bidder's Conference or personal correspondence with the client representative.

GLEAN CRITICAL RFP INFORMATION

The first step in gleaning information from the RFP is to be organized and keep all of the information concerning the response in one place. Place the RFP into a three-ring binder or create an electronic file that all of the response team can access. Placing the RFP in a central location allows it to be easily referenced, and allows other documents to be inserted into the binder or added to the electronic folder as the proposal is being developed. Placing the RFP physically into a binder allows easy marking of critical pages, paragraphs, or phrases with a highlighter or self-adhesive notes. Placing the RFP into an electronic folder allows the team to mark it with annotations and online highlights as needed. In fact, many word processing software packages have the ability to track document changes and revisions. This feature is especially useful when a team is geographically scattered.

The next step in gleaning critical information is to read the RFP at least three times. The first time is to get an overall "feel" of the request. The second is to determine key criteria requirements. You want to identify the major client issues driving the RFP. This information is placed in the *Basic Proposal Requirements Worksheet* (Worksheet 3.1). The third time you read the RFP is to identify requirements on a page-by-page, line-by-line, word-by-word basis. This third reading will be discussed in depth in Chapter 4.

Experienced professionals know that information critical to writing a winning proposal is usually scattered throughout many sections of the RFP. The following areas should be completed on the Basic Proposal Requirements Worksheet.

Basic Proposal Requirements Worksheet

Complete this worksheet based on the information in the RFP. If certain information is not available from the RFP, call the client for the requirement information. This information will assist you with the administration of the proposal writing process.

Name of Company Submitting RFP: ______________________________

RFP Reference Number (if applicable): ______________________________

RFP Contact Person: ____________________ Title: ____________________

Fax Number: ( ) - ____________ Phone Number: ( ) - ____________
E-mail: ____________________

Land Mail Address: ______________________________

Two-sentence description of problem: ______________________________

____

____

Proposal Due Date: ___/___/___ Award Decision Date: ___/___/___
Project Completion Date: ___/___/___

Proposal Delivery to Client: (circle one):
E-mail Overnight Mail Posted Marked Mail Hand Delivered

Notification of Win: ______________________________

Format Requirements: Font: ____________ Spacing: ____________

Submission Format: ____________ Page Count: ____________

Major Proposal Sections Required: ______________________________

____

Evaluation Criteria: ______________________________

____

Worksheet 3.1 This worksheet can help you to identify the basic requirements necessary for your written proposal.

Name of company submitting RFP — This is simple information. What company is submitting the RFP? It can become a little more complicated if the company is actually a subdivision of another company or part of a holding company. Knowing the exact nature of the company submitting the RFP helps determine the needs of the company and the response strategy.

RFP reference number — Some RFPs have a preassigned reference number. This number should be on the proposal submitted in response to the RFP. Make sure you record this number if it exists. Mostly they are found on government RFPs, but occasionally they can be found on commercial e-learning RFPs.

Contact person — This is the person at the client company responsible for answering questions concerning the RFP. The contact person might be the client's project manager or person overseeing the e-learning project, or it might be the procurement officer or even an external consultant. Look for land mail and an e-mail address as well as phone and fax numbers.

Two-sentence description of the problem — Providing an elegant solution begins with framing the problem simply and effectively. One method of helping everyone to understand a particular RFP is to boil down the essence of the RFP into its simplest terms. What does the client need? Writing the need in two sentences allows everyone to see the problem. Determining the exact nature of the problem and separating client needs from wants will be discussed in Chapter 4.

Proposal due date — This is the exact date and hour at which the proposal must be delivered to the requesting organization. This date is extremely important. In some cases, turning in the proposal even one minute after the requested hour is cause for disqualification. This deadline is sometimes referred to as the "closing date," "proposal date," "proposal deadline," or "submission date." Also, look for postmark requirements. Some RFPs still require a postmark by a particular date if they are mailed to the client.

Award decision date — This is the date the client will make the decision on the proposal. This date should be used to follow up with the client if you are not notified of the client's decision.

Project completion date — The RFP usually provides a date by which all of the work on the e-learning project must be completed. This date determines the deliverable timeline. It also indicates how much time is available for completion of the project. It may be stated as a date or as a number of months.

Proposal delivery to client — This describes how the client will accept the proposal. Does the client want it sent overnight? Does it need to be hand delivered? Is a fax acceptable? Is a paper copy required? How many paper copies must be submitted? Should the proposal be delivered in a sealed envelope (to protect against tampering)? Does the client want it electronically? If electronic submission is requested, what file formats are acceptable [1]? Can it be sent via e-mail or is a disk required?

Notification of win — This is a listing of how the proposal applicants will be notified of a win or a loss. Will the client representative call or e-mail the notification? This is important because sometimes the manager issuing the RFP will assume that procurement will notify the vendor of the win, and procurement assumes that the manager will notify the vendor. In the meantime, the client wonders why the winning vendor has not contacted him or her. This lets the response team know what to look for after the award decision date.

Format requirements — This is the format of the proposal. Many RFPs describe what sections are expected to be in the proposal (instructional strategies, technical recommendations, vendor company history, resumes of project team, etc.). Some RFPs include spacing and formatting requirements for the document as well as specifying a maximum page limit. Some RFPs provide a sample table of contents for the proposal, and some even include a template for the price proposal. Others require a specific number scheme for each section. This is where you write the required sections of the proposals and the numbering system if provided by the client.

Evaluation criteria — Indicates which part(s) of the proposal will be most critically evaluated. Typically price is one of the major evaluation factors, but other factors such as time to implement and innovativeness of the solution can also factor into the final decision. It is important to know how the RFP will be evaluated because that will dictate what portions of the proposal will require the most attention. Evaluation criteria are not always provided but usually consist of items such as:

- Understanding of the problem
- Feasibility of proposed schedule
- Price of solution
- Clarity of solution
- Organization of solution
- Creativity
- Similar projects
- Inclusion of all requested information
- Company experience

Here is a sample description of RFP criteria.

> *Vendor selection will be based on OilCo's assessment of four aspects of your submission:*
>
> **Product:** *Appropriateness to the need and our business and technical environments; appearance of your prototype; and innovative elements of your proposed solution.*

Project: *Quality of the people you would assign (as judged by resumes and direct contact, if any); your experience with similar projects as judged by evaluation of demonstrations and conversation with references; how you propose to handle shifts in project scope or timelines; integrity; availability of resources needed to complete the project in a timely manner; instructional design and development strategy; project management strategy; quality assurance process; and technical savvy.*

Time and cost: *They must be appropriate and reasonable.*

Proposal: *We will be looking at your organization, clarity, and brevity. Do not repeat or paraphrase our RFP. Be brief and to the point. Spare us your "boilerplate" except as appendices (e.g., company background).*

These elements are the most basic parts of the RFP you need to understand and track. You may be surprised to learn how many late proposals are submitted because the vendor misread the due date or failed to let the entire team know of a time constraint. The Basic Proposal Requirements Worksheet helps the proposal development team track the basic client requirements and ensures that all team members have an understanding of the key RFP information.

■ ■ ■

SEVEN THINGS VENDORS WISH CLIENTS WOULD PUT IN THEIR E-LEARNING RFPS

Dr. Ronald W. Berman, Vice President of Education, Interwise

INTRODUCTION

Many organizations generate an e-learning RFP for one of two reasons: One, get the price. Two, get the price with knowledge of every known product function.

Price, the most common and obvious theme, is highlighted both in importance and in visibility throughout the entire RFP process. Rarely, if ever, do the RFP authors discuss, mention, or even introduce the more important topic of actually solving the client's e-learning problem.

E-learning vendors are generally good businesspeople who understand that satisfied clients generate great references and produce significant follow-up business. Many RFP authors generate strict response guidelines often prohibiting or limiting direct communication to the institution's requesting department and prohibiting even the slightest deviation from the prescribed response format. With limited and restricted access to client personnel, vendors often miss the opportunity to understand, comment on, and ultimately determine the applicability of their own product solution to the client's needs.

The e-learning RFP should ideally be used to document the value of a vendor's solution to solve the client's business problem. Whether the technology is used for academic credit or for continuing education, there are real costs associated with its implementation and there are real benefits. The challenge the RFP authors have is to compare different technologies to determine which might offer the best solution. In most instances, this activity evolves into the creation of an elaborate product comparison spreadsheet showing every feature for every product. While this is not a bad beginning, it is often the only comparison that is done. As the questions are typically vague, the comparison is less than meaningful:

1. Does your product have two-way audio?
2. Does your white board support multiple colors?
3. Does your product automatically record live sessions?
4. Does your product support AOL users?

Vague questions produce vague answers. It should be obvious that a better approach is needed to guide product vendors to describe with greater clarity the value of their product technology and in a larger sense their ability to solve the client's e-learning problem. RFP authors need to facilitate this discussion by broadening the set of questions beyond product specifications to include the following categories: (1) course content description, (2) audience definition, (3) technical support, (4) estimate of the number of e-learning users, (5) acquisition alternatives, (6) system integration, and (7) operational cost.

CONTENT TO BE TAUGHT (WHAT)

It all starts here. What you plan to teach drives development time and cost. Without this information, a vendor cannot accurately determine how its unique technology can be best employed. For example, authoring high-quality medical content requires effortless incorporation of photographs, x-rays, video, and other high-resolution graphics. On the other hand, authoring computer science course content requires a real-time, easy-to-use technology to transmit an image of the instructor's display (and any computer application) to every remote student. Finally, the creation of management-related course content necessitates the ability to easily create thought-provoking flash animations to generate interest and to facilitate discussion. As noted above, each audience requires different types of learning materials which are best optimized by different technologies. RFP authors should describe the content and include examples of their learning materials within the RFP.

AUDIENCE (WHO)

With the content defined, next comes the audience. This is important to the vendor as different user populations may have specific and sometimes rather unique requirements (which cannot always be easily addressed by the vendor's product architecture). Knowledge of the content alone is not sufficient information as different audiences may have different learning needs. For example, the developing visual perception of younger students often requires the e-learning system to display words with large typefaces. Engineers and software designers frequently need to browse full-page images of technical manuals and require their e-learning system to display text using small fonts.

Students pursing an online degree will have different needs in terms of navigating through course materials (notes, instructor notes, homework assignments, and faculty office hours). In this instance, the e-learning system must have an easy-to-use, customizable user interface. Finally, with the audience defined, it is equally important to articulate where the audiences are located. This information may help some vendors reduce implementation cost by optimizing existing communications bandwidth.

TECHNICAL SUPPORT (HELP)

Users will always have questions. Whether the audience is defined to include business executives, teachers, consultants, high school graduates, or even elementary school students, they all need to ask questions. It is amazing how many RFPs do not access the vendor's ability and desire to provide initial customer support, which has the potential, depending upon the architecture, to significantly drive operational cost. Therefore, it is imperative to quantify this during the RFP process to reduce the likelihood of misunderstandings and to ensure that the support costs are included in the overall project plan.

USAGE/GROWTH/SCALABILITY (HOW MANY)

The number of students using the e-learning solution directly affects aggregate project costs because it influences staffing, computer resources, support, curriculum development, faculty development, compensation, and marketing. No other category is as important and yet is so frequently misstated and miscalculated. Many RFP authors have great difficulty in establishing initial and follow-up project size. In some instances, they actually omit their estimate of the number of students who will be using the system during its first year of operation. Starting with an uncertain initial user estimate, they then frequently employ broad wishful thinking growth estimates exceeding 50% per year. The combination of an uncertain initial user population plus the effect of unsubstantiated growth makes the vendor response extraordinarily problematic.

It is true that growth will occur and that usage will increase. It is therefore important to provide realistic estimates for a two-year period. In today's economic and technologically changing environment, forecasting beyond two years is often difficult with the results being unreliable. Since the time frame is two years, the RFP authors should consider developing some form of ROI formula to cross-reference the cost over two years with the anticipated benefits. ROI examples might include: reducing the cost of electronic communications, increasing marketing activities, improving student academic achievement, accelerating research initiatives through enhanced communications, reducing training cost, or providing education to home-bound students.

ACQUISITION ALTERNATIVES (HOW MUCH)

Price is important. It is often one of the final determining factors in making the client's product acquisition decision. However, to get the best price, you sometimes do not have to purchase the product; you can rent it! For example, the purchase price of a 1000-concurrent-user e-learning software product might be $1,000,000, yet the yearly rental charge based on a two-year lease for this product might be less than $150,000 per year. Reducing the two-year expenditure by $700,000 greatly improves the client's e-learning ROI.

It is not surprising that technology is constantly bringing to life new products, services, and companies. Having said this, be cautious when purchasing software and making long-term commitments which might preclude your institution from taking advantage of the next leap in e-learning technology (whatever that might be). To gain maximum flexibility, be sure to request alternative acquisition models in the RFP.

INTEGRATION (CONNECTION TO)

With the product specifications defined and with pricing established, most RFP authors conclude that their job is done. Integration of the e-learning product into existing company processes is a must and may be time consuming, technologically challenging, and expensive. Failure to define and consider this effort can doom the initiative to failure.

Successful companies integrate and share data to either gain a competitive advantage or to maintain detailed historical records, as mandated by law. The e-learning project will not exist in isolation. It never does. Therefore, it is imperative that the RFP authors review the product's capability to interface with other systems. The RFP authors should, at a minimum, define how students will enroll in class sessions, what data must be captured and stored for each student, and how students will be charged for and billed for attending class sessions (either by cost allocation or by actual monetary reimbursement).

OPERATIONAL COST SAVINGS ($$)

After selecting, acquiring, and installing the e-learning product, you are finally ready to succeed. The instructors have been trained, the curriculum has been developed, and students are enrolled. Now all you have to do is operate the system.

To your surprise, this sometimes turns out to be a much more difficult and time-consuming feat than anticipated. The RFP authors often assume that every system is operationally similar and easy to run because they view the most simplistic tasks that often only include adding and removing courses. They rarely, if ever, examine the operational requirements to run a fully deployed e-learning system in support of a large community of users. They fail to even list those features that are automatically performed without administrator or operator intervention.

Manual system functions devour IT administrator resources when not automatically performed by the e-learning product. For example, some e-learning products enable the recording of live sessions. This is a great feature in providing a refresher to those students who attended the live session and a backup for other students who were unable to attend the session. Once a client begins to record sessions, the process continues forever. For example, a client who manually recorded 50 two-hour sessions per week would certainly have to add two full-time staff members to administer this process (if the system did not perform this function automatically). Other tasks that the RFP authors should evaluate to determine if they are automatically performed include: maintenance of the user database based on a user-supplied date, conversion of course materials preserving embedded animation, distribution of student materials, user recovery upon detecting server malfunction, and load balancing based on network performance.

SUMMARY

A well-written RFP provides more information to the vendor and ultimately results in greater value to the client. It is the basis for enabling vendors to solve a client's e-learning objective within a specific time frame and at a specified cost. The cost should include both product cost and associated operational cost. To accomplish this, the client should be available to discuss the specifications and to address the type of content, characteristics of the target population, and the detail plans for user support.

■ ■ ■

THE BOTTOM LINE

Far too much business is lost in the e-learning industry because someone forgot the due date of a proposal, misread a formatting requirement, or misspelled a contact name. Unfortunately, many of these mistakes are understandable because of the poor condition of the RFP. However, as a vendor, you must work through the RFP and attempt to cover all of the bases for the client.

Failure to capture basic information can cost an e-learning firm thousands of dollars worth of business. The best method for assuring that the basic information is correct is to complete the Basic Proposal Requirements Worksheet. This single piece of paper can save your company thousands of dollars by ensuring that all of the basics are in place when the proposal is written.

This book has free materials available for download from the Web Added Value™ Resource Center at www.jrosspub.com.

4

DEFINING THE PROBLEM

INTRODUCTION

To win an e-learning contract you need a complete and thorough understanding of the client's problem. The time you spend determining and defining the client's e-learning problem will be well worth the effort when your development team sits down to write the proposal. The better you understand the problem, the better able you are to present a winning solution.

DEFINING THE PROBLEM

One of the first steps in responding to the RFP is to succinctly define the client's problem. This seems like it should be easy. The client should simply state the problem and you should simply develop a solution. As we learned in previous chapters, clients do not always come right out and tell you the problem they want solved.

Because of this lack of a definitive problem statement, you must carefully dissect the RFP and determine key pieces of information. This requires a more in-depth analysis than what is needed for the Basic Proposal Requirements Worksheet discussed in Chapter 3. You need to understand just what the client wants and the nitty-gritty details required to satisfy the needs of the project. However, this is not enough; you must also be able to read what the client did not write. You must determine what information is missing from the document and discern client needs from wants. You must "read between the lines." To understand the RFP and to be able to read between the lines, you must first understand the typical types of information within an RFP.

Scope of work — This section of the RFP contains a description of the tasks required to be completed. This portion describes what is expected of the vendor. Some of the tasks are stated specifically as deliverables and some are embedded into the project itself. For example, the RFP may request an LMS as a deliverable, but may require that the LMS contain the ability to track user registration and courses completed (embedded). You need to identify all of the embedded requirements as well as the deliverables.

Deliverables — A deliverable is a tangible product that the client expects at the end of the e-learning project or at various times throughout the project. The project may require one deliverable such as an installed LCMS or many deliverables such as ten separate Web-based courses. If possible, ascertain from the RFP the number of hours of Web-based training (WBT), the number of objectives, the number of lessons, or the number of screens that need to be produced. One of the first things you need to establish is the quantifiable aspects of the RFP. The following statement indicates quantifiable information that can be used to respond to the proposal:

> *We expect the "typical" job guide conversion to require 9, plus or minus 3, screens to present content with approximately 100 job guides.*

This means that between 600 and 1200 WBT screens need to be created. One possible method of pricing or estimating this proposal could be "price per screen."

Confidentiality arrangements — Most RFPs include language describing the expectation of confidentiality between the vendor and the requesting organization. You must honor this arrangement because often the requesting organization may divulge important proprietary information within the RFP. For example, one RFP provided the turnover rate of the company, which was a closely held piece of information. Usually the RFP indicates that the proposed solution will also be held in confidence. A simple statement describing your intention to hold everything in confidence usually satisfies this requirement.

Copyright arrangements — The RFP usually describes who owns the complete deliverables once the work is completed. Typically, the proposal work is under a "work for hire arrangement," meaning that the requesting organization retains all rights to the completed work when the project is done. While it is important to be aware of copyright arrangements, the best time to delve into the details concerning these arrangements is during the contract or SOW phase, not in the proposal.

Keeping track of all the requirements listed in the various sections of the RFP can be a daunting task. The solution is to develop a list of all requirements to help ensure that you do not overlook a requirement when developing a solution or writing the proposal. One method used by many professionals in the field is to develop a *Requirements Matrix*.

DEVELOPING A REQUIREMENTS MATRIX

A Requirements Matrix is a listing of every requirement in the RFP including page and paragraph number. The process of developing the Requirements Matrix is actually quite simple. The first step is to have each of the RFP response team members read the RFP. After each team member has read the entire RFP a number of times, he or she should develop a list of requirements. This list is referred to as a Requirements Matrix.

Once individual team members develop the matrix, the team members meet as a group and compare each list. If an item is on every list, it is definitely a requirement. If the item is on only one person's list, it needs to be revisited to determine if it is an actual requirement. You cannot go through an RFP too carefully. Make sure you do not miss a single requirement. Some RFPs can have as many as 250 separate requirements.

Example 4.1 is a Requirements Matrix for an RFP that describes the desire to have a vendor submit a proposal for the development of an online e-learning portal for truck drivers. The idea was to place the portal on the Internet and have it accessible by truck drivers from home and from kiosks in truck stops throughout Pennsylvania and, eventually, the entire country.

One method some vendors use to ensure that their proposal is "compliant" with the client's RFP is to add another column to the matrix titled "Proposal Page Number." This column lists the page in the proposal on which the RFP requirement is addressed. When all the requirements are listed in that fourth column, the proposal is complete.

Gathering all requirements is important. A seemingly minimal or unimportant requirement may be missed in the Requirements Matrix and that simple item could be important to a particular member of the client's proposal review team. Missing even one requirement can result in the client labeling your proposal as noncompliant and open to possible disqualification.

RFP ANALYSIS

Once you have examined the RFP and developed the Requirements Matrix, you need to take time to analyze each part of the RFP and determine minimum requirements and the overall goals of the requesting organization. You also need to identify the stated and embedded deliverables mentioned in the RFP.

An RFP is more than just the sum of its requirements. Rarely does an organization want to solve just a list of requirements. Instead it wants to solve a real and

Requirement	RFP Page #	Paragraph #	Proposal Page #
Executive summary	4	2	
Outline of design solution	4	4	
Time/cost to complete work	4	2	
Understanding of problem description	4	3	
Problem description	4	4	
Describe finished product	5	2	
Include prototype screens	5	3	
Project description	4	5	
Resources (client and vendor)	10	4	
Timeline	10	4	
Costs	11	3	
o Ongoing fees	11	3	
Payment schedule	11	3	
Deliverables	12	2	
Appendix	12	2	
o Project Gantt chart	12	2	
o Line-item spreadsheet to include team	4	1	
member roles, time, cost per deliverable	4	5	
	4	5	
Appendices	4	6	
Vendor references	4	4	
Resumes	4	5	
Vendor work samples	4	5	
Demos as screen shots	4	6	
Length — 40 pages, 12-pt font	4	7	
Learning portal	5	4	
User profiling (who took class, performance,	5	bulleted list	
time, company)	5	page 5	
Links to training (ten courses initially)	5	"	
Weather reports	5	"	
Mapping functionality	5	"	
Space for advertisement	5	"	
Job announcements	5	"	
Links to other sites	5	"	
Online discussion groups on various topics	5	"	
Objectives of learning portal	6	1	
Simple, easy, intuitive	10	1	
Meaningful information	6	5	
Common look for entire site	5	7	
Help assure regulatory compliance	6	2	
Reduce fines for noncompliance	6	2	
Encourage users to seek more training	10	5	

Example 4.1 *Requirements Matrix* used to help proposal writers identify all of the requirements of an RFP.

pressing problem. Usually, the requirements listed in the RFP are the client's attempt to dissect a larger problem into manageable pieces. Too many novice proposal writers focus only on the requirements of the RFP and not on the underlying need of the client's RFP.

Winning vendors expose the underlying need, define the problem from a "big picture" perspective, discern the client needs from the wants, and show complete understanding of the client's problem (sometimes better than the client).

This is possible because they do not stop the RFP analysis process at the Requirements Matrix; they go on to question and examine the client's problem from multiple perspectives to gain a clear picture of the issues confronting the client.

A number of techniques are available to help facilitate the analysis process. The goal of each technique is to encourage the RFP response team to look at the information in the RFP from several angles. Looking at the RFP from multiple viewpoints helps the team to see elements within the RFP that it may not have originally seen or understood. Three proven techniques for conducting this type of analysis are thought-provoking questions, concept map, and fishbone analysis.

THOUGHT-PROVOKING QUESTIONS

One technique available for analyzing the problem discussed in the RFP is through a series of thought-provoking questions. Answering the questions forces you to consider the problem from different angles and helps clarify the underlying causes of the problem.

This technique begins by assembling the proposal development team after it has read the proposal and developed the matrix. Begin by asking the following types of questions:

- What is the business need driving this RFP?
- What is the education need driving this RFP?
- What is the technical need driving this RFP?
- What are the "wish list" items in this RFP?
- Is this an instructional problem?
- What other organizations have solved this problem? How have they solved it?
- What is the optimal desired outcome?
- What if this e-learning problem is not addressed?
- If no constraints were involved, how could this problem be approached differently?
- Does the client really understand the problem?
- Is this e-learning needed for the client to be profitable, avoid costs, or for other reasons?
- Is the project congruent with the client's other e-learning activities?

- Is this project ahead, behind, or even with trends in the client's industry?
- Does the client have a budget large enough for this type of initiative?

Answering these tough questions forces members of the RFP response team to consider elements of the problem not previously considered. It provides the group with a chance to approach the problem from many perspectives. These questions get to the serious matter of discerning needs from wants. Then, when the proposal is written, the proposal writing team will know the needs and the wants of the client and be able to better address the RFP.

CONCEPT MAP

A more involved process for "reading between the lines" and determining the underlying need expressed in the RFP requires gathering the proposal development team together to visualize the needs expressed in the RFP. This technique of exploring different angles of the client's problem is known as developing a concept map.

The concept map technique involves writing the RFP problem in the middle of a white board so all team members can see it. Next, team members discuss and write down critical aspects of the problem. The requirements identified in the Requirements Matrix are constantly referenced to ensure that nothing is missed.

The group then considers the relationships established between the different requirements. The visual nature of the concept map allows the group to see the relationships between the various RFP requirements. Often linkages between various aspects of the problem are evidenced only through this process.

Figure 4.1 illustrates a concept map created for the Truckco RFP based on the information from the Requirements Matrix. Notice that the RFP requirement of "developing an Internet e-learning portal for truck drivers" is written in the middle and circled.

Proposal development team members contributed to the concept map process by choosing items from the Requirements Matrix to include in the map. As the relationships between items began to surface, lines were drawn to link the items together.

At the conclusion of the session, it was determined that two separate but related aspects of the kiosk needed to be developed — an information side and a learning side. These two items were written on the white board and highlighted in the two squares on the right side of the diagram. This relationship may not have been realized if not for the concept map process.

FISHBONE ANALYSIS

Another effective method for looking at all of the possible causes of a particular problem is to use the fishbone analysis. This analysis starts with a particular prob-

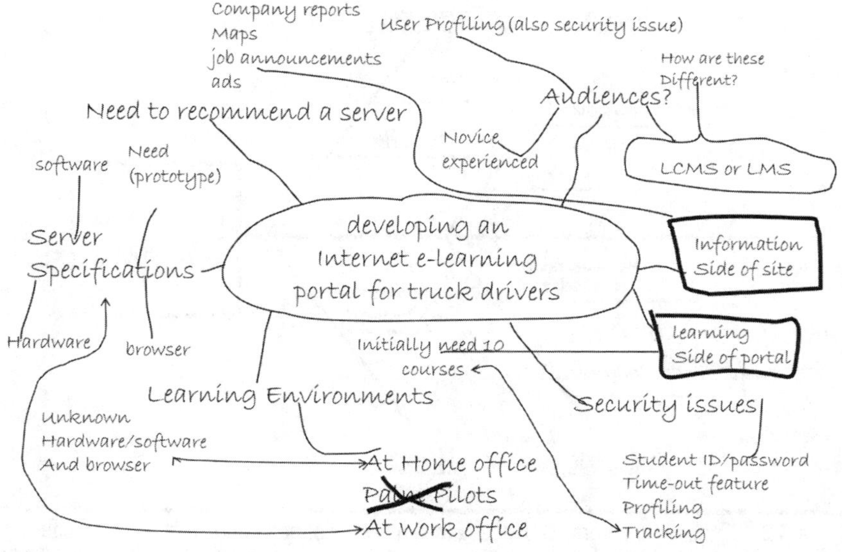

Figure 4.1 Concept map created as a result of a brainstorming session. Many of the requirements are from the Requirements Matrix.

lem and divides all the possible causes of the problem into different categories. Under each category, specific items that may be the root cause of the problem are identified. This technique is called a fishbone diagram because the completed diagram resembles a fish skeleton.

Many types of causes can be used to help categorize a problem. Major categories include people, materials, machines, methods, metrics, environment, quality, and technology. Regardless of what causes are chosen for the main categories, the goal is to break each cause down into its components to see what is really driving the problem posed by the client.

Fishboning promotes the analysis of a client problem by forcing the team to look at multiple inputs to a single problem. It helps to prevent a myopic, simplistic solution to a complex problem. It reminds the proposal development team that often problems are caused by multiple variables. Figure 4.2 illustrates a fishbone diagram used to identify possible reasons for high employee turnover, which the client viewed as "only a training problem." The proposal development team found many reasons above and beyond the need for training that drove the high level of employee turnover.

The fishbone diagram technique is especially effective when the root cause of a problem is not easily identified. It is also useful when the proposal development team has attempted to solve a particular problem with little success. Often fishboning a problem reveals several possible causes. You may want to attempt

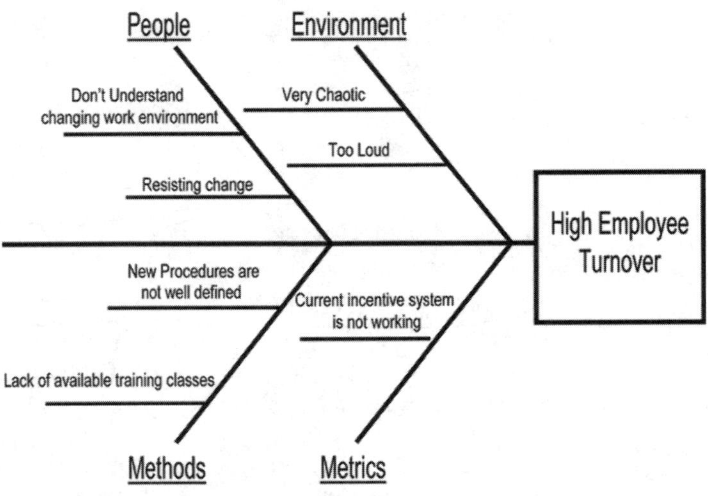

Figure 4.2 Fishbone diagram. The idea is to identify major categories that could be causing the problem and then break those categories into subcategories to find the root cause of the problem.

to solve the client's e-learning problem by addressing several of the causes listed on the diagram or you may choose to address the one you view as most critical. When analyzing processes you may want to include categories such as administrative procedures, reward structures, peer influence, processing rules, and working environment.

PULLING IT TOGETHER

While each of the above techniques is time consuming, they are also extremely important in developing a winning proposal. Most vendors stop at the Requirements Matrix and fail to further analyze the client's RFP. These vendors tend to offer a simple, one-sided solution to the client — a solution that usually does not win. Take the time to dig into the client's issues. View the problem from the client's perspective and provide insights and ideas that the client has not yet considered. To do this, you need to understand the problem described in the RFP better than the client.

PROBLEM DEFINITION WORKSHEET

Regardless of how you gain an understanding of the client's problem, the next step is to complete the *Problem Definition Worksheet* (Worksheet 4.1). This

Problem Definition
Worksheet
(Problem Definition)

After careful analysis of the RFP, write the different needs of the client in the spaces below.

Client Business Need: What business need is behind this RFP (i.e., reduce costs, increase productivity, increase market share, increase profit, government regulations, etc.)? Be careful because there can be two types of needs: those expressed by the client and those implied. Record both expressed and implied needs.

____
____
____
____

Client Educational/Training Need: What educational needs are being addressed by the RFP? Are the employees not learning under the current system? Is the current delivery of the training too cost prohibitive? Is the current training out-of-date? Are the trainee records too hard to manage?

____
____
____
____

Client Administrative Need: Does the client have a large number of trainees to track? Multiple courses running at the same time? Is the client looking for a way to ensure that an employee took a certain class and passed the required performance assessment?

____
____
____
____

Client Technical Need: Describe the technical need(s) of the client in layperson terminology. Include implied and expressed needs.

____
____
____
____

Overview of Problem: Describe the client's problem in two or three sentences encompassing all of the above-identified needs.

____
____
____
____

Worksheet 4.1 This worksheet is designed to help you clarify the problem stated in the RFP.

worksheet provides a one-page synopsis of the client's problem. When you examine the RFP and complete the worksheet, you will find that problems generally fall into four categories. Use these categories and the RFP to complete the Problem Definition Worksheet.

Business need — A business need is expressed in terms of cost reduction, increased productivity, decreased downtime, higher quality goods or services, more efficient services, reduced turnover, increased market share, increased revenues, increased profit, and cost avoidance. The business need always has a dollar value associated with it. For example, if the RFP asks for electronic delivery of instruction, the business need may be to reduce costs because the present stand-up training is too expensive. If the RFP requests training the sales force to be better negotiators, the business need might be to increase revenues. If the RFP is for training employees to be more efficient, the business need could be to have more efficient services, which means a reduction in costs to the client. You must determine the business need and separate it from other needs listed in the RFP.

Unfortunately the business need is usually not explicitly stated in the RFP. You must determine the business need from what the client writes. If the client is focused on reducing travel and eliminating expensive paper binders, the need may be cost reduction. If the client is trying to create a better orientation program, the need may be a reduction in turnover. Look for the implied need within the RFP and, when you are creating your solution, use that need to frame your proposal.

Educational/training need — The educational need of an e-learning RFP is usually clearly stated. For example, you may read a statement in the RFP such as "We need to teach our client service representatives to better handle irate clients." Other times the educational need will not be as clear.

The educational need can be a result of the fact that the current training is not working. Most of the time, the client will not tell you that the current training is not working. Instead the client includes euphemisms that mean the training is not working. Examples of such euphemisms are "our training is out-of-date" and "our training needs to be reconfigured due to recent changes in policy." Read the RFP carefully to determine the educational need. Sometimes the need is not educational at all. For example, if the client wants more cost-effective training, that does not mean the current training is not working, it just means it is too expensive.

While discussing educational needs, it is important to remember that the e-learning RFP may not have an educational need at all. In some cases an expressed need such as "reduce employee turnover" may not have anything to do with an educational need. Employees may be leaving the company for other reasons. Clients tend to like to introduce training-based solutions to problems that cannot be solved with training. Sometimes the cause of the problem is the working environment, poor quality materials, or performance metrics, all of which have nothing to do with training.

For this reason, do not assume that e-learning will automatically solve the client's problem and do not skimp on a needs analysis. You need to give yourself some room, should you win the contract, to make sure that you know what is causing the problem the client is trying to solve. The client may not realize the true cause of the problem and, therefore, not mention any other factors that are contributing to the problem. However, when you get on-site to begin the training development, you may quickly learn that the employees already know how to do the work, but just do not do it.

If you suspect something other than training is the problem, you will want to address that issue with your client or tactfully work a performance analysis and intervention into your proposal.

Administrative need — Many RFPs in the realm of e-learning have centered on LMS and LCMS because many organizations need more effective methods of managing their human resources, large amounts of corporate information, and their growing offerings of e-learning. An e-learning RFP may focus on nothing more than helping a client choose the best LMS. For organizations that are a little more complex with much internal training, they will want to manage both learners and content. These organizations want meta tags for content and methods of reusing pieces of content over and over again.

Read the RFP carefully to determine all of the administrative needs of the organization. Often the client will want to be able to manage classroom instruction and e-learning with the same LMS or LCMS. Make sure you understand the administrative requirements of the client.

Technological need — A solution for one or more of the needs above will generally create a need for some type of technology. You will have to determine if there are intranet, Internet, or extranet issues. What type of browser does the client use? Does the client need a new server? Will the e-learning solution run on the same infrastructure as mission critical applications? Do all the PCs within the company have speakers? What other applications will be running on the e-learning server? Is the company technologically savvy? Does it outsource the IT function?

You must determine which of the many technological needs requires the most attention. Usually by isolating the major need, the other needs then can be easily identified. For example, if you know that very little bandwidth is available for e-learning, you know there is no need for speakers at the users' PCs because a sound file takes up too much bandwidth and video is out of the question. Identify technological issues as early as possible when examining the RFP. It is a good idea to always request technical specifications from the client up front to determine what type of e-learning can be developed.

While a technology need is usually part of the solution, do not become caught up in it. Remember, e-learning is about learning. Too many proposals spend too much time explaining the technical aspects of the solution and not enough time explaining the anticipated educational outcomes.

BIDDER'S CONFERENCE

Often after reading and rereading the RFP, conducting a fishbone analysis, and even developing a comprehensive Requirements Matrix, questions still remain. What did they mean by that? What is the current technological infrastructure? The answers to the questions may make a difference in how you respond to the RFP. It is for this reason that many clients conduct a Bidder's Conference. The Bidder's Conference is simply a method of answering vendors' questions all at once. Sometimes the date for the Bidder's Conference will be listed in the RFP and sometimes it will be separate. The Bidder's Conference helps to ensure that all of the competing vendors receive the same response to all of the questions.

Not all clients hold a Bidder's Conference or entertain RFP questions, but many will. Even if an official Bidder's Conference is not held, it is always a good idea to call the client contact to ask clarification questions. You might receive answers that will help you to write a winning proposal and you may end up building rapport with the client contact, which may be helpful in securing the work.

Traditionally, the Bidder's Conference took place in a face-to-face setting where each competing vendor had a representative present who asked questions and listened to the other vendors' questions. Today, clients tend not to hold face-to-face Bidder's Conferences; instead, they solicit questions from vendors in writing and then send a written response to all vendors via e-mail. Other times a conference call is used to answer vendor questions. No matter how the Bidder's Conference is held, the idea is to ensure that all vendors receive the same information.

The interesting thing about a Bidder's Conference is that the vendors pay as close attention to the questions being asked by other vendors as they do to the answers. Often valuable information about a competitor's proposed solution can be gleaned from the type of questions the competitor is asking. The difficulty with a Bidder's Conference is that everyone has access to all the questions. If you have a question that will give away your solution, you may want to think twice about asking that question.

Prior to the Bidder's Conference, decide what strategy you will use when asking questions. Sometimes vendors will ask questions that have nothing to do with their solution to throw off the other vendors. Sometimes a vendor will ask a series of questions to pin the client into a corner where only one solution is possible — that particular vendor's.

Clients will also use the questioning process as a method of gaining insights into their e-learning issues. Sometimes certain questions will actually affect the RFP or change a requirement within the RFP. Insightful vendor questions can make the client think through the problem more thoroughly, which may lead to different or more refined requirements.

Another complication with the Bidder's Conference is that the client is not always forthcoming with answers. As you can see from the questions and answers below, the Bidder's Conference sometimes raises more questions than it answers.

> ***Q.*** *Is there a server or server space dedicated to training?*
> **A.** *Yes and no, we have space but are considering a new server for this e-learning.*
>
> ***Q.*** *When is this training module scheduled to be released for corporate use?*
> **A.** *Within two weeks of the completion date. We would like it as soon as possible but don't have a firm fixed date.*
>
> ***Q.*** *What is your current rate of turnover for the position that needs the e-learning?*
> **A.** *That is proprietary information.*
>
> ***Q.*** *With which specific AICC specifications do you need to comply?*
> **A.** *All that are appropriate.*

The Bidder's Conference can serve as a good mechanism for gaining additional detailed information about the client and the client's problem. However, do not expect the Bidder's Conference to provide you with all the answers. Also, remember that competitors are listening to or reading your every word.

THE BOTTOM LINE

To write an effective proposal, you must understand the client's needs and motivation for the RFP. Invest the necessary time and effort to properly identify these needs, not just the RFP requirements. When you truly understand the client's need, you have a better chance of writing a winning proposal.

This book has free materials available for download from the Web Added Value™ Resource Center at www.jrosspub.com.

5

CONCEPTUALIZING A WINNING SOLUTION

INTRODUCTION

While it is important to painstakingly identify the RFP requirements and follow the client's directions for writing the proposal as discussed in Chapter 4, these steps are not enough. Writing a winning proposal involves more. You need to develop an exciting, effective solution and present it in a unified manner with each section supporting the other sections within the proposal. Integration and unification are keys to creating a winning solution.

DEVELOPING A BALANCED SOLUTION

Development of a feasible solution begins when you define the client's problem. The next step is to develop potential solutions. Then the trick is to choose the solution most appealing to the client while simultaneously exploiting the strengths of your firm.

Your proposal must explain your e-learning solution in simple, effective terms. Straightforward, elegant solutions are the most successful. Take the client's myriad e-learning complexities and reduce them into one or two issues that your firm can easily address. The simpler, the better.

When developing a feasible solution to the client's needs, there are three general areas to address. These areas are business needs, technology requirements, and instructional design. It is not enough to address only one of these areas. An effective solution involves the seamless integration of all three.

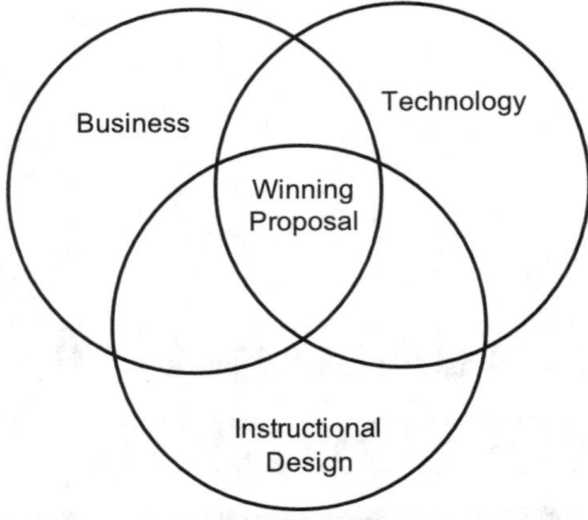

Figure 5.1 It takes a combination of business, technology, and instructional design to win an e-learning proposal.

Each area must support and agree with the other two areas. A shortcoming or disconnect between two areas may lead to the rejection of the proposal. Likewise, if one area is extremely strong and the other two are weak, the proposal also risks rejection. Strive for balance between the business needs, technology requirements, and instructional design. Figure 5.1 depicts how the merger of all three leads to a winning proposal.

BUSINESS NEEDS

The first area to address when conceptualizing possible solutions is the business need. Keep this in mind when considering possible solutions with the fishbone or mind map techniques. When an RFP is issued, it is to satisfy a business need first, a training need second. This is true even if the writer of the RFP does not realize it. Corporate training is not done for altruistic reasons; it is done to address business needs. If the e-learning does not address a legitimate need, the project will not be successful even if it is completed on time and within budget.

The more directly you tie the e-learning solution to the bottom line of the organization, the more successful you will be in securing the business. Organizations typically seek solutions that help them reduce time, increase quality, provide better client service, or reduce costs. If you do not write a proposal linked to one or more of these elements, your chances of winning are slim. Assure clients that you understand not only technology and instructional design, but their business as well. A simple method of learning which business needs impact a potential client is to research the client's industry.

Every industry has a trade association that publishes information describing the economic and competitive environment in which it operates. For example, in the manufacturing industry an organization exists called APICS — The Educational Society for Resource Management (www.apics.org). This group frequently publishes information about the current state of the manufacturing industry.

Industry-specific information can be invaluable for determining which competitive pressures are dominant and likely to impact a client. For example, if a particular client is in an industry that has a high level of turnover and you are proposing a project to train front line employees, consider how your e-learning course might aid in employee retention or shorten the training time for new employees. This can be done even if the RFP asks only for e-learning on how to operate the cash register.

TECHNOLOGY REQUIREMENTS

The second area to address when conceptualizing an e-learning solution is technology requirements. The technology used to provide your e-learning solution must be explained in an easy-to-understand manner. While you may be familiar with the technology, typically the client is not. Help your client understand how the proposed technology impacts his or her organization without letting the technological aspects of the solution outshine the instructional design aspects.

Basically, clients want to know that you are using a standard technology that will work within their environment. They want assurances that the technology chosen will not become obsolete within a few months and they want an open technological solution compliant with industry standards and norms. Often clients will ask their own IT department to have a look at the technological description of your solution and determine if it is feasible and how it would work given the client's current network configuration.

When looking for a technology solution, clients want maintainability, compatibility, usability, modularity, and accessibility. These elements of the technical solution are explained in more detail in Chapter 12.

Some clients have an elaborate staging process to test new software applications within their network environment. This process may involve a test server and a staging server, which must be tested with your e-learning application before it can be placed alongside mission critical applications. As a vendor, you need to help your client prepare for the different compatibility tests that might be required and make provisions for altering your e-learning application if necessary.

Even if you host the e-learning solution on your own servers, you may have to facilitate the process of getting the client's end users through corporate firewalls or other security measures. You may also have to assist the IT department with any browser upgrades or with the inclusion of any required plug-ins. Let the clients know that you have the technological expertise to assist them in implementing the technology portion of your e-learning solution.

INSTRUCTIONAL DESIGN

The third area to address when conceptualizing an e-learning solution is often the most overlooked. However, it is critical to success. The proposed e-learning must be instructionally sound. The proposal must discuss how you are going to use proven techniques to ensure effective instruction. You must explain the instructional design process to the client.

It is surprising, even in the training industry, how few people know or understand the instructional design process, although the numbers are growing. Many potential clients will have no idea of the steps needed to develop effective online instruction. In your proposal, you will need to explain step by step how you will convert the client's existing course content into e-learning. Do not explain the "theoretical" or "academic" instructional design process, and do not drop names of well-known instructional design models or famous theorists in the field (most clients will not know who you are talking about). Instead, explain how the instructional design process aids you in developing effective instruction for the client. Use examples that are appropriate to the client; use terms that make sense to the client. You want to educate the client on how your adherence to the instructional design process provides a better final product.

Explain the process of how you will analyze the client's needs to gain an understanding of what type of instruction is to be developed and to determine if any key content is missing. Describe how you use storyboards to design engaging instruction through the application of proven instructional strategies. Describe your development process and how you ensure quality.

Explain how you will help the client implement the e-learning solution. Finally, explain the planned evaluation process to measure the effectiveness of the instruction or the LMS implementation.

Describe to the client how you will apply the ADDIE model of instructional design to the e-learning problem. A quick explanation of the instructional design process or your version of the ADDIE model in a language the client understands is an important element in winning e-learning business.

You must also explain the instructional strategy or strategies you are going to use to design the instruction. An instructional strategy is a methodology purposefully employed to help an individual learn the desired material. Strategies are incorporated into e-learning modules to assist the learner in learning. There are different instructional strategies for learning different types of information. For example, you would employ a different strategy for teaching problem solving than you would when teaching jargon or a concept such as total quality. The elements of instructional design and the different types of instructional strategies are explained in more detail in Chapter 12.

If you are proposing an LMS or e-learning software, you may need to explain how the LMS supports the client's educational goals. For an LMS, it might be tracking employee performance or sequencing of instruction, or it might mean explaining how the system allows the training department to reduce time and effort in tracking employee performance and course registration. You may want to explain how courses can be launched from the LMS and provided to the learners at any time with bookmarking capabilities so the learner can leave the course and return to the exact same spot. If you are proposing an LCMS, you may need to explain learning objects and provide examples so the client can understand the concept. For e-learning two-way, Web-based audio software such as Interwise or Centra, you might explain how the two-way communication enhances learning and provides access to a company expert and how the ability to record sessions for later playback is an asset for future learning.

These three elements, business needs, technology requirements, and instructional design, must work together to make the proposal successful. As you design your solution, you must ensure that the instructional approach does not impede upon the due date of the project. The technology proposed must support how the instruction is going to be delivered. And, finally, the instruction must satisfy an actual business need. If these elements do not work together, the proposal has a low chance of winning.

■ ■ ■

HOW DO YOU SELL THE VALUE OF E-LEARNING?

Debra L. Newton, President, Newton Gravity Shift

When selling the value of e-learning, here are a few items to consider:

- Will the organization benefit from e-learning?
- Is the organization ready for e-learning?
- What are the long-term learning needs of the organization?
- What is the organization currently spending on non-e-learning programs? In other words, will e-learning bring any cost savings over traditional learning delivery methods?

The first step in selling the value of e-learning is to make sure that certain criteria, agreed upon by both you and the client, are met by the recommended solution. This is often the part of selling the value of e-learning that is overlooked. Generally, most people think that convincing a potential client that e-learning is the best way to conduct training and save money will seal the deal. This is a misconception you should avoid. When reviewing your solution and explaining it to your client, make sure that it meets the following criteria:

- The technology is easy to use. Remember, organizations are concerned with outcomes of the technology and are not buying it to spend a lifetime learning to use it.
- The technology is easy to access. Is this something that can be accessed through an intranet, CD-ROM, or palm device? Make sure that the delivery mechanism will meet the needs of the intended audience.
- The technology can be easily integrated into the existing infrastructure. It is also recommended to not make assumptions regarding your client's infrastructure.
- The cost of the solution will be acceptable. Sometimes it is difficult for stakeholders to see the value of e-learning when the initial investment is so great. Think big and start small. You may want to offer a pilot program before you recommend that your client purchase a learning management system. You have to walk before you can run.
- The solution meets the needs of learners and provides feedback. If the learning system is not acceptable to your audience and they do not want to use it, the value with which you started will disappear and training may suffer.

The second step in selling the value of e-learning is to gain commitment from the potential buyer that e-learning as a concept is an appropriate endeavor for the organization. This should occur well before an e-learning proposal is developed. Without that initial commitment to the concept, it will be virtually impossible to sell the value of e-learning.

To obtain commitment from management, there are several action steps that should be taken. These steps are as follows:

- Identify all of your stakeholders and choose an internal coach to help guide you through discussions with management. It is important not only to identify who the stakeholders are, but to have an internal champion act as a catalyst in obtaining the commitment as well.
- Identify the learning need. Work with your coach to identify the training priority. If you can identify the training need that is giving the client the most pain, then you will be able to provide the client with a solution that will provide relief in the right areas.
- Get to know the stakeholders. Working with your coach, set up a meeting to meet the stakeholders who will be making the decisions. You will find that each stakeholder will have a different opinion and need regard-

ing the training solution. It is your job to identify each of these needs and provide solutions for them. Feeling their pain will show much value in your solution.

- Translate needs through e-learning concepts. Now that you have identified the pain, show the group how e-learning concepts can help meet their individual needs.
- Correlate your solution to the overall learning strategy of the organization. Tying the e-learning program into the training "big picture" helps organizations overcome the phobias of e-learning in cultures not yet accustomed to delivering learning in this medium. It also helps to further communicate that your solution encourages the training goals of the organization.
- Work with your coach to create the business case. By this point you should know enough about your stakeholders' organization to present them with a business case for e-learning. Having a business case will not only show how the solution will impact the organization, but will provide support for those stakeholders who may have to sell the solution to upper management.
- Gain support. Now that you have presented your business case, work with your coach to gain the support of each member of the management team. Refine your solution as necessary to meet the needs of the group.

Thereafter, the proposal should summarize previous discussions you have had with the organization about e-learning.

Prior to the development of an e-learning proposal, you and your client will need to clearly define what e-learning is to accomplish; in other words, what are the goals of e-learning? The proposal is then a restatement of the previously agreed upon e-learning objectives. For example, is the e-learning designed to prepare learners for an in-person group learning setting, or will it be used as the end point of a training program where additional in-person sessions are not necessary?

A good e-learning proposal should include an overview of the program's features and functionality. More importantly, each feature and function should include a benefit or value statement. The value statements or benefits are what will truly sell the e-learning initiative.

Here is an example of an e-learning feature:

> *The e-learning program will be available on the Internet and can be accessed any time, day or night.*

The value of the 24/7 availability is that learners can access information at a time during the day when they are optimally prepared to concentrate and gain the most benefit from the learning. As we all have different learning styles, we all have times throughout the day when we can better understand and absorb information. Therefore, the round-the-clock availability of the learning system becomes a value to the organization.

To further enhance the success of a proposal, ROI calculations can be made to support the e-learning value statements. For example, the cost to offer live classes, 7 days a week, 24 hours a day to train factory workers may cost hundreds of thousands of dollars when the cost of a training space and instructors to support a 24/7 training environment is considered. On the other hand, the cost of e-learning virtually eliminates the need for space and instructors, provided the e-learning is a self-paced, noninstructor-led program. To further help your customers realize the ROI of an e-learning program, the solution you provide should include mechanisms that enable your customer to quantifiably demonstrate or track the effectiveness of the learning.

For example, utilizing both a pre- and post-test scenario in a learning program allows the client to perform a statistical gap analysis of learner competencies before and after the learning program is completed. This approach can help measure the effectiveness of the training and potentially identify areas that need improvement within the training content or the training audience.

Additional benefits of e-learning over other media are as follows:

E-learning vs. print-based training

- Learners can become engaged in and interact with training material.
- Steps in a process and/or functions can be demonstrated through the use of animation instead of being explained in text or shown with static graphics. This allows for a much higher level of understanding because learners can actually see how something works or how to perform a certain task.
- Eliminate planning and costs associated with printing and distribution.
- Can design training to suit various learning styles instead of just one style.

E-learning vs. stand-up training

- Save money on travel, lodging, and meals. (Learners often have to travel to a designated location to attend training sessions.)
- Provide one consistent message to all learners. (Sometimes multiple trainers will present the same training materials. They all have different styles and will not present a consistent message every time.)
- Learners can learn at their own pace. (They are not rushed through material they have not yet comprehended and do not have to sit through information they already know.)

Miscellaneous

- Can utilize online assessments tied to learning management systems that automate the test-making as well as tracking and reporting of all learners within an organization.

In summary, if you do not have the commitment from the organization that e-learning will benefit the company, then it will be virtually impossible to sell the value of e-learning. Also, if the organization is not ready for e-learning, you will not be able to sell an e-learning initiative. However, once you have gained commitment and the company sees its benefit, then you can address the value that e-learning brings to any organization. At that point, you address both the tangible and intangible benefits that e-learning provides throughout the life of a company. Whenever possible, you will want to quantify those benefits. For example, e-learning will reduce traditional training costs by x% a year. Also, when in doubt, keep this phrase in mind: "Features tell, benefits sell."

■ ■ ■

E-LEARNING PROJECT MANAGEMENT CONSIDERATIONS

Each of the three general areas of the solution (business needs, technology requirements, and instructional design) can be broken down further into various areas of project management. The essence of an e-learning proposal is actually a description of how you are going to run a project. You need to convince the reader that you can take into account business, technological, and instructional needs and bring the project to completion on time and within budget by successfully managing project elements such as quality, risk, budget, and schedule.

Effective project management consists of managing three elements with three different tools. The three elements of a project are quality, cost, and speed. Unfortunately, most clients want high-quality, low-cost solutions as quickly as possible. They want good, fast, and inexpensive e-learning. However, they can only have two. It is impossible to achieve all three. This is known as Elridge's Axiom, which states "Quality, Speed and Cost: You can have one or two, but not all three simultaneously" [1].

Each of these dimensions can be thought of as a side of a triangle. Shorten one side and the other two sides increase. This is sometimes referred to as the Good, Fast, Cheap triangle. You can have good and fast, but not cheap. You can have cheap and fast, but not good. You can have good and cheap, but not fast.

PROJECT MANAGEMENT TOOLS

To manage these three elements, three tools are available: tasks (how many things the client wants done, scope), time (you can move the due date up or back depending upon needs), and resources (the number of people involved in a project). The secret is to determine which of the three elements is most important to the client and what tools need to be manipulated to effectively achieve the client's goals. Does the client want a good, fast, or cheap solution and what is the client willing to sacrifice to get the desired outcome? A careful read of the RFP usually indicates which element is most important.

For example, if the client's first selection criterion is price, you can be sure that cost is one of the two important elements for that client. The tools that are used for helping control the price might be to reduce the number of resources on the project or cut some of the desired tasks. If that same client wants a flawless product that will run on every imaginable browser with high-resolution graphics and an imaginative interface, quality is the second dimension. If this is the case, some of the tasks may be put back into the project and the tool of time will need to be used to elongate the project. Therefore, the third dimension, time, will increase to accommodate the price and quality dimensions.

Manipulating the elements of a project to achieve the desired result for the client is a complex process. Project management consists of not just one or two elements, but several different elements that must be constantly managed, monitored, and balanced. The Project Management Institute (PMI) lists nine elements of project management. The list for e-learning uses some of those same elements, eliminates two, and adds several more for a total of ten elements of an e-learning project that must be managed. As someone writing a proposal, you must convince the reader that your firm can manage those items effectively. The ten elements fall under the three general headings of tasks, time, and resources as shown in Table 5.1.

When you write a proposal, you must describe in simple and effective terms how the following elements are going to be addressed. A client must feel comfortable that you can handle these elements with professionalism and without undue problems.

Project scope management — This includes proper identification of the scope of the project from the information in the RFP. It also includes language within the proposal to discuss what happens when the scope of the project changes.

Project quality management — The client must feel that you are providing a high-quality product. This starts with the proposal. Typographical and grammatical errors and misstatements reflect poorly upon your firm and are grounds for proposal disqualification.

Project instructional design management — The Instructional Systems Design (ISD) process is a methodology for developing instruction. Following the methodology ensures that your resulting instruction is engaging, effective, and instructionally sound. Not all clients understand the ISD process or see its value. It is your job as a vendor to explain the concept of ISD in a straightforward, easy-to-understand manner. You must describe how following the ISD process ensures a better end product. Clients need to see the process adding value to their project.

Table 5.1 You Must Convince Your Client That Your Firm Can Manage These Project Elements During the Development of the E-Learning

Tasks	Time	Resources
Scope	Time	Cost
Quality		Human Resource
Instructional Design		Technology
← Communications →		
← Risk →		
← WOW! →		

Project time management — This involves determining the amount of time it takes to perform each task as well as determining the overall time required to complete the project. The time allocated for each task must be feasible and within industry norms. One of the first things a potential client will review is the time frame indicated for the completion of the project. If the time frame does not seem reasonable, the client will not continue with the rest of the document. Clients typically have a time frame in mind for a project, and it is almost always shorter than what is really necessary to develop the requested e-learning.

Project cost management — This is the price that you present to the client. The price must not seem outrageous, but must be high enough for your firm to make a profit. The method of presenting the price has a dramatic impact on whether or not the client awards you the contract.

Project human resource management — The client wants to feel that the team assigned to the project is capable of actually performing the work outlined in the RFP. Show evidence that the team has worked together on similar projects, and that it is capable of dealing with unforeseen occurrences during the e-learning project.

Technology management — One area that confuses most potential e-learning clients is technology. Explain to the client how your technological solution works without jargon or techno-speak. Walk that fine line between showing off your technical prowess and overshooting your client's ability to understand what he or she is reading. This is made doubly difficult by the fact that the client will usually hand the technical section off to a person in the IT department who is just waiting to dissect the solution line by line. You need enough detail to satisfy the technical people without bogging down the business people.

Project communications — Clients want communication channels between vendors and themselves to be open and honest. A good idea is to develop a Web site for you and the client to post and exchange information. Project Web sites are useful because visuals and timelines can be posted and followed from a central location. Messages to all team members can be posted on the site and an area for comments can also be created.

Project risk management — All projects have risks; some are internal and some are external. It is important to let the client know that you understand the risks associated with an e-learning project and that you are capable of successfully mitigating those risks. However, your risk management section must be carefully presented. You need to present the potential risks and ways to mitigate those risks without scaring the client. If you suddenly expose a number of risk factors the client never considered, the client may get cold feet and wonder why you are pointing out all of these risks. Be careful with the risk management section of the proposal.

WOW! management — Tom Peters writes that every project should also have a WOW factor [2]. If the project does not make someone sit up and take notice, then it is not worth the effort. Peters says that mediocre successes are far worse than spectacular failures. While I would not go that far, I do believe that e-learning projects should have a certain degree of "flash and pizzazz" even if that does not add to the overall effectiveness of the learning. Remember that many people who do not understand instructional design, and who will not be taking the training, will look at the training and will either be impressed or unimpressed based solely on the look and feel of the piece. Do not forget a little WOW!

Presenting the management of an e-learning project to a potential client is not an easy task; many variables come into play during e-learning projects. Potential clients must be comfortable with your ability to successfully manage all aspects of the e-learning project.

PROPOSAL CONSIDERATION HIERARCHY

An important aspect of presenting your e-learning solution is to make sure that all of the elements under business needs, technology requirements, and instructional design as well as the ten areas of project management are adequately explained and integrated throughout the proposal. Each element that you explain in the proposal should support the other elements and, in the end, they should all support the business need you are addressing. Tie each item in the proposal back to the client's business need — from instructional strategies to usability of the software to the time required to finish the project. Each item in the proposal should support solving the client's business need. One method of visually depicting the relationship among all of these elements is via the *Proposal Consideration Hierarchy*.

The Proposal Consideration Hierarchy is a hierarchical representation of the key elements that need to be contained within an e-learning proposal. It visually depicts the relationships of all the proposal elements. The hierarchy starts with the business need of the organization, and then considers the project management aspects. After project management is considered, the technology that will be used to support the e-learning effort must be determined and must fit into the project management elements of the project. Only after these items have been considered can the instructional design model be applied.

Within the instructional systems design parameters, the most important aspect is the application of the proper instructional strategies for addressing the e-learning problem. If the proposal is for e-learning software or LMS/LCMS systems, the instructional strategies may not be as relevant. You need to apply the Proposal Consideration Hierarchy with an understanding of the business need you are addressing. Figure 5.2 illustrates the relationships between the elements.

Every step within the hierarchy should be tied to the step above and below. As you write your proposal keep these elements in mind. Mapping your solution back to the Proposal Consideration Hierarchy ensures an integrated solution.

CAPTURE STRATEGY

Unfortunately, after you have worked to develop a good, integrated solution, you are not done. Now you need to plan how to convince the client that your solution is best for them. To do this, you need a *capture strategy*. A capture strategy describes the systematic planning, management, and synchronization of all proposal elements to support a unique advantage, approach, or perspective that leads to victory [3].

The capture strategy is the plan for winning the work from the client. The strategy can revolve around having the lowest price, being the most innovative, or developing an approach to quickly solve the client's e-learning problem. The capture strategy focuses on matching the unique capabilities of your firm with the prospect's specific challenge on three levels: the business needs of the client, the technology specifications for the project, and the instructional design requirements. A capture strategy works with your solution. It supports the solution and highlights the elements of the solution that are most important to the client. It is not something you reveal to the client in the proposal; rather, it is your own internal strategy for winning the business.

The purpose of the capture strategy is to bring together all of the elements of the proposed solution under a common idea or theme. While the Proposal Consideration Hierarchy splits apart the different elements of the solution, the capture strategy unites these elements.

For example, a capture strategy may revolve around reducing costs. If that is the case, the entire proposal is written to emphasize the fact that the solution reduces costs. Low-priced software is proposed, the fact that travel can be eliminated is highlighted, and the low cost of ongoing maintenance is carefully ex-

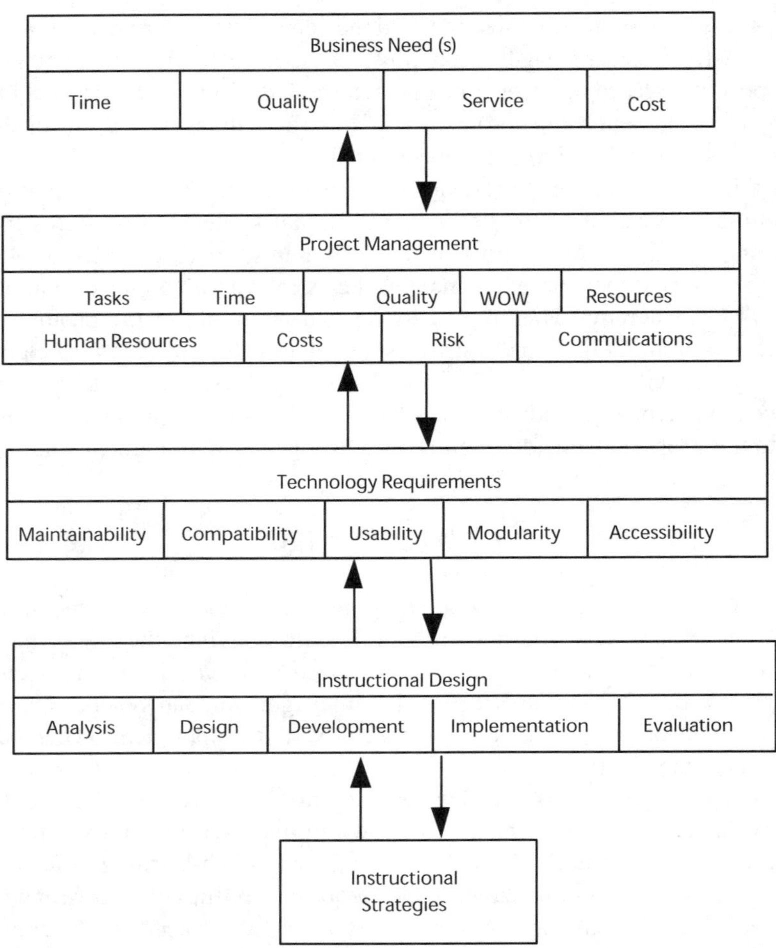

Figure 5.2 The *Proposal Consideration Hierarchy* helps ensure that you integrate all of the key elements into your proposal.

plained. The instructional strategies that are proposed are simple and easy to implement. The instructional design process is modified whenever possible to streamline the amount of effort that goes into the solution. Every item in the Proposal Consideration Hierarchy is focused on reducing costs.

If the capture strategy involves providing a high-quality product, then the emphasis would be on conducting every step in the ADDIE model to ensure quality instruction, incorporating engaging instructional strategies and using proven technologies. While these elements may be a little more expensive, the capture strategy will emphasize the quality aspects of the solution. With the "quality" capture strategy, the goal is to minimize the discussion of costs and maximize the discussion of quality.

Once the capture strategy is determined, everyone involved with writing the proposal needs to understand the strategy so that they can develop supporting substrategies. The capture strategy is a framework in which elements of the solution are placed. If it is well planned and effectively executed, the chances of winning the proposal are high.

For example, if the capture strategy is to emphasize quality, you want a substrategy in the instructional design portion of the document focusing on how the instructional design process supports quality. You want your risk mitigation discussion to focus on mitigating quality issues. You want your understanding of the solution section to revolve around quality. Every subsection has a substrategy to support the main capture strategy, which is, in this case, quality.

For any RFP, different vendors will most likely employ different capture strategies. One vendor may feel that the "hot button" of the client is cost and another may feel it is quality. Choose a capture strategy that is in line with the business requirements of the client. Carefully choosing a capture strategy can help unify your proposal and focus the client on your solution.

THEME

What separates a losing proposal with a good solution and a good capture strategy from a winning proposal? A theme. The theme of the proposal is the thread that holds the entire document together. It is like a plot in a movie. Although different, seemingly unrelated items may happen in a movie, in the end, the plot ties everything together (at least in good movies). This is the purpose of a proposal theme. The theme is woven throughout the document to hold all the disparate elements together.

The theme is different from the capture strategy because it does not reflect a business need of the client. The theme is a unifying element. It can be more whimsical than the capture strategy. An example of an effective theme would be the idea that the client has an e-learning "puzzle" and the vendor holds the missing puzzle piece. Let us see how this theme would play out.

Imagine that a client's goal is to develop interview training for front line supervisors so they will hire the best individuals for the job. The business need is to reduce turnover. Unfortunately, under the current scenario, the front line supervisors spend little time preparing for interviews because they are busy with their primary responsibility of supervising employees. The need for quick and accurate interviews can be viewed as a quality issue or a time issue, depending upon which capture strategy you employ.

The client requested that the training of the front line supervisors be a Web-based refresher course that could be reviewed 30 minutes before an interview. The work environment is hectic and only certain types of individuals are suited for the work. The client wants to hire employees who fit into the existing corporate culture with little training.

The winning vendor titled the proposal "Good Selection: Finding the Perfect Fit," and featured two interlocking puzzle pieces, one representing the client company and one representing the vendor company on the front cover of the proposal. In fact, the proposal clearly spelled out the theme the vendor was going to use for the e-learning.

> *We have developed a puzzle metaphor for the Good Selection training. This puzzle metaphor is emphasized throughout each lesson. The underlying theme is: There are many steps to finding the right employee. Skipping any step may result in a poor fit. The focus on any hiring procedure is to find the perfect fit, just like finding the missing puzzle piece. You need the correct piece to successfully complete the puzzle [4].*

For the topic, audience, and proposal, the theme was perfect. The proposal won, in part, because of the comprehensive, easy-to-understand theme. While good themes can elevate proposals to the level of winner, inappropriate themes damage a firm's possibility of winning.

In one situation, an e-learning vendor proposed developing training for a chain of convenience stores. The goal of the training was to convert existing job aids and procedural information into an online format for things such as running a meat slicer. The theme chosen by the vendor was one of a "university." The vendor named the online training the Convenience Store University (CSU). To further the theme, the vendor developed a logo and a mascot, which appeared on the front cover of the proposal. Within hours of receiving the proposal, the client rejected it.

One of the main reasons for the rejection was that the university theme was not congruent with the target audience or the information to be learned. Most of the chain's employees were either high school dropouts or senior citizens who were past the university stage of their lives. In addition, the university theme did not fit with the content. The content was mostly procedural, not conceptual or theoretical. In short, the content did not fit the theme of a university.

When choosing a theme, choose one that fits with the project's instructional content, target audience, and the client's corporate culture. Choosing the wrong theme ruins a proposal's chances of winning. However, the right theme can provide a competitive edge.

When determining the theme for your e-learning proposal, ask yourself several questions to make sure it is on target with the needs of the client:

- Is it simple?
- Is it expressed clearly?
- Has it been articulated to the potential client?
- Is it threaded through the entire proposal?
- Is it easy to grasp and remember?
- Does it relate directly to what the client wants or needs?
- Does it reflect the capture strategy?
- Is it visual as well as verbal?
- Is it congruent with the target audience and course content?

Careful consideration of these factors will help you develop an effective proposal and accompanying theme.

A theme can be focused on the proposed solution like the idea of a corporate university or it can be related to your company. For example, if your company is highly experienced in a certain area such as banking and you employ instructional designers who have all worked in the banking industry, your theme for the proposal could be "we have walked in your shoes." Even if you never mention the words "shoes" or "walked," the idea that you've "been there, seen it, done it" can be evident within the proposal. This "theme" can be evident in the Corporate Capabilities section, the Overview of the Solution section, or other sections where the firm's experience in the field of banking can be used as an asset.

A theme does not necessarily need to be articulated; it can be implied within the proposal. The use of a theme can be a tricky; you need to walk a fine line between subtlety and overdoing it. If you think incorporating a theme into your proposal is too much, then you are probably correct. When they work, themes provide an amazing competitive advantage; when they do not work, you have virtually no chance of winning. Use themes with caution.

■ ■ ■

TIPS FOR CREATING A WINNING RESPONSE

Carl Seidel, Strategic Account Manager, Newton Gravity Shift

- Visualize yourself creating a winning response in your mind. Map out your strategy and the path you will take to accomplish your goals, and write them down on a piece of paper. Congratulations, you have just taken the first step to defeat the competition.

- Make sure that participating in the RFP will result in a win/win for your organization and your client. If the situation is not a win/win, rethink why you are participating or if you really should.
- Show the client the WIIFM (What's in it for me?). A great response is one that shows the value in winning for all parties involved. Formulate a list of questions to be answered for the client before developing your solution.
- Be concise! Do not let vague abstract language take away from the brilliance and creativity of your solution. Remember, people who are most likely working on limited time are reading your solution. Present the meat and leave out the stuffing.
- Frame your solution in a manner that provides the customer with more than one option. Providing options and a price range lets the customers choose between the "silver" and "gold" versions of your solution while seeing what they get for their money. Give the client an open opportunity to barter on price, but provide the parameters in which it is done.
- Go beyond the request. Do not let the structure of the RFP keep you from delivering more than is asked. Show the client you can think outside the box and deliver a solution that goes beyond the requirements. It may be the only part of the solution that differentiates you from the competition.

■ ■ ■

PRELIMINARY SOLUTIONS DOCUMENT

The solution is determined, the capture strategy is chosen, and the theme is developed. Now what? The next step is to develop a *Preliminary Solutions Document* (PSD). The PSD is a one- or two-page document describing, at a very high level, the proposed solution, capture strategy, and theme. The PSD ensures that everyone is working with the same understanding of the solution. It is a quick and concise explanation of the RFP and the proposed solution.

Once completed, the PSD should be distributed to each team member to use as a guide for writing his or her section of the proposal. The PSD helps ensure that all team members have a common understanding of the solution and helps everyone write with the same goals in mind.

The PSD contains a number of different sections. The first is a single-sentence explanation of the purpose of the document. This section explains why this particular PSD is being written. The second section is a short description of the client's need. It provides a 30-second explanation of what the client wants. Next is a short description of the proposed solution. This is where the team describes, in general terms, what the solution will be for the client's problem. The final section is an area for any additional comments. In this case, the team made note of the client's concerns about cost. This will help team members focus on a cost-oriented capture strategy. The theme for the proposal is also indicated on the PSD. Knowledge of the theme allows each team member to incorporate the theme concept into his or her section of the document. In this case, the theme used is one of providing a "Road Map" to the online learners.

The PSD is a reference point for the proposal, prototype development, and sales presentation. Many organizations keep a copy of past PSDs to use as a reference library for generating ideas when new RFPs are received. Example 5.1 contains a sample PSD for the Truckco RFP.

THE BOTTOM LINE

Your solution must focus on the business need or needs driving the RFP and you must focus on describing how your firm will successfully manage all elements of the process. Balance the business needs, technical requirements, and instructional design elements to achieve success. Provide a comprehensive capture strategy to address all the needs in the RFP. A clever and appropriate theme will make your solution stand out. Organizations that are able to develop compelling, integrated, and exciting solutions win contracts and rapidly increase market share.

This book has free materials available for download from the Web Added Value™ Resource Center at www.jrosspub.com.

Purpose is described so everyone will know why document exists.

Client need is discussed succinctly.

Proposed solution is outlined at a high level to provide everyone contributing to the proposal with a sense of what the final solution will entail.

Capture strategy is described so writers can develop appropriate sub-strategies within their sections.

Theme is outlined so that everyone will know what element ties together the solution.

Preliminary Solutions Document

Purpose—To address the requirements for the Truckco RFP

<u>Client Need</u>

Development of a kiosk/portal for truck drivers (client actually wants a prototype of a physical kiosk as well as a web-based portal for the drivers to use at home and in truck stops via the kiosk).

<u>Our Proposed Solution</u>

We will sub-contract for the development of the physical kiosk prototype (hardware and platform).

We will develop a two-pronged approach. We will have part of the kiosk (portal) be an information site. It will be open to the public, providing information about the weather, travel maps, weather reports, job announcements, and advertisements.

The second part of the site will contain the e-learning courses. We will initially develop 10 courses. This part of the kiosk (portal) will require a password and ID for logging in. It will also track the user and do some profiling so that the user will know what classes he or she has taken in the past.

Our solution needs to run at the kiosk (where we control the hardware and software) and at the homes of truck drivers (where we do not control the hardware, software or browser used). We are recommending that palm devices not be used at this time.

The targeted audience is truck drivers in Pennsylvania, as well as truck drivers in other states. The truck drivers can be broken into two groups—novice and experienced. The solution must appeal to both of those truck-driving audiences.

<u>Capture Strategy</u>

The client's main priority seems to be price. We need to focus on keeping the costs down for the project. The entire focus of the solution should be on reducing costs to the client. Before adding an item to the solution, think of the impact on price. We will "sell" ourselves as a high-quality, low-price solution.

<u>Theme</u>

The theme for this proposal will be that of a "Road Map." We will provide a road map for Truckco's success. The web site will have a road map theme with road map icons.

Private and Confidential 1 of 1

Example 5.1 Sample of a *Preliminary Solutions Document.*

6

GOOD WRITING IS ESSENTIAL

INTRODUCTION

First and foremost, a proposal is a written document. Without good writing, the proposal cannot possibly succeed. The written proposal determines if an organization will consider your firm as a viable vendor to help it solve its training problem with e-learning.

In addition to the requirement of having an exciting, interesting, and cost-effective solution, the proposal needs to have good sentence structure, active language, effective paragraph design, and a logical thread. Each section of the proposal must support the capture strategy and aid in convincing the client to purchase your solution. Every word, sentence, and paragraph needs to add value to the proposal.

GOOD WRITING

Good writing consists of a number of elements that must be combined to achieve success. These elements start with the appropriate format. You must determine what format is required for margins, fonts, and page layout to write effectively. Next, your document must use the language of business. It must be concise and to the point, not filled with flowery sentences or superfluous adjectives. It must be written in the active voice at the appropriate level for the reader. It must contain just the right amount of redundancy so that the readers are neither lost nor bored.

The primary method of ensuring a well-written proposal is to develop paragraphs that are unified, coherent, and transition the reader easily from topic to topic. Good proposal writing starts at the fundamental levels of word choice and paragraph construction.

Finally, you must avoid bias and offensive language. You must craft sentences and paragraphs with the reader's perspective in mind. It is not enough to simply have the correct spelling, grammar, and punctuation. You must also engage, inform, and entertain the reader with innovative ideas, insights, and techniques. Carefully balancing all of these elements is the start of a winning proposal.

FORMAT

A proposal can be thrown away before it is ever read if it does not follow the prescribed format. If the RFP specifies a format, it must be followed. For example, some RFPs from the United States Office of Personnel Management (OPM) can be as long as 114 pages, specifying everything from paper size and weight to the spacing between sentences.

Fortunately, most RFPs are not that specific. The majority of e-learning RFPs are not demanding in terms of formatting requirements. Usually e-learning RFPs focus more on the specific sections to be included and not on items like font choice. This means the vendor has free rein to use any appropriate format. When no format requirements are specified, follow basic industry guidelines as described below.

- Use the outline provided in the RFP (if none is provided, use the one shown in Example 6.1).
- Single-space the document.
- Use one-inch margins (top, bottom, left, right).
- Use a standard business font such as Times New Roman or Arial for the body of the document. Often Times is used for the text and bold Arial is used for the headings and subheadings. More than three fonts is distracting and confusing to the reader.
- Use a 12-point font size for body text and 14-point for headings.
- Limit the document to approximately 20 pages.
- Include "white space" within the document. This includes the use of bulleted or numbered lists, as well as frequent headings and subheadings.
- If submitting an Adobe PDF file, when converting from word processing software to PDF format, save as RTF format and then covert to PDF format. The font to use for the bullets should be from the Lucida Console family. If you choose an item from that font, you should not have any

Outline

Cover

Cover Letter/Letter of Transmittal

Table of Contents

Legal and Confidentiality Statement

Section I.
- Executive Summary

Section II.
- Description of Problem/ Overview of Solution/Understanding of Scope

Section III. Solutions

- Instructional Approach
  - Overview
  - Detail

- Technical Approach
  - Overview
  - Detail

Section IV.
- Project Management and Schedule

Section V.
- Cost Analysis/Budget

Section VI.
- Corporate Capabilities/Profile

Appendices

NOTE:
These items are typically under one of the above headings or contained within the appendices: Deliverables, Quality Assurance Procedures, Corporate Resumes, Corporate and/or Project Organizational Chart.

Example 6.1 This is a sample outline that can be used for an e-learning proposal if none is provided by the client.

trouble. Use Adobe Distiller to allow live links with the Adobe Acrobat PDF file.

- When turning in a proposal, use the company name as the name of the document unless otherwise indicated.
- Use two spaces after all end punctuation marks (period, question mark, colon, comma). Leaving two spaces after end punctuation and colons allows readers to easily and quickly read the document.
- Use ragged or unjustified right margins.

CONTENT OUTLINE

Part of good writing is having a good outline. Most clients provide specific instructions concerning the organization of the proposal information. They indicate what section comes first, what information goes in each section, and how the proposal should flow.

Typically, you will be provided with a numbering system, section titles, and specific formatting instructions. You must follow the requirements exactly. Clients eliminate a proposal almost instantly if it does not follow the required format. If a particular section seems not to warrant information, you can put "Not Applicable" or "See Section X.X for Details." You must put something under each specified section in the RFP. This allows the client to do a side-by-side comparison of proposals received.

However, if the RFP does not specifically prescribe a format, you may want to use the one shown in Example 6.1. This format presents the solution to the client in a clear, logical fashion and provides room for all of the critical information. Use this outline as the beginning of the proposal. Assign each team member a specific section of the proposal to help shorten the proposal development time. Because everyone will have a copy of the PSD, they will understand what needs to be done to complete the first draft of the proposal.

PROPER LANGUAGE

The language in your proposal can convey confidence, knowledge, and intelligence to your reader, or it can convey sloppiness, lack of attention to detail, and apathy. The fundamental goal of a proposal is to persuade your reader that your solution is the most feasible of all the solutions he or she is reading. This is accomplished with clear, concise language, well-developed arguments, and attention to detail. The language of your proposal should lead the reader to the conclusion that your proposal is the best and most likely to achieve success for the client organization.

The proposal should not include formal or academic writing. The tone should be that of a knowledgeable professional speaking, in a conversational tone, to another knowledgeable professional. Avoid slang, excessive jargon, superlative language, and condescending verbiage. Often when the proposal is describing the instructional design solution to the reader, it can seem stilted and pedantic. This should be avoided.

Another common mistake made by many novice proposal writers is to add dramatic words in an attempt to convey a deep sense of importance to the prospective client. While it is critical to let prospective clients know you think their problem is important, do not overdo the importance. Terms such as "awesome," "imminent," "paramount," and "terrific" as well as phrases such as "hold a candle to" or "vast reservoir of knowledge" are out of place in a business proposal.

> *The need for your e-learning solution is imminent. We will provide a learning portal along with the proposed training modules that have been deemed of paramount importance.*

The use of these words is too much. They add an artificial level of importance and false sense of drama not warranted in a business proposal. Use straightforward terms that do not convey too much gravity or severity. Terms such as critical, important, and overriding can work in place of more dramatic terms. The sentence below is more appropriate for an e-learning proposal.

> *The need for your e-learning solution is critical. We will provide a learning portal along with the proposal training modules that have been deemed important.*

In summary, take great care to eliminate any writing that seems pompous. Keep the writing at a friendly, professional level and take great care to avoid the addition of dramatic words or phrases. A well-written proposal should not need the added drama.

ELIMINATING BIAS WRITING

Another area that proposal writers must consider is bias language. Writers need to take great care to avoid offending any potential clients. Many bias statements occur in proposal writing simply because the writers do not consider the factors that make writing biased. "Long-standing cultural practice can exert a powerful influence over even the most conscientious author" [1]. With business professionals coming from more and more diverse backgrounds, an effective proposal writer will take great care not to offend any potential readers.

To help avoid bias in proposal writing, the following guidelines and subsequent checklist were developed. These tools should help the proposal writer avoid bias language [2].

Be precise when referring to people — Referring to all people as "men" is not as accurate as the phrase "men and women." To describe age groups, it is better to give a specific age range such as "ages 18 to 25" instead of a broad category such as "over 18." "Oriental" is not as precise as "Korean," "Chinese," or "Vietnamese." However, if at all possible, avoid any reference to ethnic group or gender. Also, if you are developing instruction for a large population, clearly identify if you are proposing to produce materials in one or multiple languages.

Avoid associating a gender with a profession — Not all nurses are female and not all supervisors are male. Avoid sentences such as "At the XYZ clinic a nurse can choose her own method of online learning." Instead, write "At the XYZ clinic, nurses can choose their own method of online learning." Terms such as "chairman," "foreman," and "salesmanship" should not be used. Instead use terms such as "chairperson," "supervisor" "manager," and "ability to sell."

Avoid labeling a behavior or trait as belonging to a specific gender — "The masculine trait of bravado was evident in the chemical plant supervisor." "As females usually do, she enjoyed learning." These types of phrases should be avoided.

Do not classify people by a label — Calling a group of people "subordinates" or "techies" is not appropriate. Instead, it would be better to use the terms "employees who work for managers" or "technically skilled people." Keep in mind that you are referring to people and not to the categories by which those people may be known.

Avoid culturally specific references — Certain holidays such as Christmas and Thanksgiving are not universal and should not be referenced in the proposal (although time should be appropriately accounted for in the development schedule if the days are legal holidays). Also, avoid symbols of nationalism (for example, referring to the Statue of Liberty as a symbol of freedom may not hold much meaning for individuals from other countries).

Do not unfairly mix gender terms — The phrases "girls and men," "ladies and men," or "man and wife" are not appropriate. Each of these phrases implies superiority of one gender over the other. It would be better to write "women and men," "girls and boys," and "husband and wife."

Do not unfairly describe a population or person — Using the term "smart supervisor" or "astute manager" implies that other managers or supervisors are not smart or astute. Also avoid phrases such as "the articulate female executive." This implies that typical female executives are not articulate.

Avoid language that implies sexual orientation or innuendo — It is never appropriate to indicate sexual orientation, preference, or innuendo in proposals. Avoid phrases such as "I'm going to reproduce" when referring to making copies in a copy machine. Avoid suggestions of sexual behavior and orientation as well as any sexual undertones. This can sometimes happen accidentally, so make sure you have others reread your proposal so no undertones or double meanings are evident.

Avoid emotionally charged expressions — A term such as "underling" or "secretary" can sometimes carry with it negative overtones and should be avoided. Phrases such as "ignorant factory workers" or "untrained assistants" should not be used. Instead use phrases like "employee working for" or "factory workers who are not aware of" or "assistants who were not trained."

The goal is to use language that is universally appropriate in a variety of business environments. Even if you are familiar with the client, you never know who may end up reading the proposal. Keep the language simple, professional, unbiased, and at a level everyone can understand. Use Worksheet 6.1 to help you avoid bias language in your proposals.

READING LEVEL

The proposal should be written at a ninth-grade reading level. Most word processing software programs offer readability formulas with spelling and grammar check. The two offered with MS Word are the Flesch Reading Ease score and the Flesch-Kincaid Grade Level score. Both of these scores take into consideration average sentence length and the number of syllables per word.

The Flesch Reading Ease score rates text on a 100-point scale; the higher the score, the easier it is to understand the document. For most proposals, you should aim for a score of approximately 60 to 70.

The Flesch-Kincaid Grade Level score rates text on a U.S. grade-school level. A score of 8.0 means an eighth grader can understand the document. Proposals should have a score of approximately 8.0 to 9.0.

Use the "reading level" function of your word processing software to check your proposal before sending it to the client. You can bring down the reading level of a document by reducing the length of sentences, using more common words, and avoiding too much jargon.

THE IMPORTANCE OF REDUNDANCY

A proposal is not read in a linear fashion, one section after another. It is read randomly because each person on the evaluation team is interested in a different part of the document. For example, the information systems manager is interested in the technical solution, while the training manager is interested in the instructional design portion. Therefore, you must repeat the essence of your solution in

Checklist for Unbiased Proposal Writing

When reviewing the final proposal follow this checklist. If you answered "No" to any of the questions you will need to rewrite that part of the proposal to ensure that it does not contain bias language or content.

Question	Yes	No
Is the language precise when referring to specific people or groups of people?	Yes ☐	No ☐
Does the proposal avoid associating a gender with a profession?	Yes ☐	No ☐
Does the proposal avoid labeling a behavior/trait as belonging to one gender?	Yes ☐	No ☐
Does the proposal avoid classifying people by illness or age?	Yes ☐	No ☐
Does the proposal avoid culturally specific references?	Yes ☐	No ☐
Does the proposal avoid unfairly mixing gender terms?	Yes ☐	No ☐
Does the proposal avoid unfairly describing a population or person?	Yes ☐	No ☐
Does the proposal avoid language that implies sexual orientation and/or innuendos?	Yes ☐	No ☐
Does the proposal avoid emotionally charged expressions?	Yes ☐	No ☐
Does the proposal contain any phrases or statements that may be deemed offensive?	Yes ☐	No ☐
Has proposal been reviewed specifically to eliminate any bias writing?	Yes ☐	No ☐

Worksheet 6.1 Use the *Checklist for Unbiased Proposal Writing* to ensure that you write a bias-free proposal.

every section of your document without seeming redundant. This can be a difficult task.

One effective method of adding redundancy without being boring is to frame the solution into the context of the proposal section. Using this method, you repeat your main solution as it relates to the section.

In the instructional design section:

> The instructional solution we are offering is effective because it is delivered using Active Server Pages (ASP) technology. This enables us to provide dynamic Web sites in an almost infinite combination to the learner while freeing the front-line trainer from security and maintenance issues, allowing him or her to concentrate on delivering knowledge and not the underlying technology necessary for the e-learning to be successful.

Another effective method is to refer directly to a previous section of the proposal. This ties together the sections of the proposal and lets the reader know that you know the proposal has some redundancy.

In the technical section:

> As described in the Overview of the Solution Section, our technical solution is to provide an ASP (Active Server Pages) environment to meet your security, instructional, and maintenance needs.

You can also paraphrase your solution by altering the words you use to refer to the elements of the solution. In this case, the term "security" was changed to "secure access." This may seem minor but it helps someone reading through the entire document to avoid boredom.

In the budget section:

> The budget was developed to support the concept of ASP (Active Server Pages). The carefully developed budget meets the needs of secure access, instructional integrity, and ease of maintenance in a cost-effective manner.

A question usually arises concerning how often the words of an acronym should be repeated. For example, in the last three paragraphs the acronym "ASP" is linked with the words "Active Server Pages" in every section.

A good rule of thumb is to repeat the words of the acronym at the beginning of each section and use the acronym throughout the rest of the section. This is important because few evaluators read an e-learning proposal cover to cover and do not want to thumb through the entire document to learn what the letters of an acronym represent.

CRISP, CONCISE WRITING

Busy professionals are constantly under deadlines and time pressure. They do not want to spend extra time reading verbose, long-winded proposals. Too many words or unnecessary redundancies result in boring, hard to read proposals. Avoid wordiness.

Unfortunately, wordiness is a common problem with proposal writing; often the author of a proposal is writing to impress the reader rather than conveying meaning. The desire to impress the reader typically results in unnecessary words, a formal stiff tone, and the inclusion of meaningless buzzwords.

The goal of a proposal is not to impress the reader. It is to convince the reader of the feasibility of your e-learning solution. Impress the reader by succinctly making your point and selling him or her on your solution. Remember, "save the words."

Extra words clutter sentences and hide meaning. Make a conscious effort to "trim" words from sentences. Each word must be able to stand on its own. Simple words, paragraphs, and concepts are good. Complexity is bad. Avoid it.

Write as you speak. Ask yourself how you would say it if you were talking to the prospective client [3]. You want to formally address the person in a professional manner but you do not want to inundate them with too many buzzwords, jargon, or superfluous language. By the same token, you do not want to appear uneducated, ill-informed, or unprofessional. Consider the following:

Would you really say this?

> *The fundamental impediment to your organization's successful implementation of a technocentric learning strategy is the inadequate technological infrastructure throughout your company.*

Or would it be more like this?

> *Your company's main obstacle for implementing e-learning is the lack of an adequate computer network.*

Or like this?

> *Your network stinks.*

(This is going too far. You want to keep it simple but maintain a professional tone.)

The most effective proposals do not contain buzzwords, confusing sentences, or techo-speak. Instead, they are short and to the point. They strive for simple sentences and simple words.

The better a perspective client understands your proposal, the higher your chance of success. Do not fall into the trap of turning a word like "use" into "utilize" because it sounds more professional or businesslike. Keep it simple.

Use sentences that are no more than 15 or 20 words long and paragraphs that

Table 6.1 List of Wordy Sentences and Their Shortened Versions

Wordy sentence
It is the e-learning portal *that* tracks employee scores.
Shortened sentence
The e-learning portal tracks employee scores.

Wordy sentence
There are many OSHA-approved e-learning classes *that* are available.
Shortened sentence
Many OSHA-approved e-learning classes are available.

Wordy sentence
The consultant who was subcontracted is experienced with JAVA.
Shortened sentence
The subcontracted consultant is experienced with JAVA.

Wordy sentence
The solution appears *to be* necessary for growth.
Shortened sentence
The solution appears necessary for growth.

Wordy sentence
Our e-learning courses state the *exact date of revision.*
Shortened sentence
Our e-learning courses state the *exact revision date.*

are 100 words or less [4–6]. Look for the two or three words that carry meaning in your sentence and try to eliminate all other words such as which, by, is, of, to be, who, whom, it is, and that. Table 6.1 provides examples of wordy sentences that have been condensed into simpler, more effective sentences. Table 6.2 lists "wordy" phrases often found in proposals and the shortened version of each phrase.

The proposal writer must weigh each word to determine if it is needed. If the word is not needed, eliminate it.

USE ACTIVE VOICE

One place in which wordiness invades a document is through the use of passive voice: *The test data is secured by the user login.* Overuse of passive voice is boring, impersonal, wordy, and unnecessary. Instead, use the active voice to make your point: *The user login secures the test data.* Active voice is more direct and easier to read, two virtues in proposal writing.

Table 6.2 List of Wordy Phrases and the Shortened Version of Each Phrase [7–10]

Wordy Phrase	Shortened Version
Absolutely essential	Essential
Adequate enough	Enough
Advance notice	Notice
Advance warning	Warning
Ahead of schedule	Early
A large number of	Many
At all times	Always
At an early date	Soon
At the present time	Now
Basic fundamentals	Fundamentals
By means of	By
During the time that	While
Each and every	Each
Each separate lesson	Lesson
Exactly identical	Identical
For the purpose of	For
In order to	To
In regard to	Regarding
In relation to	With
It is clear that	Clearly
Long in size	Long
Many different ways	Many ways
Mutual cooperation	Cooperation
Necessary prerequisite	Prerequisite
Of a peculiar kind	Peculiar
Of an indefinite nature	Indefinite
Of great importance	Important
Out-of-date	Dated
Paramount importance	Important
Prior to	Before
Puzzling in nature	Puzzling
Refer back	Refer
Repeat again	Repeat
Take into consideration	Consider
True facts	Facts
Until such time as	Until
Wide variety	Variety
With reference to (with regard to)	About

In the active voice the action is in the verb, whereas in the passive voice the action is in the form of the helping verb "to be" [11].

Any form of the word "is" may reveal the passive voice. In sentences written in the passive voice, the subject of the sentence is being acted upon. To determine if a sentence is in active or passive voice, identify the subject of the sentence and decide if the subject is doing the action or if it is being acted upon.

For example, in the sentence "The kickoff meeting was made for September 25" the subject is *kickoff meeting*. The subject is being acted upon; therefore, the verb (*was made*) is passive. Another method to determine passive-voice verbs is to look for "to be" verbs, such as *is*, *are*, *was*, *were*, *be*, or *been*.

For example, the sentence "The proposal was submitted before the June 1st deadline" is written in the passive voice with an emphasis on the word *was*. In an active-voice sentence, the subject is the doer of the action. The subject makes something happen. If we rewrite the sentence to read "Exoset Interactive submitted the proposal before the June 1st deadline," the main focus is on "submitted." It moves the sentence into an "active" frame of reference. It implies confidence, action, and precision.

In the first version of the sentence, the passive-voice verb emphasizes the proposal. In sentences with passive-voice verbs, the doer of the action is typically unknown. For example, in the first version of the sentence, it is not stated what company or individual completed the proposal. In contrast, the second version of the sentence uses an active-voice verb emphasizing Exoset Interactive, the company that submitted the proposal.

Active verbs are appropriate for proposal writing because such verbs tell the reader what the action is and who or what is performing the action [12]. The sentence "The kiosk will be able to be accessed by truck drivers at truck stops" is not as effective as "Truck drivers access the kiosk at truck stops."

PARAGRAPH FORMAT

You must design each paragraph carefully for maximum impact. A well-written proposal informs and persuades the reader through careful paragraph design. Well-designed paragraphs have the characteristics of unity and coherence [13, 14]. These two characteristics make it easy for the reader to understand what you are writing.

UNITY

Each paragraph should embody one idea, topic, or concept expressed within the topic sentence. Each sentence within the paragraph should support the topic sentence. When writers introduce other ideas or topics into a paragraph, they violate the unity of the paragraph. When paragraph unity is violated, the reader becomes disoriented or confused.

Here is an example of a paragraph that lacks unity. In fact, the paragraph contains at least three different disjointed thoughts. The sentences do not flow and the transitions between sentences are nonexistent.

> It is assumed that both new and experienced truck drivers are over 18 years of age. These drivers have at least a 6th grade reading level. Research indicates that approximately half of all truck drivers own computers. For novice users, SoluTeach offers a complimentary Introduction to Computers training course for distribution by Truckco.

Notice that the writer begins to discuss both new and experienced truck drivers and their reading level and then immediately discusses that half of all truck drivers who own a computer. There is no transition between reading level and truck drivers' computer ownership. The last sentence ignores the experienced truck drivers and just discusses the novice drivers. This paragraph needs to have a link between one sentence and the next.

> It is assumed that both new and experienced truck drivers are over 18 years of age and have at least a 6th grade reading level. In addition, research indicates that approximately half of all truck drivers own computers. For the 50% of drivers who are new to computers, SoluTeach will offer a complimentary Introduction to Computers training course for distribution by Truckco. This course is specifically written at a 6th grade level and is geared toward users over the age of 18.

In this example, one important item to note is that the effort of unifying the paragraph increased the number of words from 53 to 84. This seems to be in direct contradiction to the earlier discussion on reducing wordiness. This is where the "art" of proposal writing comes into play.

A good proposal writer balances all the elements of good writing to create the desired effect. Sometimes wordiness is sacrificed for unity and sometimes passive voice seems more appropriate than active voice. The art of writing a good proposal is balancing the elements. Guidelines can help in this area, but to build the skill you must write and rewrite, evaluate the effort, and gain the unbiased input of others. Do not treat these guidelines as set in stone; instead, treat them as sound advice that needs to be weighed, considered, and acted upon carefully.

COHERENCE

Coherence is the quality that makes it easy for the reader to follow the writer's train of thought from sentence to sentence and idea to idea. Coherence is the tendency of the paragraph to lead the reader from point to point in a logical, clear manner. It is the arrangement of the writer's thoughts into clear, established order. Notice in the previous paragraph how the first and the last sentences use the idea of truck drivers being over the age of 18 and having at least a 6th grade reading level. The first and last sentences tie the paragraph together — they make it coherent.

Coherence can be achieved by using certain conventions throughout a paragraph. Although not all conventions should be used in every paragraph, careful use of the coherence conventions can make your entire proposal more readable.

REPEAT KEY WORDS

In the following paragraph, notice that the words *firewall* and *security* are the links from sentence to sentence.

> The first line of security is to place the trainee database server behind a *firewall*. The *firewall* we recommend has three levels of *security*. These three *security* levels protect the server from unauthorized access either internally or externally. The secure *firewall* protects your critical data from hackers, e-mail viruses, and computer worms.

USE SIMPLE CONNECTING WORDS

Use pronouns for key nouns. Pronouns gain meaning from the noun in the previous sentence. Also use words such as *it*, *that*, *this*, *these*, *those*, *most*, *several*, *many*, and *they*.

> Docent Enterprise 4.7 Learning Management System is our recommended solution. We have been using *it* since the release of version 3.2 and, therefore, have a clear understanding of *its* capabilities and maintenance requirements.

> We recommend the creation of four separate modules. *These* modules will have the following characteristics. The first is an objectives page. *This* page will contain a listing of each objective and its performance measure.

USE THOUGHT-CONNECTING WORDS

Use thought-connecting words such as *however*, *unless*, *therefore*, *on the other hand*, and *in turn*.

> SoluTeach anticipates that the number of users, both drivers and general public, accessing the portal will increase substantially in the coming years. *Therefore*, the recommended server is scalable to meet the needs of the present audience.

Another effective technique is to arrange sentences in a perceptible order. There are basically three different methods of ordering ideas in sentences: chronological, descriptive, and logical.

USE TIME OR CHRONOLOGICAL ORDER

This is used when attempting to establish a time frame or to link information to a specific due date for a deliverable.

> In the *first* month of the project, we will hold team meetings at each of the different plants to determine the learning needs of the entire organization. In the *second* month of the project, the development team will perform a task analysis of the top five tasks identified during the first month of the project. In the *third* month, the team will design the training.

USE DESCRIPTIVE ORDER

Descriptive order is used to paint a mental picture in the mind of the reader concerning what something will look like. It is used effectively for describing parts of a lesson, a design strategy, a procedure, or pages of a Web site.

> The lesson will have *three distinct sections*. The initial section includes graphics designed to gain the attention of the user. The *next section* contains the concepts and procedures the user must learn. The *final section* contains a practice exercise.

USE LOGICAL ORDER

This technique is usually used to describe a concept, procedure, model, strategy, or project plan. The writer of the paragraph establishes a sequence or relationship between sentences to describe how all of the ideas of the paragraph fit together.

The techniques used to establish a logical order include using the idea of cause and effect, general to specific, whole to part, familiar to unfamiliar, sequencing from one idea to another, or dividing a concept into different parts and then describing how individual parts work together to accomplish a goal.

EXAMPLE OF SEQUENCING

> The *first line* of security is to place the database server behind a firewall. The *second line* of security is the addition of password and login encryption. The *third line* of security is physical.

EXAMPLE OF DESCRIBING HOW INDIVIDUAL PARTS WORK TOGETHER TO ACCOMPLISH A GOAL

> The reason phase two of the project is scheduled for six months is because the design of the instruction is in that phase. Designing instruction requires the development of the course outline by the design staff. The course outline must then be converted into a flow chart and storyboards. The flow chart details the screen-by-screen progression of the course. The storyboards provide a detailed explanation of what appears on each screen.

TRANSITIONAL WORDS

Coherence can also be established by using words to move the reader from one thought to another. These words are typically called transitional words. Transitional words help make the document "flow" and make it easy for the reader to move from idea to idea. Transitional words include [15, 16] *and, or, but, for example, although, unless, instead, for instance, because, before, in fact, finally, since, after, first, second, third…, consequently, provided, meanwhile, next, until, when, whenever, for this reason, furthermore, in addition, nevertheless, on the other hand, for example*, and *however.*

CONSIDER YOUR READERS

Consider your audience as a mixed group of intelligent and reasonable professionals who do not understand instructional technology, e-learning, or the multimedia development process. These professionals know and understand business and may even understand training but usually are not well versed in all aspects of e-learning. Try to imagine what they may ask and what their objections to your solution may be. Address those potential objections in your writing.

After reviewing the executive summary, most proposal readers will look at the budget and the timeline. Almost everything else is secondary. Make sure these sections are well written. If these items are satisfactory, then the other items (project management, technical solution, and instructional design) will be read. Each section must contribute to the entire solution within the proposal, but must also stand alone because often readers will not read a proposal cover to cover. They read only one to two sections.

The key to good writing is rewriting. Do not be afraid to review and revise the document again and again until you have a well-written proposal. However, do not spend all of the allowed time just writing the proposal. A proposal will never really be complete — you can always add "just one more thing." But at some point, you must consider the fact that the reader will be better off with a well-edited, nicely polished document than a sloppy proposal with "everything" in it. At some point, draw a line and do not make any more revisions to the document. Instead, use the time for grammar and spelling corrections. The time will be well spent.

THE BOTTOM LINE

Many people, especially in the training field, will gladly take a red pen to a document and mark every mistake, typo, and grammatical error. Do not give them the opportunity. Take the time for quality control. Remember, the proposal is sometimes the first and only impression the client has of your organization. Make sure the impression is one of neatness and attention to detail.

7

CHARTS, GRAPHS, ILLUSTRATIONS, AND OTHER EYE CATCHERS

Richard Peck, Institute for Interactive Technologies

INTRODUCTION

Part of the requirements of an e-learning vendor is to make difficult information understandable and boring information interesting. Your proposal must demonstrate your firm's ability to convert mere information into knowledge and instruction. If you cannot do that in your proposal, chances are you will not be able to do that online. Clients judge your firm by the "look and feel" of your proposal. They want a crisp, clean document that elegantly conveys information in an eye-pleasing format. Many clients glance through proposals looking for diagrams, illustrations, and tables before even reading any of the text. Your use of graphics must catch the client's eye and draw the client in.

WHY ARE GRAPHICS IMPORTANT?

Including graphics in your proposal enhances it in a number of ways. They add appeal and character, motivate the client, and assist with the visualization of your solution. Clients do not like to read page after page of text. It is tiring. By providing graphics, you give readers a place to rest and relax their eyes. Graphics reduce the fatigue that occurs when reading too much text.

There are cognitive benefits as well. Graphics can explain difficult concepts or relationships with one image where it may take four or five text pages. Graphics arrange information quickly and provide a clear message. By providing graphics, you increase the chance of readers retaining and comprehending the information being presented. Clear explanations of concepts or topics give you an added advantage over your competitors.

While the use of graphics is important, you need to keep in mind the first principle of instructional graphics: "There are times when pictures can aid learning, times when pictures do not aid learning but do no harm, and times when pictures do not aid learning and are distracting" [1]. You want the picture or graphics within your e-learning proposal to, at the least, not distract your reader and, at the most, add value.

To understand how graphics can add value to your proposal, you need to understand the different types of graphics and the most appropriate format for each type.

TYPES OF GRAPHICS

There are many types of graphics you can include in your proposal. Regardless of the type, the goals of each are the same — succinctly and effectively convey the right message. Do not include graphics simply for the sake of visuals. Each graphic must have a meaning, a purpose, and a message even if it is just to give the reader a break.

One method of identifying items to be visualized is to look for areas of complexity or confusion. When portions of the proposed solution are difficult to grasp, graphics can usually add clarity. Graphics provide a concise explanation of a topic and help to organize the reader's thoughts.

Graphics for e-learning proposals can be divided into different categories according to the type of information being explained. The categories are:

- Photographs/drawings
- Tables
- Charts and graphs
- Flow charts
- Screen captures

PHOTOGRAPHS AND DRAWINGS

Objects can be visualized through the use of photographs or drawings. Sometimes it is valuable to display a concrete item such as a laptop, kiosk, or personal digital assistant (PDA) to a potential client. We all liked picture books as children

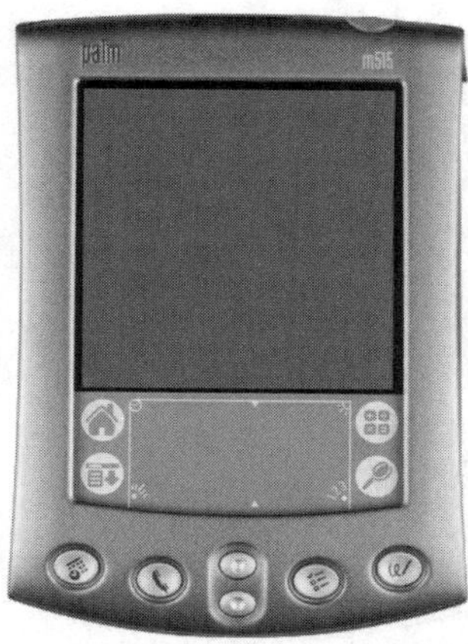

Figure 7.1 Photograph of a personal digital assistant (PDA).

and we tend to like pictures of one sort or another within e-learning proposals. The use of photographs and drawings can be especially effective for drawing attention to a piece of hardware that you are planning to recommend.

For example, imagine you are designing an e-learning training module for delivery to field engineers over a wireless network through a PDA. It may help your potential client to visualize the use of the PDA by including a photograph of it within the proposal as shown in Figure 7.1. The reader of the proposal then has an exact vision of what the PDA looks like. There is little chance of confusion or misunderstanding concerning the type of PDA being recommended.

While photographs provide a high level of detail, they do have some drawbacks. The first is that they do not photocopy very well. Often a proposal is photocopied and distributed among the client's evaluation team. If the photograph loses clarity or becomes hard to read, key information that you are trying to convey could be lost. This could then reflect poorly on your firm.

Second, a photograph may contain more detail than the client needs. You may only want the client to concentrate on one or two aspects of the photograph and not on the entire image.

It is for these reasons that sometimes it is more effective to use a diagram to show the object you want to represent. A diagram is a line drawing of an object displaying pertinent details. Figure 7.2 shows a diagram of a PDA with certain features highlighted. Diagrams tend to photocopy with more clarity than photographs and provide the chance to add a feature on the item that does not currently exist. You can use a line drawing to "invent" new items where photographs provide an image of "the real thing." A hardware prototype is an excellent candidate for a diagram.

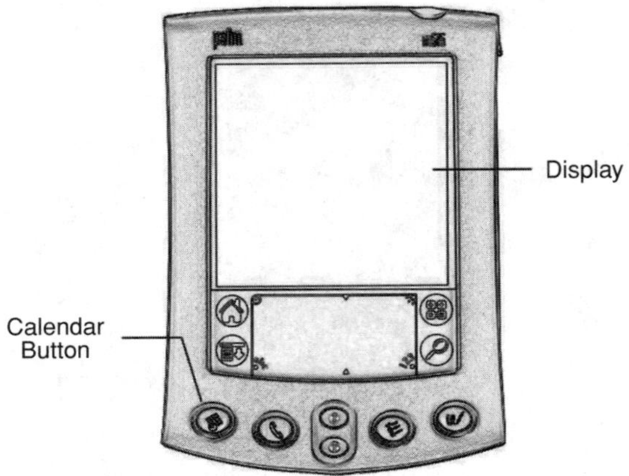

Figure 7.2 Line drawing of a PDA.

TABLES

Tables are an effective method for presenting information within a proposal. They can be used to convey a relationship between two or more items or to show different dimensions of a relationship. Tables 7.1 and 7.2 demonstrate how tables can be used to describe information concerning the relationship between various items. Table 7.1 shows the relationship between the tasks of the project and the individuals performing the tasks and who has primary responsibility for a task and who is the backup. Table 7.2 shows the different elements of e-learning solutions that have been performed for various clients.

Tables are excellent tools for showing numeric data. Many tables within a proposal are composed of a series of rows and columns. A distinct advantage of a table over a chart or graph for presenting numeric data is that it is precise. The reader can see the exact numbers being referenced. For example, if you want to show a breakdown of the amount of time each member of your project team spent on a project, you may decide to include the data as a table as shown in Table 7.3, which illustrates a budget table from a proposal.

Using tables in your proposals allows your client to quickly find and access the information being presented. Regardless of whether your tables contain numbers or show relationships, make sure they are simple. Overly complex tables may confuse your reader and lead to questions.

A popular type of table to include within a proposal is a comparison between two or more items or solutions. This is frequently included within the budget section. For example, you may compare the cost of having the e-learning hosted on your own servers vs. the cost of the client hosting the e-learning solution.

Table 7.1 Using a Table to Show Relationships

	Person Assigned to the Task					
Project Tasks	**Project Manager**	**Senior Instructional Designer**	**Junior Instructional Designer**	**Quality Assurance Manager**	**Web Developer**	**Graphic Artist**
Facilitate kickoff meeting	▲	△				
Development of needs analysis questionnaire		▲	△			
Meeting with Subject Matter Expert (SME)	▲	△				
Development of HTML training template					▲	△
Creating static graphics for instructional unit		△				▲
Complete quality checklist for each module	△			▲		

▲ = Primary responsibility △ = Secondary responsibility

Table 7.2 Using a Table to Show Different Types of Information

	Area of Focus					
Client	**Needs Analysis**	**Course Development**	**Blended Learning**	**LMS Implementation**	**Streaming Video**	**Online Collaboration**
HealthCo	⊙		●			
Xpress Airlines		⊙			●	
Truckco	●			⊙		
Shazam Consulting			⊙			●
Super HealthCare		●		⊙		
Institute of Technology		●	⊙			

● = Primary focus of project ⊙ = Secondary focus of project

Table 7.3 Numeric Information

	Excluding Kiosk	Including Kiosk	Date Due
Initial payment (40%)	170,232.00	181,317.20	4/23/01
Summary of development (25%)	106,395.00	113,323.25	6/11/01
End of Phase 2 (25%)	106,395.00	113,323.25	8/20/01
End of Phase 3 (10%)	42,558.00	45,329.30	10/01/01
	425,580.00	**452,293.00**	

Table 7.4 Comparison of Two Different Types of Learning Delivery Methods

Traditional approach to new employee training and maintenance	[Classroom instruction] Corporate overview	[Classroom instruction] Job-specific training	[Classroom instruction] Refresher training	[Conference call] Supervisor follow-up
Blended approach to new employee training and maintenance	[Web-based instruction] Corporate overview	[Classroom instruction] Job-specific training	[Web-based instruction] Refresher training	[Conference call] Supervisor follow-up

Key: [Classroom icon] = Classroom instruction [Computer icon] = Web-based instruction [Telephone icon] = Conference call

You can also use a table to show the relationship of one type of solution to another. Table 7.4 illustrates a table that compares a traditional training solution with a blended learning solution.

CHARTS AND GRAPHS

While charts and graphs are not as precise for showing numeric data as a table, they are excellent for displaying trends and relationships. A number of chart types are available for presenting numeric information [2]. Table 7.5 illustrates the different types of charts and when it is appropriate to use each. It is also a good example of how a table can be used to present information clearly and concisely.

Charts are powerful tools because they convey much meaning in a small space and they are more visual than tables. A quick glance will usually tell you the nature of the information. Figures 7.3 and 7.4 show an effective use of two of the chart types to make a point about trends in the use of HTML in Web-based training and the increase in the number of students within a particular industry enrolled in Web-based courses.

Table 7.5 Different Charts and Graphs That Can Be Used to Display Information in an E-Learning Proposal

Type of Chart	Type of Relationship	Chart Visual
Pie chart	Part to whole/components of whole	
Bar chart (above line)	Item to item	
Bar chart (both sides of line)	Correlation	
Column chart	Time series and frequency	
Line chart	Time series and frequency	
Dot chart	Correlation	

Figure 7.5 shows the use of a bar graph to convey information about the timeline for the project. The chart simply and effectively informs the client of how long each phase of the project will last and when the entire project will be completed.

Figure 7.6 shows the use of a pie chart to indicate what percentage of the project each phase of the instructional design process will take. The pie chart provides the reader with a quick look at the project phases and what percentage of effort will go into each phase.

If you decide to use charts and graphs in your proposal, there are certain items that must be included. For one, always include a title with the chart or graph. A well-titled chart tells the reader of your proposal the nature of the information being presented. When creating a chart or graph, do not forget to include a key or legend. The key functions as a translator, telling the reader what the different shades, colors, or patterns mean in the chart or graph. Be sure to include axis labels with charts and graphs.

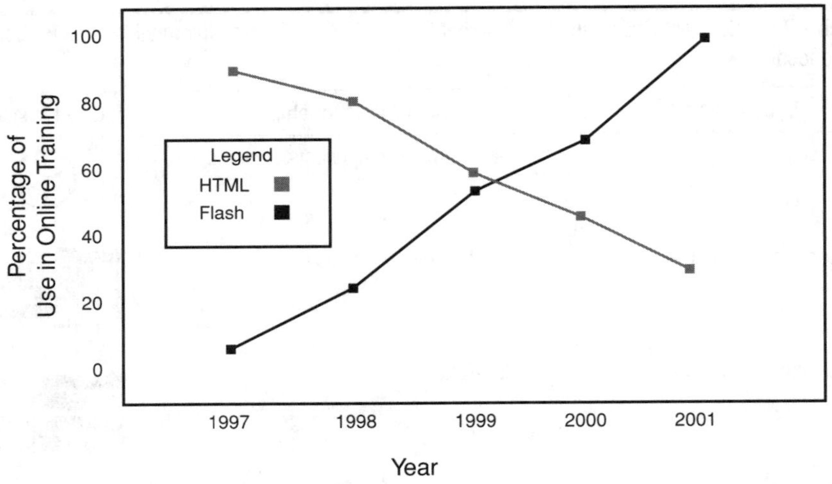

Figure 7.3 Use of a line graph to display numeric information.

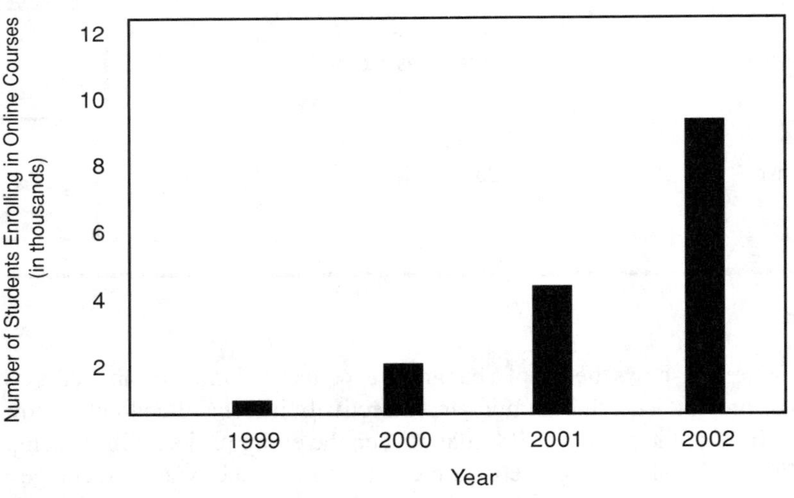

Figure 7.4 Use of a bar chart to display numeric information.

FLOW CHARTS

Flow charts can be used to help the reader visualize concepts or hierarchical arrangements. They can show a sequence of operations, processes, or navigation through a particular situation. Flow charts can also show the relationship between different items.

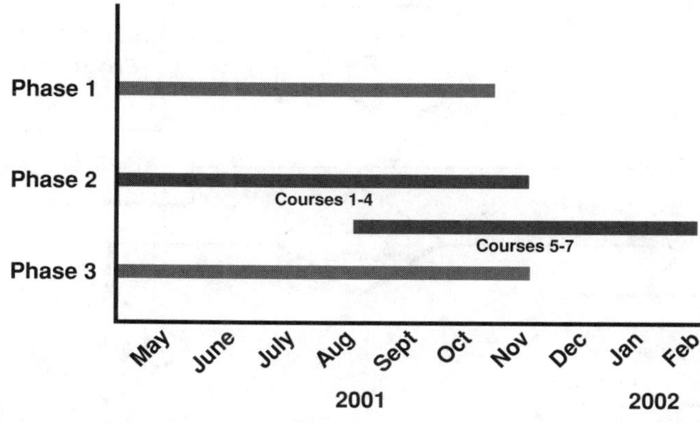

Figure 7.5 Bar chart used to display timeline information for a project.

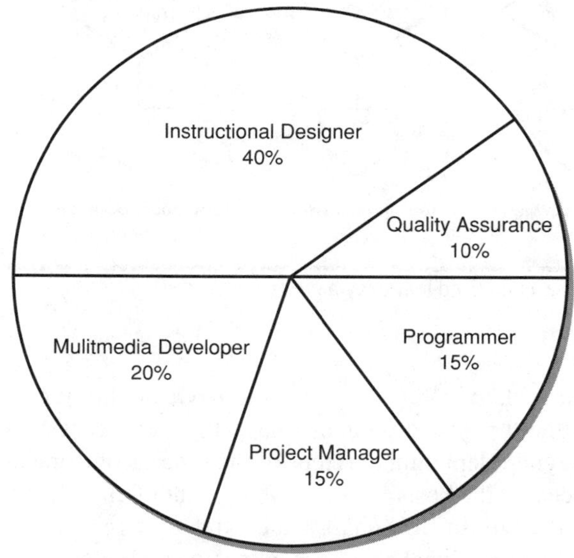

Figure 7.6 Pie chart used to display information about a project.

In manufacturing, flow charts are used to visually show the flow of goods or materials as they are being manufactured. For an e-learning project, flow charts can be used to show the user's path through a program or can be used to show the movement of information from one server to another. Flow charts are effective for any situation where you want to show movement from one area to another.

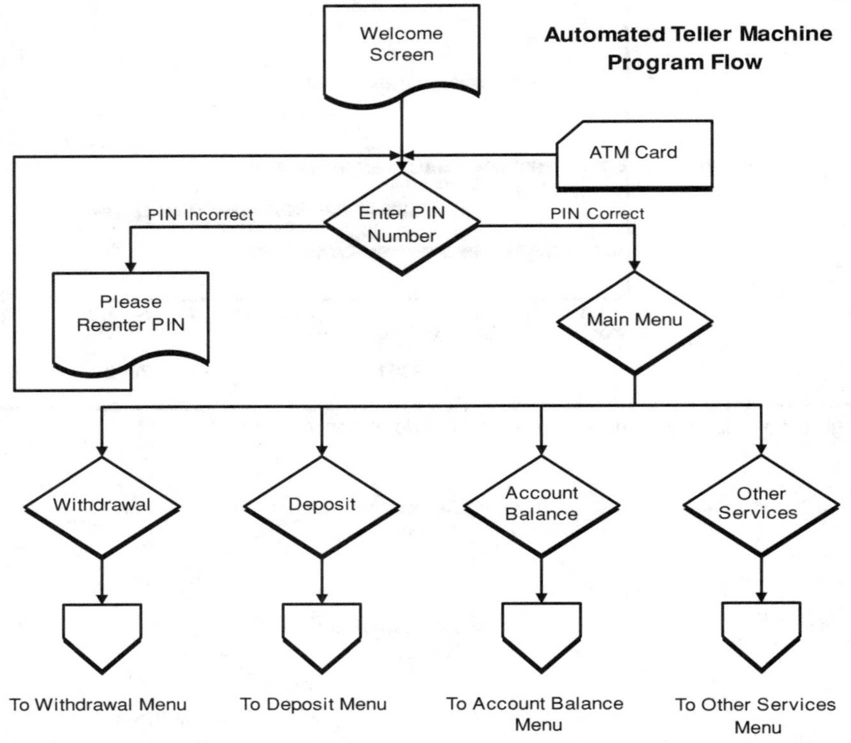

Figure 7.7 Flow chart used to display a process.

The use of flow charts allows the reader to navigate through a particular process or section without physically interacting with that process or section. Figure 7.7 shows a flow chart depicting the steps of the process of using an ATM card. This flow chart became the basis for the development of an online tutorial.

One specific type of flow chart that is often used in a proposal is an organizational chart. Organizational charts visually depict who reports to whom within an organization. When developing a proposal, you may wish to visually show the structure of your development team. Your goal when creating an organizational chart within a proposal is to show the structure of the persons directly involved with the project team. Creating a detailed chart showing more of the firm will only add complexity to the chart. Figure 7.8 shows an organizational chart for an e-learning project team.

Another unique type of flow chart is a model. You might want to include a model within your proposal showing the interrelationship and flow of informa-

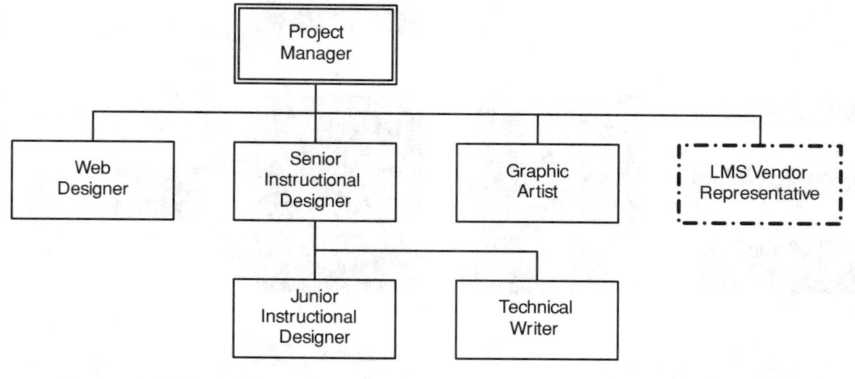

Figure 7.8 An organizational chart used to show the project team reporting structure.

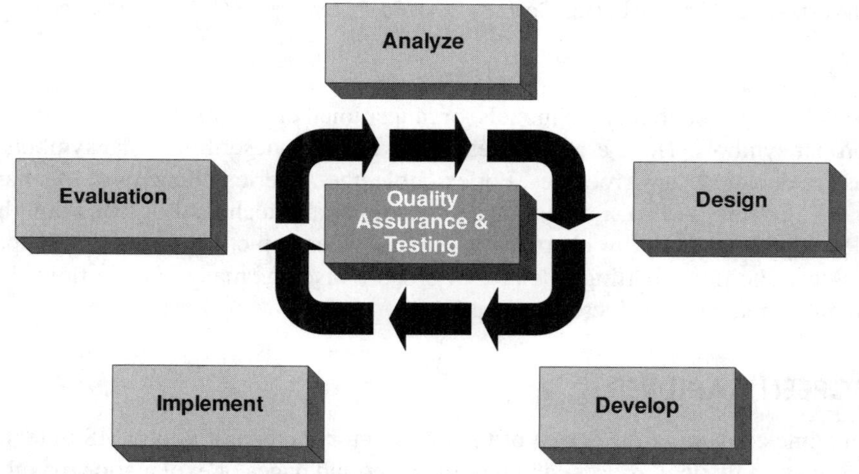

Figure 7.9 Use of a chart to show the instructional design process to a client. (Courtesy Karyn Gandenberger, copyright 2002. With permission.)

tion from one step in the model to the next. The advantage of using a visual model is that it can show relationships that are difficult to describe in text and that are difficult to convey using other types of visuals. Figure 7.9 illustrates an instructional design model.

Another flow chart often used in an e-learning proposal is one showing the relationship of the e-learning system to other systems within the organization and to the end user. Figure 7.10 shows the relationship between the end learner, an LMS, and an LCMS.

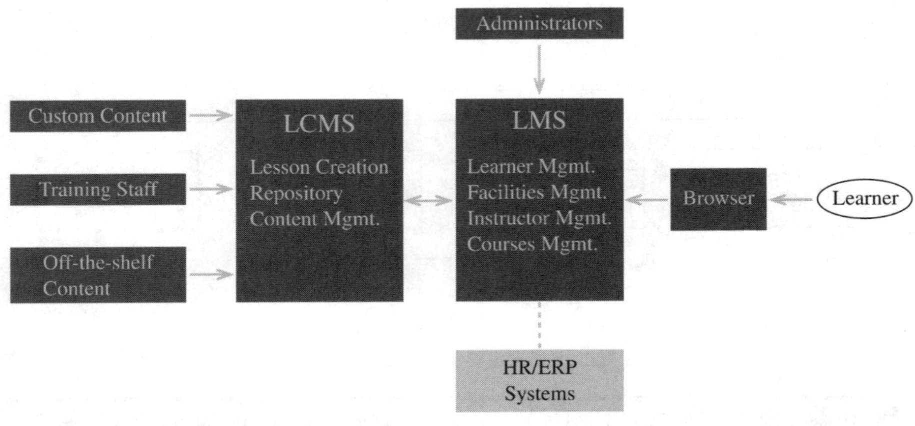

Figure 7.10 Use of a chart to show the relationship between various systems within an organization and between an LMS and LCMS. (Courtesy Divjot Punia, copyright 2002. With permission.)

If you decide to include models, organizational charts, or flow charts, use the proper symbols. There are many resources available describing what symbols to use to depict certain processes. For example, the American Society of Mechanical Engineers (ASME), a nonprofit educational and technical organization, has developed standard flow chart symbols to use when depicting manufacturing processes. The flow charting software Microsoft Viso has many built-in flow chart symbols that are considered standard.

SCREEN CAPTURES

Imagine explaining the layout of the introductory screen of your LMS in text. It would be a difficult process and require pages and pages of explanation, trying to explain what the page looks like, where the menu items are located, and how the banner includes the client's logo. One simple screen capture could explain the introductory screen quickly and easily.

Figure 7.11 shows a screen layout for an LMS. When you have the chance, include a screen layout in your proposal. It helps the client to visualize your solution and understand how your software functions.

PREPARING GRAPHICS FOR PROPOSALS

Before diving into creating the graphics for your proposal, there are a few items you need to consider. A good rule of thumb is "simple is best." Remember, graphics should be used to reinforce or explain already difficult concepts or topics. Com-

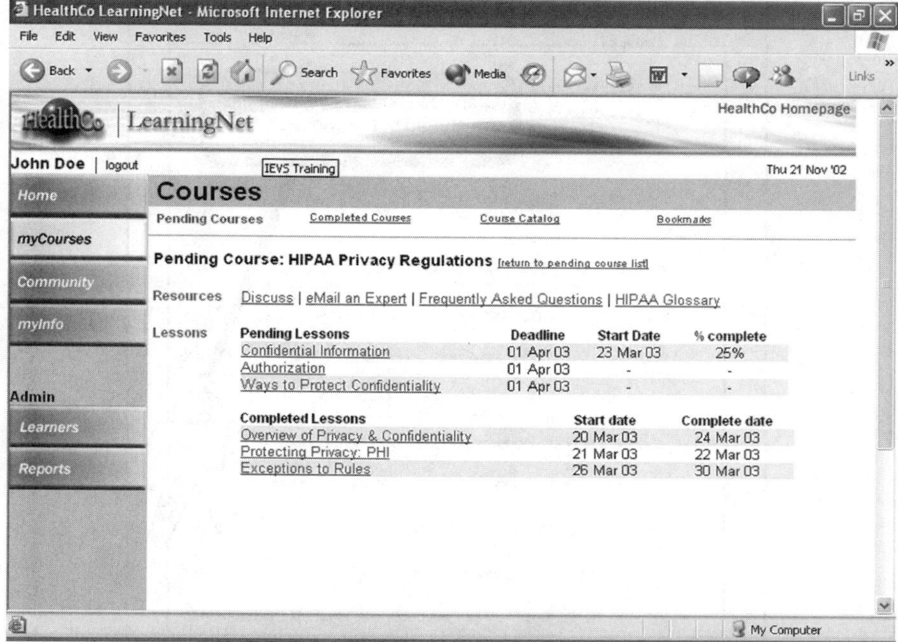

Figure 7.11 Screen capture from an LMS system. (Courtesy Divjot Punia, copyright 2002. With permission.)

plex graphics will only add to the need for explanation. Therefore, try to keep your graphics as simple as possible while still providing a valuable explanation. The goal of any graphic placed in a proposal is to reinforce or display pertinent information, not to dazzle the audience with your graphical ability.

When you are ready to tackle the task of creating the graphical elements for your proposal, you have to make a decision. Will you be creating the graphics yourself or will you hire a graphic artist to create the graphics for you? Hiring a graphic artist will add to the expense of writing the proposal and time frame. However, this approach allows the writer to focus on the textual content in the proposal.

If you are graphically oriented, you may decide to create the graphics for the proposal yourself. Look for graphics software that contains templates for creating models, flow charts, and other images.

PAGE SIZE OF GRAPHICS

Visual aids are meant to support the text of the proposal, not to overtake the proposal content. When creating graphics for your proposal, consideration should

Figure 7.12 Keep the graphical images you use within the margins of the page.

be given to the size of the graphic. Graphics should be sized to easily allow the reader to see the information being presented without taking away from the text of the page. The bounds of the graphic should not extend past the margins of the page. Resize graphics to fit between the margins while still maintaining the readability of the graphic as shown in Figure 7.12. Text information accompanying the graphic should also be formatted for readability. Choose a font size and style that allow the user to read the text easily without straining his or her eyes at the same time. Anything less than 10-point font size is not recommended.

COLOR SELECTION

Creating colorful graphics for your proposals can really enhance the look of the written work. However, more often than not, your proposal will be reproduced in black and white. This is commonly done on a photocopying machine. The vivid colors in your visual aids may not print correctly in black and white and may degrade even further when photocopied. It is important to use colors in your graphics that will reproduce effectively on modern photocopy machines. Experiment with different colors and shades to determine which color combinations will accurately reproduce on the photocopy machine. If you want to ensure that your graphics reproduce exactly as they are, limit your graphics to black and white.

ALTERNATIVE METHODS FOR CREATING GRAPHICS

Including visual aids in your proposal does not mean you have to spend hours creating the graphic from scratch. There are other methods for acquiring graphics. One alternate method of acquiring graphics is to photocopy a graphic that already exists. When using this method, be sure to scale the graphic so that it fits within the bounds of the page. Scanning is also another method that you may choose to use. When scanning, pay attention to the scale and resolution of the scanned image. Adjust these settings to produce a properly sized image at a resolution suitable for printing.

THE BOTTOM LINE

Adding graphics to your proposal will greatly benefit the reader. Visual aids have a profound impact on the way readers interpret information. These aids not only assist in the explanation of content, but also add appeal and character to the written work. Remember, visual aids are not meant to be a display of graphical ability. Use them to enhance and promote the textual content of the written proposal.

8

TEAM WRITING

INTRODUCTION

Writing a proposal is seldom a solo task. Often an ad hoc team is formed to write the proposal. Sometimes the team is the same one that will actually develop the instruction and other times it is whomever is available. When writing a proposal as a team, the team needs to work together to accomplish the goal of winning the business. Several factors contribute to a successful proposal writing team.

TEAM WRITING

Writing as a team is important. The different levels of expertise needed to complete the various sections of the RFP require input from several individuals. The input can range from giving estimates to writing entire sections.

No matter how many people contribute to the completed document, it still must "read" as if it were written by one person. One major reason for the rejection of proposals is that they read as if many people have written the document without any discussions among themselves. Strive for a single voice within the proposal.

To obtain the goal of a single voice, the proposal team must have certain ground rules. If a team spends time at the beginning of the proposal writing process creating the ground rules and discussing how it will approach the proposal, success can be achieved. If the team rushes into writing the proposal without spending time establishing processes and procedures, the likelihood of success is greatly diminished. The writing team must establish the following:

- Clear vision of proposed solution
- Defined roles
- Development process
- Accountability for actions
- Communication plan
- Version control process
- Format plan
- Trust

CLEAR VISION OF PROPOSED SOLUTION

The proposal development team needs to have a clear vision of the proposed solution. If each member of the team has a slightly different vision, the proposal suffers. It becomes choppy, illogical, and difficult to understand, which leads to possible rejection.

To avoid rejection, the proposal team must spend a considerable amount of time discussing the solution even before one word is written. This discussion should focus the team on the solution. Different possible scenarios should be discussed as well as the "ideal" solution and the "minimal" solution. However, simply discussing the proposed solution is not enough. Once a solution is determined, the team must create a vision document.

The vision document is a simple, straightforward statement of one or two pages explaining what the team will propose to the client. The development and adoption of a vision document help each member of the team understand the goal and general direction of the proposal. The vision document serves as a road map during the writing process.

Often proposal development teams become overwhelmed by the needs of the RFP, the research requirements to find the right solution, and the pressure to have the document developed quickly. When this occurs, team members lose focus. The technical person recommends a server too large for the instructional solution. The instructional designer recommends a learning methodology not supported by the technology. The budget person proposes an hourly rate incongruent with the talent needed to develop a 3D simulation. Productivity drops and the proposal becomes confusing and mismatched.

The vision document keeps team members focused and continually reminds them of the shape and form of the final solution. It keeps everyone "on the same page" when they are developing their proposal sections. The vision document keeps the proposal cohesive. When writing, each member keeps the statement in front of him or her and does not "forget" what was said in a meeting or what was decided about the instructional solution. It is written down for everyone to see.

One word of caution: the vision document does not have to be an anvil around the neck of the development team. Occasionally, based on research or other discoveries, the vision document changes. When this occurs, a meeting is held, the new changes are discussed, and each member is given a revised vision document.

The important contribution of the vision document is that it serves as a framework for the larger proposal. It is a clear reminder to the team of the purpose and direction of the proposal. Proposal teams must take the time to discuss the proposed solution and to record that solution. When time is taken early in the process to focus on the vision, time and headaches are saved when the proposal deadline approaches.

DEFINED ROLES

Team members require explicit roles to function effectively. If roles are not defined at the beginning of the writing project, unintended roles develop. Often, these unintended roles are counterproductive. The team must establish clear roles at the beginning of the project. Roles keep team members focused and establish lines of communication, research, and responsibility.

A proposal development team typically includes several of the following roles; however, each team will be structured differently depending on the needs of the RFP and the organization of the vendor. Many different team structures are possible and lead to success. The important thing to remember is that each organization needs to determine, within itself, the roles needed for its success for each different RFP. Different RFPs require different writing teams.

The roles can be broken into two categories, process and functional. The process roles involve the team process. How are team members going to relate to one another? Who will lead? How will decisions be made? Process roles are typically assigned after the team meets for the first time. During the first meeting, each member discusses his or her strengths and weaknesses and indicates a desired role. If the team agrees, then the individual assumes that process role.

Occasionally upper management or some other external person already defines a process role such as team leader or proposal writer. Then the team simply has to decide who will fill the other process roles such as recorder and facilitator.

The functional roles are the specific areas of expertise for each member. Someone will know more about budgeting than any of the other members. He or she will be the budget specialist. Another person will understand instructional strategies and will be the instructional designer. Typically, the functional roles of each team member are defined externally prior to anyone joining the team. These are the jobs for which the team members were hired by the firm. Some possible roles include:

Process role	**Functional role**
Project leader/manager	Instructional designer
Team recorder	Technical expert
Team facilitator	Web designer
Proposal writer	Interface designer
Team member	Programmer
	Quality assurance specialist
	Graphic artist
	Budget specialist

Each of these roles (process and functional) and the members fulfilling them should have a written job description outlining the obligations and responsibilities. While job descriptions are a common practice when hiring new employees, they are seldom used internally.

However, when individuals are faced with the difficult task of developing and writing a proposal, detailed job descriptions help them understand what is expected throughout the proposal development process. The roles work best when the individual team members define them. When the roles of each team member are defined, the individuals can refer to their job descriptions when discrepancies arise. Job descriptions can also diagnose areas of concern when the writing process falls behind schedule.

Roles should not be cast in stone. Allow flexibility within the team. Assigning roles and writing job descriptions for each role is an important component of team growth. It forces the issue of accountability. However, the goal of assigning team roles is not to restrict the team members in any way; rather, it is to allow the team to establish norms and parameters by which it operates. It is always acceptable to ease up on team roles and job descriptions after they have been firmly established. It is difficult to apply strict roles when a team has been run loosely for some time.

Be careful not to overlook a critical element in the development of the proposal because it was not in your job description. The element of flexibility discussed above should help to avoid this situation but it is important for the entire team to remember that roles are the baseline of responsibility and not the entire scope of a team member's responsibility. Many tasks are required of the proposal development team that cannot possibly be foreseen at the beginning of the process.

Each member of the team is important because of his or her role and because of his or her contribution as a team member. Some general tasks and responsibilities of each team member are discussed below.

Project leader — The first role to consider is "project leader" or "project manager." The individual in charge of the proposal development must be part manager and part leader. He or she must be able to keep the writing team on task, must be able to negotiate disagreements, and must be able to keep meetings on track. However, more is required than mere management. Project leaders must inspire, cajole, and drive team members toward success. All of the visioning in the world will not lead to success unless the project leader can inspire his or her team to create a proposal with a clear focus and a sound methodology.

The role of the leader is fundamentally different from any of the project contributor roles. The leader must create a sense of shared ownership. Professionals working on the proposal want to feel as if they are part owners of the process and not just employees. "The best group leaders see themselves as catalysts. They expect to achieve a great deal, but know they can do little without the efforts of others" [1].

The project leader must plan the proposal development process, follow up on assigned tasks, spend time motivating team members, solve team process problems, communicate regularly with team members and possibly the client, keep the vision document up-to-date, and handle any unforeseen problems or issues. The project leader needs to have the final say on all decisions and needs to lead in a manner that is nondictatorial. Leaders who are able to place the team before themselves achieve success. Leaders who let egos or personalities get in the way of progress are dooming their teams to failure.

One of the most important tasks of a team leader is delegation. There are literally hundreds of tasks that must be accomplished for a proposal to be successfully written. The project leader must develop methods of delegating those tasks to other team members and then follow up on those tasks to make sure they were completed. If the tasks are not completed, the project leader must deal with those individuals and determine how to get the tasks completed.

Team recorder — The team recorder is the person responsible for documenting the decisions of the team. Every team needs a recorder because when decisions are made, instructional solutions are determined, and the direction of the proposal is set, not every team member will remember exactly what was agreed upon. Worse, different team members may remember the team decisions differently. To avoid misunderstandings, a recorder is needed. The job of the recorder is to take notes during a meeting, record the rationale for controversial decisions, and assemble a list of action items for each team member after the meeting. The team recorder may also create and distribute the agenda for upcoming meetings based on input from the project leader.

Team facilitator — The facilitator's duty is to keep the team process functioning. Effective writing requires certain team elements to be successful. These elements include having an agenda, giving someone the floor when speaking, not interrupting, involving all team members in a decision, allowing all members to express their thoughts, fairly distributing proposal sections to each person, applying conflict resolution strategies, and other team maintenance issues. While many of the duties may overlap with the team leader, the main difference is that the leader is focused on the final written proposal while the team facilitator focuses on how the team is functioning.

Dysfunctional teams can still (sometimes) achieve their goals while in the process alienating others, destroying careers, stealing the work of others, plagiarizing works, and generally ruining the chance of the team ever working together again. Therefore, the goal of the team facilitator is to keep the team process on track while the team leader keeps the goal in sight. This dual focus on the team process and the team goal helps keep each person's role separate and more focused. The team leader can concentrate on the proposal and the team facilitator can worry about who participated in the final decision to use one instructional strategy over another.

Proposal writer — Some teams have an assigned proposal writer. His or her job is to take the input from the other group members and develop the final written document. Although this role can relieve some of the burden of individual team members, the presence of the proposal writer does not diminish the need for each member's contribution. The proposal writer needs to have a clear understanding of the team's vision of the proposed solution. The clarity and congruence of the proposal depend on how well the proposal writer understands the proposed solution. The proposal writer listens to the group, takes notes, and asks many questions. Sometimes individual team members will write sections of the proposal and the proposal writer will merge the sections into a single cohesive document. The proposal writer's job is basically wordsmithing and not developing a comprehensive document after only one meeting with the proposal development team. A two-way communication path must be established for the proposal to make sense and be effective. The team and the proposal writer must clearly understand each other.

Team member — Each team member plays a critical role in the final development of the proposal. Members who do not have a specific process role certainly have a functional role, and each team member must honor his or her commitment to the team. Team members need to be able to put aside professional and personal differences and work to accomplish a desired goal. Team members will need to perform the specific tasks required to write a successful document. Team members must arrive at meetings on time. They must perform the desired work, and they must be willing to contribute ideas and insights to the writing of the proposal. If they cannot perform these basic functions, they should not be on the team.

Functional roles — The functional roles are established to contribute the necessary expertise to the writing process. When addressing an e-learning RFP, there are many issues to consider. Each individual brings his or her functional expertise to the table. Including a wide range of functions ensures that the various aspects of a client's RFP are considered and that the writing team determines how a decision in one area of the proposal impacts the other areas. For example, the decision to incorporate games and interactivity into a lesson impacts development time, level of talent needed, and project budget.

One effective method of tracking who plays what role within the proposal development process is to have a *Team Role Sheet*. The Team Role Sheet as shown in Worksheet 8.1 indicates who is playing what role. When this worksheet is posted in a prominent place, everyone knows who is doing what and there is no confusion about roles.

DEVELOPMENT PROCESS

Every team needs to have certain rules and parameters under which it functions — a proposal development process. This proposal development process, enforced by the team facilitator, will help the team function together as a cohesive unit. Once this process is established for one proposal, it can be used for all subsequent proposal writing projects.

One method is to develop a list of working rules in the early stages of the project. The rules can then be posted and referred to when necessary. The rules can include basic "rules of fairness" such as:

- Always respect another's opinion even if you disagree with it.
- Do not speak while another person is speaking.
- No idea is too outrageous to suggest.
- If an idea is controversial, a vote will be taken.
- All votes are final and an issue may not be addressed again if vetoed.
- Focus on the problem or behavior, not the person.

These types of rules help team meetings run smoothly and they remind the team that basic rules are important for reaching decisions.

In addition to rules concerning fairness, rules of conduct should be established. The rules of conduct should include:

- Meetings will be held at an established day and time each week.
- Have an agenda for every meeting.
- Always start meetings on time.
- Important items brought up but not on the agenda will be placed off to the side for later discussion.

Team Role Sheet

Complete this sheet to identify which role each person in the group is assuming. The sheet should then be distributed to all the team members and upper management so everyone has a clear understanding of his or her responsibilities to the team during the proposal development process.

Proposal Name:

Process Role	**Name of Person**	**E-Mail**	**Phone Number**
Team Leader			
Team Recorder			
Team Facilitator			
Proposal Writer			
Functional Role	**Name of Person**	**E-Mail**	**Phone Number**

Worksheet 8.1 Use the *Team Role Sheet* to assign a role to each member of the proposal development team.

- Minutes will be taken at each meeting.
- Action item lists will be distributed within one day of a meeting.

Without specific rules, the team becomes embroiled in its own problems and conflicts and loses sight of writing the proposal.

Teams should also understand that there are only two reasons to have a meeting. One is to collaborate on ideas and the other is to coordinate activities. Any other purpose for a meeting is nonvalue-added.

"Coordination is the process of connecting together the actions of the group so that they remain focused on a specific goal" [2]. These meetings should be short and to the point. It is not uncommon to have a coordination meeting that lasts less than 15 minutes. The coordination meeting simply covers who is doing what, where they are in terms of assigned tasks, what they need help with from other team members, and what the next task is. These meetings can be conference calls, virtual chats, or face-to-face meetings. Coordination meetings are urgency driven, meaning that their frequency should reflect the pressures of the project schedule. There is no need to have a coordination meeting every week if the project is progressing at the proper rate [2].

Collaboration meetings are for sharing knowledge, determining trade-offs, arbitrating decisions, and solving technical or instructional problems. These meetings should not last more than two hours. Any meeting over two hours is counterproductive in terms of morale and tasks accomplished. The collaboration meeting should be driven by need. This means that it should be scheduled based on a specific task within the development of the proposal.

A collaboration meeting may involve only a few specific individuals, whereas a coordination meeting is most effective when all interested parties are involved [2]. Using both the collaboration and coordination meetings properly leads to increased team productivity and less stress on team members.

ACCOUNTABILITY FOR ACTIONS

Each proposal development team member must be held accountable for his or her actions. Upper management will, and should, step into the proposal development process if the team is not doing its job (i.e., not finishing proposals or not winning proposals).

Because writing a proposal is a complex process, teams can get bogged down and not make any progress or create subpar proposals. The development team members may be busy working on things related to the proposal, conducting research, and holding meetings, but the proposal is not moving forward. The team must develop or be given a timeline for the completion of the proposal and then each member must be held responsible for meeting those dates. Upper management and the project leader must then use those dates as a tool for helping the team to proceed at a reasonable rate.

Often a "drop-dead" date is established for the team, which is earlier than the date stated on the RFP. The team should backward schedule from that date by determining what needs to be done in what sequence to make that date. Upper management must not allow the team to push that date back unless a compelling reason is presented. This hard-line approach helps to keep the team on track and focused on achieving the goal.

If the team sets intermittent dates or milestones, and is communicating regularly with upper management, then the state-of-readiness of the proposal will not be a secret to upper management. Accountability keeps the team on track and helps everything run smoothly. If a team member feels that he or she is not accountable to the team, he or she will not contribute. If someone knows that another team member will "pick up the slack," he or she may not perform and will let others do the work.

Each team member must be actively involved in the project. If a member is unable to be involved for any reason, then that member must be excused from the team. The project team has too many tasks and responsibilities to carry a noncontributing member. Even though it may result in more work for the other team members until a replacement is found, it must be done.

One method of making the removal process a little easier is to have established criteria indicating when a member can be removed from the team. If that type of rule is established, the individual who is not contributing may volunteer to leave the team because he or she cannot abide by that rule. This allows for a graceful exit for the team and the individual.

Another method is to have the project leader speak to the person individually to avoid a situation where the entire team is confronting one individual. When an entire team confronts one person, that person may feel as if he or she is being "ganged up on" and may resent the team for its actions. If this occurs, the team has just developed a very powerful enemy. Imagine the impact on the rest of the company of having a former team member bad-mouthing the proposal development team. Handle team exits with care and only as a last resort.

COMMUNICATION PLAN

The team must establish methods of communicating between and among team members. The team needs to determine the best method of getting information to and from each member. In addition to the weekly meeting, communication channels must be established. The team can use written memos, e-mails, or voice mails. The team must use the communication channel that is most effective for all members. It is recommended that some sort of written communication such as e-mail or memorandums be utilized. If written forms of communication are used, the team recorder should be copied on this information so he or she can keep the information for team reference.

The use of project management software packages can also help with the proposal development process. The team leader can establish milestones for the proposal writing process, place that information into the project management software, and generate reports and charts to communicate the progress of the proposal writing for all team members to see.

One important element of communication to remember is the face-to-face meeting. Face-to-face meetings convey many feelings, emotions, and impressions that are impossible to detect using other forms of communication. A reader can often misconstrue anger or confusion in an e-mail, especially if it is written in all capital letters. Many times people will write messages in an e-mail that they would not say in a telephone conversation or in a face-to-face discussion. For this reason, it is important to periodically have face-to-face meetings to make sure everyone is conveying what they intend while using other forms of communication.

Communication is critical to the success of the proposal development team. Team members must communicate continuously, accurately, and honestly with each other. Open, honest communication leads to a well-written proposal.

VERSION CONTROL PROCESS

When multiple people are contributing to a single document, the issue of version control becomes critical. It is far too easy for edits to be made to older versions of the document or to submit the wrong document to the client because of a misunderstanding of which is the latest version. One of the first steps the proposal development team should take is the establishment of a version control process. The proposal team needs to determine a method for ensuring that two people are not editing the proposal at the same time and inadvertently overwriting each other's comments.

One effective group editing process is to use the "Review/Edit or Routing" function of most word processing software. Regardless of the name, when this function is activated, it allows different users to record comments and to make changes in different colors. The instructional designer writes in blue while the Web interface designer writes in green. When words are deleted or altered, the software puts a line through the words instead of removing them. The software will also date the change and allow the person making the revision to add a note to the revision. This method allows everyone to see all of the changes made to the document, while keeping track of all the comments and critiques of the team members.

As a final step, the proposal team needs a single person (proposal writer) to be responsible for consolidating and reconciling the comments within the document and to make the editing changes needed for the final version of the proposal.

FORMAT PLAN

The writing team can avoid massive edits and rewrites of entire sections of the proposal and problems combining multiple documents by establishing a format plan prior to writing. A format plan is basically a style sheet customized to each RFP because different RFPs have different requirements in terms of spacing, margins, naming conventions, etc. The RFP specific style sheet establishes rules of punctuation, capitalization, use of terms, and other important writing conventions such as spacing after a sentence or when to use italics or underline. While these items seem trivial compared to creating the concept of the proposal and the written response, they become monumental when the document must be assembled at the last minute.

A format plan helps to ensure that everyone contributing to the proposal is using the same conventions. For example, you may determine that you should refer to the client as *ABC Corporation* instead of *ABC Corp.* or that the term *instructor-led training* will be used instead of *classroom instruction*.

TRUST

A winning proposal cannot be written in an atmosphere of distrust. Not all team members need to like each other or get along socially but they all need to respect each other's work and trust that it will get done as promised. Team members must trust each other and upper management in order to perform their jobs properly. It is trust that allows team members to take chances and to suggest radical new ideas. The team members need to know that what is said in confidence during a team meeting stays confidential. Members need to know they can count on each other for assistance. They need to know that upper management will not be reversing critical decisions they have made concerning the implementation. Team members must be honest with each other and take responsibility for their actions.

Mistakes, problems, and miscues will inevitably occur throughout the entire proposal development process. The team must realize that without some mistakes progress cannot be achieved. The team must expect mistakes to happen, learn from those mistakes, and then not let them happen again.

THE BOTTOM LINE

Most often a proposal is written by a team, but it must read as if one individual wrote it. This can only be accomplished if the proposal development team works together to resolve whatever differences members may have. Clients want easy-to-read proposals that are cohesive and make sense. Avoid miscues by taking the time to ensure that the proposal development team knows how to write with a single voice.

PART II: THE PROPOSAL DOCUMENT

9

FRONT MATTER

INTRODUCTION

Imagine your potential clients staring at a stack of proposals sitting on their desks. They all look the same. Where to start? Wait, one catches their eye; it has an interesting, colorful cover. They open it. They glance at the introductory letter containing a compelling overview of your innovative e-learning solution. They are intrigued; they turn to the table of contents and comment aloud about its effective organization. They quickly glance over the confidentiality statement and understand that your firm has invested a great deal of intellectual capital in this proposal. They decide it is worth reading. They push the others aside and read your firm's proposal cover to cover. This is precisely the reaction you want.

To get this reaction, you need to pay particular attention to the beginning material of your proposal. You need to make sure you have an attractive cover, an effective introductory letter, a confidentiality statement, and a well-organized table of contents. These items are known as *Front Matter* and can be the difference between having your proposal ignored and having it read with enthusiasm. While the front matter of your proposal may seem boring and perfunctory, it is not.

WHY THIS SECTION IS NECESSARY

The front matter of your proposal is an opportunity to impress the client. Just like you want your house to have a nice, impressive entryway, you want your proposal to have nice, well-organized front matter. Usually, a potential client skims through the first few pages of a proposal to determine if it is worth reading. In a short period of time, the client glances at the cover, reads the introductory letter, and looks over the table of contents. During that time, you need to draw the client into your proposal and encourage him or her to read the entire document. With planning and careful thought, the front matter of your proposal serves to differentiate your firm from other competing firms.

To capitalize on this competitive advantage, you need to make the front matter a priority in your proposal development process. All too often, front matter is treated as an afterthought. When the proposal development team is scrambling to put the finishing touches on the proposal, the front matter gets forgotten. Consequently, it is thrown together at the last minute even though it is the first thing a client sees.

Do not allow this to happen. Set aside time specifically for the development of the proposal's front matter. When you put time and effort into the development of the proposal's front matter, you encourage the client to read the entire proposal. This increases your chances of winning.

WHAT SHOULD BE IN THIS SECTION

Typically, the front matter of your proposal contains the cover, an introductory letter (better known as a letter of transmittal), the table of contents, and some type of legal statement concerning confidentiality. These elements provide the reader with an introduction to your company and an entrance into your proposal. Each of these elements serves an important purpose in attracting the client to the document and encouraging him or her to read on.

PROPOSAL COVER

The first exposure a client has to your e-learning firm may be your proposal cover; it is certainly the first item the client sees upon receipt of the proposal. The cover needs to be attractive and functional. It should reflect the fact that your firm is capable of effectively and attractively arranging information. It should grab the client's attention and draw him or her into your document. "A good cover may win significant psychological advantage by its impact and provide a chance to gain points even before the proposal is opened" [1].

Part of the challenge of designing a cover is that it needs to be attractive while containing key pieces of identification and contact information. Do not sacrifice information for attractiveness. When your cover has no identifying information on it, the client cannot tell what it is. Covers with no information are annoying and time consuming. The client must now open the proposal every time he or she wants to send an e-mail or make a phone call; this is a waste of time for the client. It is a good proposal design strategy to include key identification and contact information on the front cover.

Make the cover "user friendly." Show the client that your firm can make information easy to use, easy to access, and attractive. To ensure ease of use, include the following information on the cover:

- **Client name** — This needs to be prominent on the cover and can include the client's logo.
- **Name of RFP** — This should include the project or RFP number, if one is given, or can simply be the name of the project from the RFP for which you are submitting the proposal. This is important because the client may be dealing with multiple projects.
- **Name of your firm and logo**
- **Date of proposal submittal** — This is the due date indicated in the RFP.
- **Contact information** — You should include as many means of contacting your firm as possible. Include a phone number, e-mail, fax number, and Web site address as well as the name of a contact person at your firm.

While it is important to have key information on the front cover, do not go to the other extreme and ignore the aesthetics of a good cover. Good cover design requires a balance between attractiveness and functionality.

Example 9.1 illustrates a proposal cover that has all the right elements but lacks attractiveness. Technically, this cover does the job. It conveys the necessary information and introduces the reader to the document but it lacks attractiveness. This cover does not turn heads or beg attention.

To gain the reader's attention, your proposal needs to be attractive and inviting. Think of your proposal lying on a desk with six other proposals and all the client can see are the covers. The cover that attracts attention will be the proposal the client reads. A plain white cover does not provide the same positive impact as the careful use of color or graphics.

When designing your cover, think of ways to give it curb appeal and to make it stand out from the crowd while maintaining a professional image. You can make the cover florescent orange and it would stand out from the crowd, but it would not be professional. A proposal is a professional representation of your firm. Keep it elegant, informative, attractive, and simple.

There are a number of techniques you can use to develop an attractive, informative cover. These include the use of corporate logos, the effective use of color, and the incorporation of proposal-specific graphics to represent the theme of your proposal.

A simple method of increasing the curb appeal of your proposal cover is to use logos. You can use your logo and the client's logo to add visual appeal, balance, and color. Place the two logos on the page in a balanced arrangement and incorporate the key information around the logos. Example 9.2 shows an effective use of logos on a cover.

Indicates client's name in large font.

Proposal to:

EZ Electronics Manufacturing Corp.

Specifically identifies title of the RFP to which this is a response (exact wording from RFP).

For:
The Development of a Web-Based Learning Management System

Indicates the firm that has prepared this proposal.

Prepared by:
PowerPlay Multimedia

Date the proposal is due to the client.

Date:
June 12, 2005

Provides a specific person and multiple methods of contact.

Contact:
Joe K. Elliot, CFPIM, CIRM
Institute for Interactive Technologies
Bloomsburg, PA 17815-1301
Phone (555) 555-5555
Fax (555) 555-5555
Jelliot@bloomedu.edu

Example 9.1 Plain proposal cover with no graphics.

You can usually obtain a client logo from the client's Web site or you can ask the client directly for the logo. If you get the logo from the client's Web site, you may have to deal with resizing issues or poor print resolution. If you decide to use the client's logo, make sure it looks good when it is printed on the cover. You may also want to check with the client to see if it is permissible to use the logo on your document. Some clients are very restrictive with the use of their logo and may become offended if it is used without their permission.

Uses client's logo to add some appeal to the cover.

Specifically identifies title of the RFP to which this is a response (exact wording from RFP).

Line separates client information from vendor information.

Uses logo of vendor's firm to indicate name and add some energy to the cover.

Provides contact information as well as a web address so client can look up vendor's web site if desired.

Date proposal is due to the client.

Response to Request for Proposal by:

Proposal for:

Creation of Courses and a Learning Portal for Training Truck Drivers

---

Proposed by:

Nancy Jameson
Director of Learning Architecture
1325 West King Street, Suite 501
Alexandria, VA 22313
Phone – 703-385-5715
Fax – 703-385-5716
Email:info@workforceint.com
www.workforceint.com

MARCH 31, 2001

Example 9.2 Proposal cover incorporating logos to add appeal.

The careful use of color can make a proposal cover attractive. Use strong colors that represent positive symbols. Green is a good color; it represents stability and financial security. Blue is a solid color representing strength and integrity. However, colors like yellow, light blue, and pink should be avoided. Lighter colors do not typically convey a sense of professionalism or confidence. Always strive for professionalism and an image of confidence, authority, and credibility.

One caution about using colors on the cover — you may want to check to see if the client's evaluation team will be viewing the proposal in color. If the client's team will be viewing the proposal in black and white, you may not want to concentrate on an elaborate color scheme. Color copying and printing of proposals at the client's place of business is still a rare event. While many clients have top-of-the-line black and white photocopy machines, subtle color differences and shadings do not translate well when photocopied. If you e-mail your proposal to a client, you may have no control over whether the client evaluation team sees the proposal in color or in black and white. If you are worried about the distribution of black and white copies, you may want to supply enough hard copy color proposals for everyone on the client's evaluation team. You will need to check the client's proposal submission guidelines to see if that is an option. If it is not, your elaborate color scheme that looked great on the computer screen may lose impact when viewed in black and white.

Along with the creation of a colorful cover, you may also develop an original graphic to draw attention to the ideas within your proposal. Consider using a graphic that incorporates the theme of your proposal.

For example, one organization was using the theme of fitting together puzzle pieces to solve a client's problem. The cover contained an illustration of a puzzle being completed with a hand putting in the last puzzle piece with the vendor's logo on it. Use original graphics that convey a sense of energy, uniqueness, and excitement about your proposal.

In addition to the use of logos, colors, or original graphics, another method of adding curb appeal is to pay attention to the type of cover and binding that you provide if you create hard copy versions. A good solid cover and binding can add value to your proposal.

The binding of the proposal has an impact. If you cheaply bind the proposal and it falls apart on the client's desk, it does not reflect favorably upon your firm. When binding the proposal, use plastic comb binding or spiral binding. It looks professional and keeps the pages together. A three-ring binder is not advisable because it is bulky and tends not to look as professional.

The paper for the cover should be card stock or other heavy paper. The card stock should be included as both the front and back cover. This adds weight and durability to the proposal. It might be a little more expensive than plain white paper, but a client who is paying a lot of money for a solution expects professional documents from the vendor. Another attractive alternative is to use a clear plastic cover for the front of the proposal. This provides protection and a nice professional look.

Your proposal cover conveys an important initial message. It is an excellent opportunity to add visual appeal to your proposal. But remember, it also needs to convey key contact information. If crafted carefully and thoughtfully, the cover is an important element in your overall sales effort. When designing your proposal cover, think informative, think balanced, think careful use of color.

INTRODUCTORY LETTER/LETTER OF TRANSMITTAL

The next item that appears in the proposal is the introductory letter. This letter is better known as the *Cover Letter* or *Letter of Transmittal*. Many e-learning firms place the letter of transmittal as the first page of the proposal. This allows anyone reading the proposal to have an opportunity to read the letter of transmittal rather than including one letter as a separate document sent along with the proposal.

The letter of transmittal presents the proposal to and informs the client of your firm's enthusiasm and expertise concerning the project. The letter of transmittal "is probably next in importance to the proposal cover in stimulating the evaluator to read further" [2]. Because of the letter's importance, it must be carefully written and well planned. A well-designed and well-written letter of transmittal helps you to win the e-learning business. To win the business, the letter must convey two messages to members of the client's evaluation team.

The first message it should convey is that your firm is a professional organization that cares about details, following standards, and properly designing information. Before any word of the letter is read, the client notices how the letter looks. Is it attractive? Does it look heavy or gray? Does it look crisp and clean? Is white space effectively used? Is it centered? Are the margins correct? Are all the standard letter elements present? Does it look professional? Does it follow the proper format? Sloppy or carelessly designed letters send the wrong message. Your letter should have an attractive appearance and follow established guidelines for good letter writing.

After judging the appearance of your letter of transmittal, the client reads it. Therefore, your letter must do more than simply announce the arrival of the proposal. It must highlight your capture strategy, introduce your theme, and lead the reader to specific items of interest. The second message your letter should convey is one of quiet confidence in your firm's ability to solve the client's e-learning problem.

A well-written letter of transmittal influences the reading of the proposal. For example, if you want to stress the idea of forming a strategic partnership, emphasize that point in the letter of transmittal. Then, everything the client reads will be in reference to the concept of forming a partnership. The goal of the letter is to provide an "advanced organizer" to guide what the client reads and remembers about your solution.

PROFESSIONALLY DESIGNING THE LETTER

Because the appearance of the letter of transmittal is important for success, a number of letter-writing conventions and formats need to be followed. The first is that the letter should be written on your firm's letterhead. Letterhead conveys a

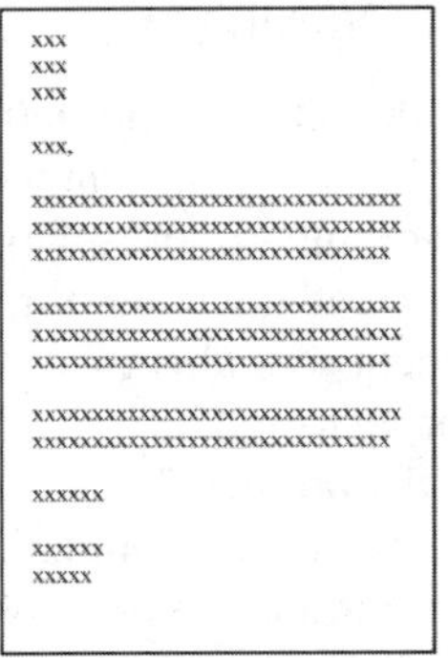

Figure 9.1 Block format (left) and modified block format (right).

sense of identity and gives the impression of an established, credible organization. It helps brand your firm whether you win the proposal or not.

Next, you should use a standard letter format. You need to include a date, inside address, salutation, complimentary close, and signature block. For the format of the letter, you can use one of two acceptable layouts: block or modified block. Figure 9.1 shows the two layout options.

The block layout consists of the date, inside address, salutation, body paragraphs, and signature line aligned on the left-hand side of the letter, as shown in Example 9.3. In the modified block layout, the date and the signature information appear centered, as shown in Example 9.4. The first line of each paragraph can begin at either the left margin or the first tab (5 or 10 spaces). Either of these two letter layouts is acceptable. Choose one layout and then follow the conventions that are expected within that particular layout.

When you look at the letter of transmittal, the first item that you will see below the corporate letterhead is the date. This date should be the date that the proposal is due. The name of the month should be spelled out. The number of the day should be written without any additional punctuation. You should not use numbers such as 1st, 2nd, 3rd, or 4th. Examples of the proper date format are *April 3, 2001* and *October 9, 2005.*

The next item is the inside address. This should be the address of the person who is receiving the proposal and, consequently, the letter of transmittal. You can typically find this information within the RFP. If you cannot find it, contact the client organization. They can tell you to whom you should mail or e-mail the proposal.

After the inside address is the salutation. Make sure you use the proper courtesy title such as Dr., Mr., Mrs., or Ms. If you are unsure as to the title or gender of the individual, call the client to find out. People are often offended when courtesy titles are misused or names are misspelled.

March 30, 2001

Dr. Karl Kapp
Learning Consultant
2221 McCormick Center
Bloomsburg, PA 17815

Dear Dr. Kapp:

Confirms the proposal is in response to a specific RFP.

On behalf of Workforce Interactive I am pleased to offer this proposal to Trucko in response to your Request for Proposal titled *Creation of Courses and a Learning Portal for Training Truck Drivers*. The proposal includes a project plan and budget for the development of a learning portal, and an on-line catalog, as well as the development of six web-based lessons.

Indicates effectivity dates of proposal.

In addition, we have included an innovative method for motivating drivers to attend and complete the training called Truckco Dollars. Our proposal meets the requirements set forth in your Request for Proposal and is effective from March 30, 2001 to May 1, 2001.

Discusses experience and capabilities of the company.

Our experienced professionals, proven instructional design process, and state-of-the-industry learning management system make Workforce Interactive an excellent choice for completing the project on time and within budget. We have developed corporate training solutions for clients such as PepsiCo, Roadway Express and Federal Express. Our intranet-based training and orientation program created for Roadway Express earned us the 1998 Distinguished Contribution to Workplace Learning and Performance Award.

Use final paragraph to ask for a specific action, preview an upcoming meeting, and/or offer an invitation for further discussion.

Workforce Interactive's core design and development team is looking forward to meeting with you on April 19, 2001 to discuss the enclosed document. In the meantime, if you have any questions or concerns, please do not hesitate to contact me at 555-3200 or via email at jmcclain@WI.com. Workforce Interactive is fully committed to helping Truckco reach its educational goals. We look forward to working with you in the near future.

Sincerely,

Jack McClain

Jack McClain
President/CEO
Workforce Interactive

Example 9.3 *Letter of Transmittal* covering the basic information required.

August 30, 2001

Dear Dr. Kapp

Indicates date of RFP and RFP title to which this proposal corresponds.

I am contacting you today in regard to Xpress Airlines' request for proposal, dated July 19, 2001. On behalf of the skilled men and women of Exoset Strategic Consulting Group, it is my pleasure to submit to you our solution to Xpress Airlines' need for the *Creation of Courses and an Interactive Kiosk Network for Flight Service Personnel*. The proposal offer is effective from August 30, 2001 to September 19, 2001.

Provides a sense of project. Lists critical factors of proposal.

After personally reviewing the proposal with management, key staff, as well as the selected project team, I am confident that the enclosed solution is both sensible and empowering. As you will see, our solution clearly defines how critical factors such as Kiosk Design, Security, Technical Infrastructure, Learning Model, Environment and Accessibility will be addressed.

In addition to the aforementioned factors, Exoset has identified three "fundamental" factors that we believe will be critical to the future of this project. We have used these factors as the litmus test for our solution. Those factors are:

Highlights three major areas for emphasis. These three "themes" are carried throughout the proposal.

Scalability:
It is critical that this proposal not be short sighted. Pennsylvania is only an initial site for testing of the concept. Any proposal must be easily scalable, and any vendor must have a clear plan for addressing the issue of scalability.

Strategic Partners:
Exoset believes that an economic and developmental partnership is in the best interest of our two organizations and will add the most value to this project.

Profitability:
The results of this project must be profitable to both Xpress Airlines as well as Exoset.

Emphasis on partnership and relationship, encourages contact.

I truly believe you will find our proposal to be unique. At Exoset, we believe in fostering relationships, and look forward to building a strategic tie between our two companies and concentrating on the fundamentals required to make this relationship productive for both organizations. I know the staff of Exoset is excited about the prospect of working with the fine people at Xpress Airlines—as am I. If I can be of any further help in this matter, please don't hesitate to call me at 555-5555 or email me at JC@exoset.com. I look forward to speaking with you soon.

Sincerely

Jocelyn Cruz

Jocelyn Cruz
VP. Customer Relationships

Example 9.4 *Letter of Transmittal* highlighting the capture strategy of scalability, partnership, and profitability.

The inclusion or exclusion of the colon in the salutation as well as the comma in the complimentary close has to do with the style of the letter. Punctuation for the letter of transmittal is either *open* or *mixed.*

With the open punctuation style, there is no punctuation after the salutation or the complimentary close of the letter. This style is shown in Example 9.4. The mixed punctuation style includes a colon after the salutation and a comma after the complimentary closing. This style is shown in Example 9.3. While both styles are acceptable, the more commonly used style is mixed punctuation. This is because mixed punctuation is more formal and proposals are considered formal documents.

Regardless of which format you choose, you must leave two spaces after all end punctuation marks (period, question mark, colon, comma). This facilitates reading the letter faster. Use ragged or unjustified right margins.

For the complimentary close, your options are limited. You can use either *Sincerely* or *Regards*. You can get creative with the close, but keep in mind your client's potential reaction to whatever words or phrases you use. After the close, sign the letter and include the name and title of the individual submitting the proposal. This person will be the contact for the client. If the letter is submitted as part of an electronic document, consider scanning a signature to include in the letter.

CONTENT OF THE LETTER

While the format and appearance of the letter of transmittal are important, it is the content and message within the letter that will grab and hold the client's attention. A well-written letter contains information of interest to the client as well as basic administrative information.

For the letter of transmittal to be effective, it needs to contain eight elements. These elements are as follows [3, 4]:

1. Indication that the proposal is in response to a specific RFP. You may want to include a project number if one is given within the RFP.
2. Statement indicating that the proposal meets all of the client's selection criteria.
3. Statement indicating that the proposal offer is good for a specified period of time such as 90 days or until June 3, 2006. This is usually referred to as "effectivity dates."
4. Statement that the author of the letter is authorized to make the attached offer on behalf of his or her e-learning firm.
5. Invitation to communicate with the author of the letter should more information or a formal presentation be desired.
6. Mention of the firm's ability to successfully complete the project.

7. Pledge of support from the firm's upper management for the project.
8. Introduction to the capture strategy and theme of the proposal.

The trick is to present all of the above information in an exciting and enthusiastic manner. You must cover the basics while persuading the client to read the remainder of the proposal. If you simply provide "just the facts," the letter will not convince the client to read further.

The letter of transmittal in Example 9.3 contains most of the required information. It contains a statement about which RFP the proposal is addressing, the effective dates for the proposal, and specifically asks for action in the last paragraph. However, it fails to mention either a capture strategy or a proposal theme. The author of this letter is missing an opportunity to draw the client's attention to the key elements of the proposal and to position the firm strategically through the message in the letter.

In contrast, the letter of transmittal in Example 9.4 clearly highlights this firm's capture strategy. It is obvious from the letter that the capture strategy consists of three elements: (1) emphasis on scalability, (2) a strategic partnership, and (3) mutual profitability. The client can easily and quickly see that these three elements are going to be discussed throughout the proposal. Everything the client reads within the proposal will now be seen through the filter of scalability, partnership, and profitability.

Creating an effective letter of transmittal can be accomplished by asking a few key questions. What is the main theme of the proposal? What is the capture strategy? How can the solution be succinctly summarized? What is the client looking for in terms of the solution? How can I convince the client to read the remainder of the proposal? Have I included all of the basic information required in the letter of transmittal? Worksheet 9.1 provides a handy tool for developing an effective letter of transmittal.

TABLE OF CONTENTS

The table of contents (TOC) is one of the first examples the client has of your firm's ability to organize information. Because a proposal is seldom read cover to cover, clients rely on the TOC to guide them through the document. A good TOC enables the client to find what he or she is looking for quickly and easily.

While the TOC is an important item to the client, the proposal development team often overlooks it. In many cases, not much thought or effort is put into its appearance or format. To have an effective e-learning proposal, you need to spend the necessary time to develop an effective TOC.

Fortunately, designing an effective TOC requires only a few simple guidelines. These guidelines will help you avoid a poorly designed TOC like the one shown in Example 9.5.

Letter of Transmittal/Cover Letter Worksheet

Convey your company's strengths to the client as well as ask for action such as a meeting date, an in-depth discussion of the proposal, or a presentation of your solution. Be brief, concise, and to the point, but you must cover specific items like what RFP this proposal is in response to, the effectivity dates of the proposal, the firm's commitment to the project, and that the individual signing the letter is authorized to commit the company to the project. Use letterhead.

Greeting: It is never acceptable to skip the greeting or to address the letter to "sir" or "madam." Address the letter to the person indicated within the RFP. If no one is indicated, call and ask. Double-check spellings, titles, and address information.

____

____

____

Introduction: Open by indicating how excited or pleased your firm is to respond to the RFP. Indicate the title or number of RFP to which you are responding. Provide a list of deliverables you are supplying to the client upon completion of the project (this list could be in bullet form). Highlight unique or innovative elements of the proposal.

____

____

____

Body of the Letter: Give examples of relevant past experience. Explain why your company can complete this project within the requested budget and time frame. List any themes or capture strategies you are employing. Indicate proposal effectivity dates. Indicate that your solution meets all the criteria in the RFP.

____

____

____

Closing: Ask for specific action like a meeting or phone call. Always provide contact information (phone number and e-mail) even if it is on the letterhead (do not make the client search for information). Indicate company commitment to the project.

____

____

____

Signature: Do not skip the signature (even if the document is electronic). Scan in the signature of the executive and include it in the document. The letter can be sent from a high-ranking official who speaks directly for the firm.

____

____

____

Worksheet 9.1 Development worksheet for the letter of transmittal.

Title not centered.

No dot leaders linking section name to page number. Makes it hard to match section with page number.

Can't tell the difference between sections and subsections, poor use of white space. Need to use some indents to clearly differentiate between sections and subsections.

Page number is not a roman numeral.

Table of Contents

Executive Summary	1
Summary of Requirements	3
Instructional	3
Technical	4
Background of Current Situation	5
Functional Requirements for Internet Training Web Site	8
Implementation and Ongoing Support	9
Price Schedule	25
Vendor Profile	27
RFP Response Guidelines	28
Appendices	29
Resumes	31
Past Work Experience	32
Project Chart	33
Sample Network Architecture	34

1

Example 9.5 A poorly designed table of contents.

1. Center the title. This helps to balance the page and make it look neat.
2. List each main topic on the left side of the page with leader dots running from the end of the section name to the other side of the page followed by the page number.
3. Under each main topic, indent and list the appropriate subtopics. This provides a quick outline of the proposal.

4. If the RFP indicates a numbering scheme for each section and subtopic, make sure your TOC reflects that numbering scheme.
5. The font for the TOC should be the same as that used in the proposal.
6. The TOC is part of the front matter of the document and therefore should include a page number using roman numerals. Properly number each page after the letter of transmittal with a centered roman numeral in the footer of the page until you begin the formal document on the first page after the executive summary.
7. Make sure you double- or triple-check the page numbers in the TOC with the page numbers in the document. When items are added to the proposal at the last minute, pages can be shuffled and renumbered. If time is not taken to check the page numbers, mistakes will occur.

The TOC is an important element in the overall look and feel of your proposal. Set aside the appropriate amount of time to ensure that it is well designed and that it appropriately represents your firm. Example 9.6 illustrates a well-designed TOC. Compare the TOC in Example 9.5 to the one in Example 9.6. Notice how appealing Example 9.6 is as compared to Example 9.5.

LEGAL STATEMENT AND ASSOCIATED ISSUES

Within the body of your e-learning proposal, much information is described which can be considered sensitive to your organization: how business is conducted, how projects are managed, how your software functions, your pricing structure, and other valuable pieces of information. In short, your proposal contains a wealth of intellectual capital. When you send your proposal to a potential client, you need to consider issues of confidentiality and copyright ownership.

In addition, if you win the business, your e-learning proposal can serve as an agreement between your firm and your client or it could be an addendum to the contract between the two organizations. Therefore, it is in your firm's best interest to know something about the legal ramifications of sending your proposal to a potential client. There are a number of items you may want to include within your proposal to help mitigate the risk of intellectual property theft or potential contract disputes.

CONFIDENTIALITY STATEMENT

One of the first things you should consider is adding a confidentiality statement to your e-learning proposal. This statement can be contained on a separate page within the front matter or it can be included at the bottom of the TOC. The actual location of the statement may depend on page count restrictions, layout of the proposal, and company policy. The confidentiality statement reminds the client

Title is centered.

Section headings are numbered to match RFP numbering scheme.

Subheadings are indented to show relationship to main topics.

Dot leaders link section name to page number.

Section headings are well spaced and easy to read.

Section 8.0 had to be included as per the RFP.

Uses a roman numeral for the page number.

Table of Contents

iv

Example 9.6 A well-designed table of contents.

Table 9.1 Different Options for Confidentiality Statement Wording to Protect the Intellectual Capital within Your Proposal

This proposal is the property of PowerPlay Interactive. Any copy, use or distribution of the information in this document without the written consent of PowerPlay Interactive is strictly prohibited.
Not for disclosure outside ABC Corp. except under written agreement.
The information contained in this document is proprietary to Maverick Multimedia, Inc. No part of this document shall be used or released to any third party without the express written consent of Maverick Multimedia, Inc.
The contents of this proposal are proprietary and confidential and are not to be copied or duplicated in any manner with out the expressed written consent of PowerPlay Interactive.
Copyright 2006 © Workforce Interactive. All Rights Reserved.

of the sensitive and proprietary nature of your proposal. The statements in Table 9.1 provide different versions of language that you may want to include in your front matter. Your goal is to gently remind clients that they are holding a valuable document containing a great deal of intellectual capital and that they should keep it to themselves. In addition to including a confidentiality statement at the beginning of your proposal, you should also include a statement in the footer of your document indicating that it is confidential and proprietary.

PROPOSAL COPYRIGHT ISSUES

Any proposal sent to a potential client is protected by copyright. This means that the expression of your work, the written words on the paper, is protected from unauthorized copying. Even though it seems to happen all the time, it is a copyright violation for a client to photocopy and distribute your proposal without your permission. When faced with unauthorized photocopies of your proposal, you need to decide if it is worth it to alert the client to the violation or to let it slide. To make that decision, you need to weigh your confidence level in winning the work, your comfort level with the client, and the value of the intellectual capital within that particular proposal. In most cases, clients do not even realize that they have done anything improper.

While copyright law covers the written words in your e-learning proposal, it is important to note that the copyright protection does not extend to the *ideas* within the proposal. Copyright laws do not protect ideas or innovative thoughts, only the *expression* of those thoughts or ideas. If the client hires another e-learning firm to develop an e-learning solution based on the ideas within your proposal, it is not considered a copyright infringement.

It is unfortunate, but this type of intellectual capital theft does occur. Therefore, another consideration when writing your proposal is to decide how much information you want to reveal to the potential client. You may want to include just enough so your potential client understands the possibilities, but not enough so that he or she can take your idea and begin development internally or with another firm. You must constantly balance the need to guard your intellectual property against your knowledge of the potential client and your need to present enough information to win the work.

PROPOSAL IS NOT A CONTRACT

Typically after the vendor is awarded an e-learning project, a contract is written between the two organizations. While basic information contained in the proposal is typically transferred to the contract, such as timelines, due dates, price, etc., the contract is usually based on a more detailed Statement of Work (SOW). The SOW is agreed upon by both organizations after a careful discussion of the constraints, demands, and resources impacting the project. The SOW provides specific details about the number and size of deliverables as well as the obligations and responsibilities of each organization.

While a proposal is not a contract, it may be added to the contract as an addendum or the contract may specifically reference the proposal. In either case, you want to make sure that everything you have included within the proposal is specifically defined within the SOW. If the two disagree, you could encounter problems in the future if a contract dispute arises. Therefore, it is a good idea to make sure that all key items from the proposal are mentioned within the SOW. A well-written SOW will help your firm to avoid misunderstandings.

NO REIMBURSEMENT FOR PROPOSAL DEVELOPMENT COSTS

If your firm responds to an RFP but does not win, it has no legal basis for reimbursement of the costs for creating the proposal. In fact, even if you win, you cannot directly bill the client for the development of the proposal. The costs of creating a proposal are an investment in future business. Sometimes the investment pays off and sometimes it does not.

One method of partially recovering the proposal development costs is to keep a library of old proposals. The library may prove useful when writing future proposals. If you can use part of an old proposal in a new proposal, you may recover some of your investment in terms of saved effort.

■ ■ ■

LEGAL CONSIDERATIONS WHEN WRITING A PROPOSAL

Linda Carroll Smith, Esq., Contract Partner, Dilworth Paxson LLP

An RFP has been defined by some courts as a "quasi-offer" or an "invitation for an offer." The RFP is not a contract or a contractual offer. In fact, the wording in many RFPs specifically states that it may be withdrawn. Even if not specifically stated, the RFP may be withdrawn and not result in a contract with any vendor organization. Another way to view the RFP is that it is the first step in a negotiation process. The award of the contract at the end of an RFP process is based on technical expertise as well as cost. In that regard, it is distinguishable from a competitive bid.

The competitive bid process is based solely on price for a clearly and specifically defined item or service. A competitive bid is the submission of prices by persons, firms, or corporations competing for a contract to provide supplies or services under a procedure in which the contracting authority does not negotiate prices. Awards in the competitive bid process are based solely on the lowest price.

Most government agencies or authorities that employ the RFP process do so under statute, ordinance, or policy governing the procedure. It is very prudent for one participating in the process to obtain a copy of the governing statute, ordinance, or policy. A Model Procurement Code for State and Local Government forms the basis for many of these statutes, ordinances, and policies, which ensures similarity in the process from one jurisdiction to another. However, there can be differences as well and the prudent contractor should be aware of his or her rights and obligations when involving himself or herself or the company in the RFP process of a given governmental body, agency, or authority. Fair and equitable treatment is a cornerstone of most statutes, ordinances, and policies defining the RFP process.

Corporations, both large and small, for-profit and nonprofit, have also adopted the RFP process. A prudent contractor would ask if the corporation has a policy governing its RFP process; however, the smaller the organization, the less likely it is to have a formal policy to guide its RFP process.

An RFP must be read carefully. Those intending to respond to an RFP should not only determine if there are any laws or policies governing the process of which they should be aware, but they should also know if their response will be disqualified if they fail to respond to all requirements or fail to meet all criteria as well. A statement about meeting all criteria or responding to all requirements may be included in the RFP itself. The RFP may also include a provision that will allow the issuer to withdraw the RFP. The RFP may also indicate if it will be incorporated by reference into any final contract. Whether the RFP becomes part of the contract or not could significantly impact on the rights and obligations of the parties. Not understanding or overlooking any of these provisions can lead to an expensive error on the part of the contractor or loss of the opportunity to contract. Provisions unique to a specific RFP can significantly impact process; hence, a careful reading of the RFP can avoid problems.

Subsequent to the issuance of a written RFP, the issuer frequently will hold a "Question and Answer," "Q & A," or "Bidder's Conference." This is an opportunity to gain a greater understanding of the goals and objectives of the issuer and to ask any questions prompted by a reading of the RFP. Whether the RFP becomes part of the contract, whether all criteria must be met or disqualification results, and whether there is a policy or law that governs the process are all questions that might be asked at this session which are not answered in the RFP. This session provides an opportunity to clear up ambiguities or lapses in the RFP and to gain a better understanding of the expectations of the issuer. The responses given in the Bidder's Conference may be transcribed. In such cases, they may be incorporated into any final contract by reference. In the absence of a Bidder's Conference, some issuers will allow interested parties to call them with any questions. A prudent contractor will take full advantage of attending a Bidder's Conference or otherwise contact the issuer with any questions. Making assumptions rather than asking a question can prove to be a very expensive error.

It is not unusual for a question by a contractor to prompt an actual amendment to the RFP. Because the RFP process is used to solve a "problem" and is awarded based on the "expertise" of the responding parties as well as cost, its stands to reason that the responding contractors have much greater expertise than the drafters of the RFP. An RFP can include two completely contradictory criteria based on a misunderstanding of the drafters. A Bidder's Conference may shed light on this kind of error and result in a resolution that eliminates one of the criteria. Failure to attend the Bidder's Conference or failure to obtain a written copy of the questions and answers may result in a proposal that misses the target, which results in a loss of a contract.

After the Bidder's Conference, the issuer reviews all responses submitted by the due date. Rarely does one person make a decision on who will be selected as the winning contractor. Usually a group of people review the submitted RFPs, with each individual having a different area of expertise. An issuer's accountant, lawyer, executive, and technical staff generally participate in the process at some point. Once selected, the winning contractor will begin a one-on-one negotiation process.

The need for a one-on-one negotiation process is inherent to the process itself. Because the issuer is seeking a solution to a problem, the suggested solutions may have undesirable parts. On the other hand, the winning contractor may not have included an option that was included by a losing contractor but which the client wants added to the contract. The negotiation process allows for the response to be fine-tuned. Other terms and conditions of the contract need to be discussed, such as insurance, what happens if a key person becomes unavailable, if there is an "act of God" or other disaster, and terms and conditions that must be developed in direct response to alternatives that were found desirable but were unanticipated by the issuer. For example, the original time schedule for completion of tasks might be altered because of the nature of the proposals. The negotiation process is required to finalize what is a very fluid and flexible process. By comparison, a competitive bid process does not include a negotiation process. The negotiation process provides a final means to achieving a "meeting of the minds," which is memorialized in a written contract.

Although the RFP process is a useful tool and results in successful contracts for both issuers and contractors, disputes can and do arise. After an executed contract is entered into, traditional contract law governs any dispute. If the contract incorporates by reference the RFP, the proposal, and the transcript from the Bidder's Conference, these documents will be evidence in any lawsuit over the contract along with the actual contract. If these documents are not incorporated, whether they are admissible as parole evidence will largely depend on the jurisdiction in which the lawsuit takes place.*

Some jurisdictions are more willing to admit such evidence in contractual disputes than others. Frequently, the jurisdiction to hear any dispute over the contract is named in the contract itself. This is one of the key provisions that is negotiated after the winning contractor is selected. Because the issuer of the RFP has more leverage, the jurisdiction is almost always selected by the issuer. Therefore, careful attention should be paid to that arrangement to make sure it is acceptable to the responding contractor and the possible risks associated with that commitment. The contract might be entered into in one state, but the jurisdiction for purposes of a lawsuit might be in a state across the country where the company is headquartered. It would be much more expensive and difficult to sue or be sued across the country than it is in your own backyard. Sometimes binding arbitration is required by the contract and the risks associated with this must also be assessed based on the jurisdiction.

---

*The actual contract will be the primary document subject to interpretation by a court or arbitration panel. Ambiguous provisions or provisions otherwise unclear in the contract itself may result in an examination of the attachments to the contract that are incorporated by reference. For example, if an RFP required ten lessons, but the proposal offered seven lessons of a larger size that covered twice the material, a dispute could result. If the contract itself failed to identify the number of lessons, the court would examine prior documents and would likely conclude that because the proposal for seven lessons was accepted, the proposal would stand. If only the RFP was included in the contract and the proposal was not incorporated, the result could very well be different. The court would look at the RFP and the contract and find ten lessons. The e-learning contractor would then have to try to get the proposal accepted as parole evidence to change the outcome.

In summary, the RFP process is an investment of time and money for any contractor. The results can be very lucrative or, if mishandled, can cost a company a great deal of money. Up-front analysis of the RFP should include a very careful reading of the RFP, a very careful assessment of costs, and knowledge of the laws or policies governing the RFP process as well as some knowledge of contract law in the relevant jurisdiction. The time for an inexperienced company to seek the advice of lawyers, accountants, and other outside professionals is at the beginning of the process when a problem can be identified and avoided, rather than when a contract has been signed and a dispute has arisen.

■ ■ ■

THE BOTTOM LINE

The front matter of your proposal makes a first impression on your client, and first impressions are lasting. Keep it aesthetically pleasing, informative, and easy to use but do not neglect to protect your investment in the intellectual capital of your proposal. Make sure you present an attractive, enticing entry into your proposal. Do not forget to allocate time to the effective design of your front matter. You only get one chance to make a first impression — make it count.

10

EXECUTIVE SUMMARY

INTRODUCTION

Busy executives have precious little time to read lengthy, complicated e-learning proposals. Yet, when faced with choosing an e-learning vendor, the executive usually makes a final decision costing hundreds of thousands of dollars and impacting his or her organization for years to come. Executives need a quick overview of the facts to make an informed decision.

A well-written *Executive Summary* provides that overview for busy executives to intelligently discuss the proposal with line managers, trainers, and IT staff. The executive summary must be a concise, persuasive document that is interesting and informative. It must contain the salient points of the proposal and encourage executives to read on or choose it outright as the winner.

WHY THIS SECTION IS NEEDED

The executive summary frames the rest of the document and makes an important impression on the reader. Although you may spend days writing a proposal, if it does not make a positive impression in less than five minutes it will be rejected. The executive summary needs to "sell" the reader on the benefits of the proposal. Successful executive summaries lead readers into the proposal; unsuccessful summaries lead the proposal into the trash. The executive summary is the most important one or two pages in your proposal — write it with care.

While executives are typically thought to be the ones who read an executive summary, in reality everyone who reads the proposal begins with the executive summary. In many cases, this is the only part of the proposal read before a manager, trainer, or staff person sits in on your e-learning sales presentation. You can be assured that everyone reads the executive summary. This makes the executive summary even more critical because many clients will initially judge your organization solely on the merits of your executive summary. Take advantage of the fact that everyone reads the executive summary and make it count.

A well-written executive summary provides you with an opportunity to:

- Establish a good first impression
- Focus on the main points of interest to the reader
- Highlight the strengths of the proposal
- "Frame" the proposal in the desired context
- Assure the reader that your firm is capable of successfully completing the project

Your e-learning executive summary should be a concise, persuasive document that is interesting to read. It must summarize the creative and innovative aspects of your proposal while establishing your ability to successfully complete the project. You must also provide a brief overview of your creative team and the attributes that make it capable of completing the project on time and within budget. Example 10.1 illustrates a one-page executive summary.

WHAT SHOULD BE IN THIS SECTION

The major sections of the proposal serve as subheadings for the executive summary. This means that each section of the executive summary corresponds to the sequence of information in the body of the document. Following is a list of typical sections in an executive summary. It should be noted that not all executive summaries contain all of these sections.

- Description of problem
- Overview of solution
- Instructional solution
- Technical solution
- Project management and schedule
- Deliverables
- Budget
- Project team
- Corporate capabilities

Executive summaries usually start with a succinct review of the problem posed by the client. This is called the *Description of Problem.* This review establishes the fact that you understand the industry and the client's needs and desires. Cli-

Conveys a sense of excitement by calling the RFP a challenge. Also creates a sense of "working together."

Executive Summary

Challenge:

Personnel Selection Corporation's (PSC) challenge to Brilliant Performance Interactive (BPI) is to propose a means of developing and producing an interactive multimedia training program for an interview training course called *Good Employee Selection*. This program will be delivered on either CD-ROMs or an intranet and will serve as a self-study certification course, as a content and skills refresher for previously trained interviewers, and as a just in time (JIT) prep tool for interview preparation.

Solution:

Solution is divided into two areas, instructional and technical.

Instructional

BPI has built an instructional solution for PSC based on experience. The final product has been designed to provide two pathways through the learning environment. For first time learners, the instruction will be presented in a linear fashion starting with the fundamentals and moving onto higher skill levels as the learner gains confidence and experience. More experienced learners will be allowed to "jump" from section to section and to access key areas whenever they are needed. The instructional design will provide a learning experience that is thorough, proactive, motivational and interactive for both new and experienced learners.

Technical

BPI has decided that, due to PSC's plans to incorporate large amounts of video into the *Good Employee Selection* product, the best technical solution is to develop the training in HTML for initial distribution on CD-ROMs and package the material for the Internet Explorer 5.0 browser. This approach provides for quick viewing of large amounts of video and provides an upgrade path for Internet or intranet release when bandwidth issues are addressed.

Deliverables:

Each item that will be received by the client is listed as well as client training.

BPI can begin work on *Good Employee Selection* by December 15, 2000. A beta version of the program will be available for evaluation by November 14, 2001, and the final product will be available by December 15, 2001. In addition to the final mastered CD-ROM and the source code of the program, BPI will deliver a printed manual, instructional design documents, storyboards, flowcharts, camera-ready graphics, and the final mastered video and audio. BPI will prepare *Good Employee Selection* for packaging and will train PSC personnel on the basics of HTML for small changes or edits to the product.

Price:

Price of the project is clearly stated.

The proposed cost for BPI to meet the challenges of PSC will be $750,800.

Project Team:

Each team member is listed by name along with his or her area of responsibility.

BPI has prepared a team of experienced professionals which includes: Brian Jones (project manager), Carol Lipski (instructional designer), Pam Bearman (instructional designer), Curvin Collin (media specialist), Bill Collins (programmer) and Andy Jaeager (programmer/technical specialist).

Example 10.1 A one-page *Executive Summary* [1].

ents feel comfortable with a vendor when they know that the vendor understands them and their industry.

The next section is the *Overview of the Solution*. This section provides the client with a high-level overview of the steps you are going to take to solve the e-learning problem. In this section, innovative or creative ideas must be stressed. This is where the client learns how your organization solves instructional technology problems. Present your best strategies and ideas in this section.

The next two sections are the *Instructional* and the *Technical Solutions*. Often these two sections are combined under an *Overview of the Solution* section, but they can be highlighted separately if you have important information in one or both of these areas that you would like to stress. The *Instructional Solution* section explains how you plan to develop the requested instruction for the client. This is where you describe your instructional strategies and your approach for developing exciting and engaging instruction.

The *Technical Solution* section describes the technology that supports the instructional solution and makes it viable. This is not the place to show off an array of technical jargon. The goal of this section is to convey to the client that you understand the technical needs of the project and are prepared to meet those needs.

The next section is the *Project Management and Schedule* section. Here you describe how you will manage the project to complete it on time and within budget. Clients want to know that not only can you recommend an innovative solution, but you can make that solution happen.

Clearly provide the estimated time to completion (six months) as well as the estimated date of completion (January 15, 2005). Do not play games or try to hide this information. Make it clear when the project will start and finish and how long it will take.

Next is the list of *Deliverables*. These are the items you will provide (or deliver) to the client during and/or at the conclusion of project. You can list the deliverables in a bulleted format or in a paragraph. Make sure the list matches what was requested in the RFP and that you do not leave out any items. An omission of a critical item at this point in the proposal could get the proposal thrown out. Strive to mention each major item requested by the client.

The *Budget* is the most critical item in the executive summary. Make sure you present the budget as clearly as possible. This is critically important if you have different options or different add-ons that impact the final price of your solution. If you have several deliverables that you are supplying to the client, you may want to list their prices separately (learning portal $120,000, first five online courses $96,000). However, provide a total of all items (total $216,000). Do not make the client add up the final budget. Also, make sure that the budget number in the executive summary matches the budget number in the budget section of the document.

The *Project Team* section is next. This section is meant to instill in the client a sense of confidence that you have the people you need to complete the project. This is where the core team of individuals who will be working on the project is listed. You may list their individual names or simply list their positions. Listing specific names and positions of team members is a powerful sales tool, but if you cannot guarantee who will be working on the project, do not name names.

The final section is typically the *Corporate Capabilities* section. This is where you establish the credibility of your firm. For large e-learning firms, sometimes name recognition is enough. For smaller firms, you need to describe your company's history within the e-learning industry and within the client's industry. Explain how your experiences will benefit the client on this project.

Each section within the executive summary must be able to stand alone. Make sure that all information contained in the summary is relevant and important to the reader. Avoid using hyperbole and fluff. Include solid statements backed up with facts and figures within each section of the proposal.

Also, make sure that all sections of the executive summary are in agreement with the proposal For example, the executive summary may include information on a *four*-person development team while the body of the proposal discusses a *six*-person development team. In some cases the budget number in the executive summary may not match the number in the proposal. Other times the development software described in the executive summary is different from the development software mentioned in the proposal. The executive summary should be cross-referenced to the proposal in order to avoid any disagreement. Make sure that the information in the executive summary exactly matches the information within the proposal.

Worksheet 10.1 will assist you with developing an effective executive summary. It contains a step-by-step listing of the sections of a typical executive summary and an explanation of what should be in each section.

FORMAT OF EXECUTIVE SUMMARY

When writing the executive summary, you need to realize that it is rarely read in an ideal environment. Picture your client on an airplane at 9:30 at night after a long day of training. She reaches up and turns on the dim overhead light, casting an eerie shadow over your proposal lying on the not-so-clean dinner tray. As she begins to read the executive summary, the plane hits a little turbulence. She looks up and thinks, "Only four more proposals to read and I'll be done." If that does not work, picture your client in a busy office with the phone ringing every ten minutes, e-mail beeping, and a line of people outside his door waiting to see him. These are examples of the environments in which most people read proposals.

Executive Summary Worksheet (page one)

Take the highlights from each section of the proposal and address the topics and questions listed below. You must be brief, concise, and to the point. Cover each topic in three or four sentences or use a short bulleted list. Use original sentences; do not "copy and paste" from the proposal. To help the reader quickly proceed through the summary, use headings, organized lists, and plenty of white space. If needed, certain topics can be combined. For example the "Overview of the Solution," "Instructional Solution," and "Technical Solution" can be grouped under one heading titled "Solution."

Description of Problem: Describe the need(s) of the organization. Provide any insights your organization has concerning the need of the client. Don't be afraid to list the needs using bullets. This section of the executive summary establishes that your company "knows the client's industry" and can understand the client's unique and individual needs within the greater context of that industry (use of industry statistics can be effective in this section).

____

____

____

____

Overview of Solution: Write a high-level synopsis of your solution. Since this is the opening description of your solution, provide any innovative or creative detail that makes your solution unique. You may want to list the items that you will provide to address the client's need.

____

____

____

____

Instructional Solution: Provide information on how you plan to design, develop, and deliver the instructional aspects of the solution. You may want to indicate the number of hours of instruction you will develop or the number of screens or objectives addressed.

____

____

____

____

Worksheet 10.1 Use the *Executive Summary Worksheet* to create your executive summary after you have written the rest of your proposal.

Therefore, when you write your executive summary, you must use a format and style that is easy on the eyes, easy to understand, and makes a quick impact. You want to make the executive summary a joy to read, not a burden.

Executive Summary
Worksheet
(page two)

Technical Solution: Describe the technical aspects of the solution in layperson terminology. Provide enough detail so that a person can understand the basics of the technology involved but spare the techno-speak. This section should provide the executives and managers enough detail so that your solution seems reasonable but not too complex.

____

____

____

____

Deliverables: This section describes what tangible items the client will own once the project is complete. This section is sometimes combined with the "Project Management and Schedule" section. It can be a simple bulleted list of items or it can be a paragraph explaining what will be delivered upon completion of the project.

____

____

____

____

Project Management and Schedule: This section conveys to the client that your organization not only understands and can describe how to solve the needs of the client but that you can actually implement your solution. This section includes mention of the duration of the project (start and end dates). It also discusses briefly how you plan to manage the project in terms of communicating with the client. If the project is broken into phases or steps, this is a good place to briefly describe each step or phase. Don't provide too much detail, just enough to encourage the potential client to read the rest of the proposal.

____

____

____

____

Worksheet 10.1 (continued).

LENGTH

The first question of format is almost always, "How long should it be?" The answer is simple: "Long enough to do the job." The executive summary must make all the points needed to persuade the reader to further explore your proposal or to award you the contract. If you need a little extra space to drive home an idea, concept, or innovative solution, then use the space. However, do not fill the executive summary with "fluff" just to reach an imaginary page limit.

Executive Summary Worksheet (page three)

Budget: What is the price of the project? Put the price of the project into the executive summary; otherwise, it looks like you have something to hide. You may want to refer to the price as an investment; however, the title of this section needs to match the title or heading for the budget contained within the RFP. If there are multiple pricing options, list each option. To make the price more palatable, you may want to break the budget into smaller increments (i.e., one price for the learning portal and one price for the developed lessons). However, provide a "Grand Total" or several totaled options of all items proposed. Don't make clients add up the numbers—that annoys them.

____

____

____

____

Project Team: Who will be performing the work on the project? Describe how long the members of the project team have worked together (i.e., how many projects they have completed together, how many years they have combined in the industry or in the area of instructional design). You may want to provide titles as well as the name of each individual on the core team. If a large team is involved, simply mention the key team members and their unique role throughout the life of the project. You want to convey to the client that the team is competent, talented, and capable of completing the project on time and within budget.

____

____

____

____

Corporate Capabilities: What is the background and reputation of the company? What other project has the company successfully completed? Name some large, well-known customers served by the company. Explain the company's experience in supplying solutions similar to your client's or similar solutions to different types of clients. You may want to include quality assurance and risk mitigation information.

____

____

____

____

Worksheet 10.1 (continued).

In practical terms, the executive summary should be one page unless you have some compelling reason to stretch it to two pages. However, if it does go to two pages, use the entire second page. One or two lines on the second page of an executive summary looks sloppy — like you could not be efficient enough to make it fit on one page. On the other hand, a two-page bulleted executive summary might be easier to read than a one-page narrative summary. Example 10.2 shows a two-page executive summary.

FONT AND FORMAT

The executive summary should be single-spaced in a 12-point font. The font chosen should either be Times New Roman or Arial. Whatever font you use, it should be the same as the rest of the proposal. The executive summary is part of the proposal and should be treated as such. The summary must be free of all grammatical and spelling errors and must accurately portray the recommended solution.

If the client indicates a specific format for the executive summary or that it contain certain sections, follow the instructions. It would not be unheard of for a client to dismiss a proposal just because the proper format was not followed in the executive summary.

BULLETS AND WHITE SPACE

It is acceptable to use bulleted lists and white space to make the executive summary more attractive to the reader. Adding white space, bullets, and headings greatly increases the readability of your executive summary. Remember, the reader wants quick access to the important points in the document. Bulleted or numbered lists can provide that quick access. Example 10.3 shows a bulleted executive summary.

Example 10.4 is a paragraph that has been taken from an executive summary and made a little easier to read. Read the *before* and *after* and note the difference. Keep in mind that the executive summary must be appealing to a busy, somewhat hurried client. The first paragraph is difficult to read and not too appealing. The second paragraph contains the same information but it is arranged in a user-friendly format.

EXECUTIVE SUMMARY WRITING PROCESS (2)

Try to think of the executive summary as a sales document. The focus should be on sales and on providing information about the e-learning solution in a concise, easy-to-read document. The executive summary should be a "proposal in a proposal."

Combined sections as per RFP.

Shows understanding of industry and problem.

Provides synopsis of solution.

Keeping costs to a minimum shows an understanding of client's business needs.

List of what client will receive at the end of the project.

Response to Truckco's Request for Proposal

Executive Summary

UNDERSTANDING OF THE PROBLEM/OVERVIEW OF SOLUTION

Workforce Interactive understands there is a need to provide regulatory and non-regulatory training to professional truck drivers in an environment that meets their chaotic schedules. We realize that truck drivers today are using the Internet to remain informed, purchase supplies, match loads, and communicate with customers, family, and associates. We understand that an online community that provides consistent training to truck drivers, job-related information, and shopping opportunities can add value to this target market.

In response to Truckco's request, Workforce Interactive proposes to develop a user-friendly and convenient online portal for the trucking community, *Truckco Online*. *Truckco Online* will consist of an Information Center, Training Center, and Shopping Center that will be accessed from home computers, laptops on the road, and truck stop kiosks.

Since Internet kiosks already exist at many truck stops in Pennsylvania and other states, Workforce Interactive recommends that Truckco develop a relationship with an Internet kiosk provider. Assuming that Truckco wants to minimize startup costs and ongoing maintenance fees, a partnership will allow Truckco to add *Truckco Online* to existing technology at minimal cost. We propose developing a subscription program where subscribers to *Truckco Online* will be eligible for benefits within the portal through an incentive program called Truckco Rewards.

PROPOSED SOLUTIONS AND PRODUCT

Truckco Online will consist of an Information Center, Training Center, and Shopping Center. The Information Center will consist of a "Freeway" and "Tollway." The Freeway will provide free access to information such as weather reports, while the Tollway will consist of Internet access, games, sports, etc.

The Training Center will initially contain seven courses developed by Workforce Interactive in addition to providing access to information on Truckco's instructor-led training courses. As part of our instructional and technical solution, we will use our Learning Management System to provide learners with the training they need to better perform their jobs and enhance the overall capabilities of their organization.

Truckco Online will also provide an online catalog in the Shopping Center where truck drivers can purchase merchandise ranging from apparel to truck parts. Subscribers to *Truckco Online* will be eligible for *Truckco Rewards*, and will receive discounts and special offers in the Shopping Center. Revenue to Truckco will be generated through the Shopping Center, subscriptions to *Truckco Online*, course registration, and advertising.

Confidential v

Example 10.2 This is an example of a two-page *Executive Summary*.

Response to Truckco's Request for Proposal

Executive Summary (continued)

PROJECT MANAGEMENT AND SCHEDULE

Workforce Interactive will hand select each member of the core project team to work with Truckco. We will manage this project by utilizing our core team members and the resources of Truckco, such as the subject matter expert, usability testers, and course content.

Describes how the project will be broken down.

Provides some detail about each phase.

This project will be broken into four phases with a portal prototype being created prior to the development of any of the centers. Development of all three centers will begin simultaneously with key team members performing their respective tasks. Throughout the process our quality assurance procedures will guarantee Truckco's satisfaction with each phase of the project, while keeping Workforce Interactive on task. We will address potential risks by managing resources wisely and using effective communication with Truckco.

BUDGET

Provides price for project. Indicates what price includes and when payments are due.

Truckco's investment for this project is $452,118. This price includes development of the portal and the instructional courseware. The project will be broken down into four phases and will be completed in approximately nine months. Payment will be due upon completion of each phase. Prior to payment, the client will have the opportunity to review and sign-off all materials.

PROJECT TEAM

Establishes team history, credibility, and member roles.

Might have included name of project manager in this section.

Members of our core project team have been working together since 1995 and have over 50 years of combined experience in the multimedia and instructional technology field. Our senior members, who include the project manager, instructional designer, web developer, multimedia specialist, and technical specialist, work together to develop creative and effective instructional products.

This team has collaborated on numerous projects including the award-winning Roadway Express intranet-based training and orientation program. We are confident that this experience will benefit Truckco as well.

CORPORATE CAPABILITIES

Lists major clients as well as successfully completed projects.

Workforce Interactive is a single-source provider of training to the trucking industry. We have successfully developed web-based learning solutions, CD-ROM training, instructor-led seminars, kiosk-based instruction, and standardized courseware for companies such as Roadway Express, Allied Van Lines, NetTrans, The National Private Truck Council, and FedEx. Our experience also includes e-commerce and portal development for Tewel Corporation.

We also have, in place, many risk mitigation strategies that help ensure that we will complete your project on time and within our stated budget. We are able to offer this type of insurance because we have worked on many projects and are capable of addressing your e-learning needs.

Confidential vi

Example 10.2 (continued).

Executive Summary

Description of Need:

Quickly lists the needs of the client as listed in the RFP.

Athena Healthcare needs to train its 8,000 employees in proper handling of hazardous medical materials in accordance with OSHA regulations in a fast and efficient manner in the following topics:

- Benzene Safety
- Bloodborne Pathogens
- Hazardous Materials Transportation—Bulk Loading/Unloading
- Hazardous Materials—Waste Handling
- Isolation Precautions
- Radiation Safety for Fluoroscopy Procedures
- Respiratory Protection

Solution:

Solution is divided into two areas, goal of the project and elements of the LMS.

The goals of our proposed solution are to:
- Educate Athena clients in the proper standards of OSHA
- Provide efficient and affordable on-line training for all 8,000 Athena employees
- Provide bilingual educational offerings when needed
- Track individual employee performance on specific training criteria
- Implement the LMS into Athena's existing intranet with minimal interruptions.

Terse and to the point.

We propose to deliver and implement a Medical Library Learning Management System (MLLMS) that contains the above titles along with 22 other important OSHA topics. The LMS will provide:
- Tracking of individual employee progress
- Bookmarking features
- Administrative reporting
- Recording of when refresher training is needed
- Ability for Athena personnel to create courses

Price:

Price of the project is clearly stated in terms of initial and ongoing costs.

The price for the MLLMS is $500,000. Each title in the library is approximately $75 per user per year.

Satisfied Customers:

Instead of "Corporate Capabilities," the section is "Satisfied Customers" because the product is an "off-the-shelf" item, not custom e-learning development.

Our list of satisfied customers includes:
- Albert Einstein Medical Hospital in Philadelphia
- New York City Hospital
- Hospital of New Brunswick
- Thomas Jefferson Hospital
- Medical Hospital of New York

Example 10.3 Bulleted *Executive Summary.*

Before

Together, Manufacturing Education Corporation (MEC) and Digital Ingenuity will develop an interactive training program for individuals seeking certification in inventory control and ERP implementation. Individuals using this interactive web-based training will have the advantage of being able to take the class from any location and to access relevant supplementary information as needed. They will also have the ability to interact with MEC experts who can offer advice and guidance and interact with other individuals who are taking the training class. Students will also be able to work with the MEC body of knowledge while engaged in real-life, work-related scenarios. The system will also provide individual record keeping and personalized instruction.

After

Overview of Solution

Collaborative Partnership

Together, Manufacturing Education Corporation (MEC) and Digital Ingenuity will develop an interactive training program for individuals seeking certification in inventory control and ERP implementation.

Advantages of Our Solution

Individuals using this interactive web-based training will have the following advantages:

- Freedom from location restraints
- Quick, easy access to relevant supplementary information
- Access to MEC experts
- On-line interactions with fellow classmates
- Participation in real-life, work related scenarios
- Personalized instruction
- Individualized record keeping

Example 10.4 This shows a paragraph from an *Executive Summary* before and after it was formatted for easier reading.

The proposal development team should have a documented approach for writing a successful executive summary. Unfortunately, many firms have no such approach and just throw it together at the last minute. The following describes a successful approach used by many.

The first step in developing the executive summary is to finish the proposal. The proposal must be written before it can be summarized. Write the proposal first. This helps ensure that the executive summary matches the solution in the proposal. An executive summary should be a summary of the proposal.

The next step is to write the executive summary with no regard to length. The idea is to write down all the main points, ideas, and recommendations. You can prune the length later. If you attempt to limit the page length from the beginning, important points and connections between different parts of the proposal may be lost. The act of writing often spawns new ideas and insights, and artificially limiting the page length may cause many of those idea and relationships to be lost.

Now that a draft of your executive summary has been written, the third step is to begin pruning the summary from the perspective of the *client*. Too often the executive summary emphasizes the vendor's company and not the needs of the client. The executive summary must sell the ideas, innovations, and concepts within the document. This is done by appealing to the client, telling them how you will solve their problem. You also need to develop an executive summary that adds excitement and energy to the proposal without sounding flowery or overhyped.

The final step in the process of writing the executive summary is to proofread. Several people should proofread the executive summary. Few things can ruin the chances of winning e-learning business faster than typographical and grammatical errors in the executive summary — the first description your client reads of your entire solution. Make every effort to avoid errors in the executive summary.

COMMON EXECUTIVE SUMMARY MISTAKES

Unfortunately, typographical and grammatical errors are not the only kinds of mistakes that are made in the executive summary. Awareness of the types of mistakes that are commonly made will help you to avoid them. They are listed below. Keep these in mind when you are proofreading your executive summary.

- **Too salesy** — The executive summary is not a sales brochure; it is a summary of a business document. Do not make it sound like a brochure. While you do need to sell your solution in the summary, do not overdo it. Phrases such as "the one-and-only solution you'll ever need" are not appropriate. You can run into this problem if you are not providing enough substance in your executive summary. Your summary should contain concrete information explaining how you are going to help the client.
- **Wrong budget number in the summary** — If one person is preparing the executive summary and another person is preparing the budget, there could be miscommunication concerning the final budget number. Double-check all places where the budget number appears.
- **Too much "gray" space on the page** — Use white space effectively. An executive summary that looks crammed turns off a potential reader.

- **Too technical or too detailed** — This is not the place to go into the technical details. Provide a broad overview of the solution. The details should be in the body of the proposal.
- **Too vague** — If you provide too much of a high-level overview, the client will not know anything about your solution. Your summary will sound more like sales literature and not like a solution to the client's actual e-learning problem.
- **Not really a summary** — The executive summary should be a summary of the proposal. Do not copy and paste paragraphs from the body of your proposal into the executive summary. It annoys the client who decides to read the entire proposal. Copying and pasting limits your ability to be creative or convincing within the executive summary. The summary is an opportunity to restate the material from the proposal in a clear, concise, and exciting manner.
- **Too wordy** — The following paragraph is nothing but fluff:

  Pinnacle Interactive has extensively reviewed and researched the proposal set forth by Xpress Airlines. These efforts have produced an excellent solution to your training needs. Additionally, these efforts have allowed us to provide you with detailed information and responses to all areas in your Request for Proposal.

  The paragraph does not add any insight into the solution or provide the client with any information that can be of value in making a decision about this vendor.
- **Vendor focused** — Your executive summary needs to focus on the client's need, not on your firm. Do not spend too much time discussing your firm; instead, discuss what you can do to satisfy the client's needs.

These types of mistakes can occur for a variety of reasons. You need to look for these mistakes within your executive summary and make sure that they do not appear in your final version. Again, check and recheck your executive summary.

THE BOTTOM LINE

The executive summary is critical to the success of your proposal. Everyone reads the executive summary first. It sells the rest of the proposal and either encourages the readers to continue reading or causes the document to be thrown out. Great care must be taken to write the proposal in a manner that attracts the reader and builds excitement for your solution. Use your executive summary to draw in the client and encourage him or her to read the entire proposal.

11

DESCRIPTION OF PROBLEM/ OVERVIEW OF SOLUTION

INTRODUCTION

Clients do not always take the time to clearly define their own e-learning needs. This may be due to the fact that the client is caught up in the day-to-day struggle of running a training department, the client is dealing with several issues at once, or the client is unable to pinpoint the exact need. The client may know that "something has to be done" but is not sure what. Other times, the client might be so close to the problem he or she cannot view it objectively. Clients need your help to define their e-learning need.

The client's need is typically defined in the *Description of the Problem/Overview of the Solution*. This can also be called *Understanding the Scope, Statement of Scope*, or *Solution Overview*. Other titles can also be used.

Regardless of the exact title, this section of the proposal is where you show clients that you understand and can define their e-learning need. Clients need to know that the vendor has a clear picture of the e-learning need facing them. The main purpose of this section from the client's perspective is to see if you understand the client's need. The main purpose from your perspective is to define the client's e-learning need so that only your firm can solve it.

WHY THIS SECTION IS NEEDED

In this section of the proposal you provide a description of the client's e-learning need as you see it. You take the time to think through the problem for the client. You then describe the need and an overview of your recommended solution. The remainder of the proposal details *your* solution to *your* definition of the client's need. The *Description of the Problem/Overview of Solution* section allows you to frame the problem in a manner that makes it easy for your company to solve the client need because you have defined it to suit your firm's capabilities.

This is not to say that you force a square peg in a round hole. If your firm's capabilities do not fit the client need, do not respond to the RFP. You cannot fool clients into thinking that your solution is appropriate for them when clearly it is not. Before providing your firm's definition of the client's e-learning need, make sure you have an honest, workable solution. If you are dishonest with the client, your reputation of dishonesty will grow and your firm will soon be in trouble.

If your solution fits the client's need, then define the client's need from your perspective. Just keep in mind that if you go too far afield from the client's perspective you will most likely not be considered a viable contender. You need to balance the abilities of your firm with the actual needs of the client. Frame the client's e-learning need in a manner that makes sense to both your firm and the client.

One method of accomplishing this goal is to frame the need described in the RFP into a larger strategic context. Most training departments have many projects occurring simultaneously; see if your solution can fit into the overall training strategy of the client. Show how your LMS not only helps with current training needs but can be expanded to address future needs or how it can be accessed by the client's customers in the future. Discuss how your use of templates will allow the client to expand the course offerings easily and quickly. Think outside the box when you consider the client's e-learning need. Think of the strategic implications of your solution, not just the tactical aspects.

Your job is to frame the client's problem accurately and honestly in light of your firm's capabilities. E-learning problems can be approached and solved by many different methods. Define the client's e-learning need in such a manner that your firm is uniquely qualified to meet it.

If you can, position your firm and your solution to not only solve the current need but future e-learning needs as well. Show the value of your solution and what it can do for the client. Example 11.1 shows the *Description of the Problem/ Overview of Solution* section from an RFP. In this case, the vendor called the section *Understanding of the Problem*. Notice how the vendor succinctly captures the essence of the client's e-learning problem by writing *Training must be efficient, convenient, and maximize the driver's time*. This statement provides the client with a concise goal for the training.

Response to Truckco's Request for Proposal

Describes what the vendor, Workforce Interactive, views as the problem.

UNDERSTANDING OF THE PROBLEM

Workforce Interactive understands that there is a need to train truck drivers. Special training is needed to optimize a truck driver's performance. Tasks of truck drivers are multiple, from safety inspections to load securement. Truck drivers have deadlines to meet; therefore, time is valuable. Training must be efficient, convenient, and maximize the driver's time.

In addition to the need for providing drivers training on trucking-related topics, we understand Truckco's need to provide a one-stop community for truck drivers while on the road and at home. An online community will provide truck drivers with a gateway to training courses and information such as weather, trucking-related products, news, and a forum for drivers to communicate with other drivers on industry topics. The community will also allow them to shop and purchase trucking-related items.

According to Truckco, the training needs to be online in an environment that promotes optimum job performance while working within the chaotic schedule of truck drivers. This environment includes home computers, truck stop kiosks, and wireless devices.

OVERVIEW OF SOLUTION

In response to your request, Workforce Interactive will design a systematic and personal approach to develop a one-stop, user-friendly portal for the trucking community called *Truckco Online. Truckco Online* will consist of an Information Center, Training Center, and Shopping Center. Truck drivers can access the proposed portal from their home computers, laptops on the road, and Internet kiosks at truck stops. It is our understanding that Truckco will generate revenue through various parts of the portal, such as advertising and other training course contributors.

This solution adds value to Truckco's customers, initially Pennsylvania truck drivers, in the following ways. The Information Center will benefit the drivers by providing pertinent information that will increase their efficiency in performing their job. In addition, it will offer entertainment opportunities to the trucking community. The Training Center will increase the safety of professional truck drivers, assure regulatory compliance, and reduce fines for non-regulatory compliance. The Shopping Center will allow the driver to conveniently purchase products related to the trucking industry using an online catalog.

Since Internet kiosks already exist at many truck stops in Pennsylvania and other states, Workforce Interactive recommends that Truckco develop a relationship with an Internet kiosk provider. Assuming that Truckco wants to minimize startup costs and ongoing maintenance fees, a partnership will allow Truckco to add *Truckco Online* to existing technology at minimal cost. We propose developing a subscription program where subscribers to *Truckco Online* will be eligible for benefits within the portal through an incentive program called *Truckco Rewards.*

Confidential 1

Example 11.1 This is an example of a vendor providing an overview of the client's problem statement in a section titled *Understanding of the Problem.*

WHAT SHOULD BE IN THIS SECTION

This section of the proposal needs to convince the client that you understand the e-learning problem and that you have a viable solution. In this section restate the client's need in your own words. Demonstrate to the client that you understand the essence of the need and that you agree with the client's own vague concept of the problem but that you have a unique and interesting method of solving it. This section demonstrates to the client that you have truly analyzed the RFP and have put some effort into thinking about the client's e-learning problem. Basically, this section needs to do three things:

- Demonstrate that you have a clear understanding of the client's actual business need (whether clearly stated in the RFP or not).
- Frame the client's problem in a manner favorable to your proposed solution.
- Divulge enough of your solution to encourage the reader to continue reading without getting into too many details.

One mistake many proposal writers make is to simply mimic the words found in the RFP. In fact, many novice proposal writers wonder why this section is even needed. "Everyone understands the problem, it's described in the RFP," they protest. However, the problem described in the RFP may not even be a problem. It may only be a symptom of a problem.

For example, a convenience store chain issued an RFP to develop Web-based training for all of its franchisees. The problem, as stated in the RFP, was a high turnover rate of clerks. The solution, as the convenience store executives defined it, was to provide more training to the clerks via e-learning. The executives believed that when the clerks received more training, they would feel more comfortable in their position and, therefore, not leave the company.

Several vendors took the client at its word. These vendors described the problem as one of employee training. This mimicked exactly what was stated in the RFP but it was not the "real" problem. These vendors all proposed Web-based training for clerks as the client anticipated. None of these vendors won the business.

The winning vendor determined that Web-based training for clerks would not entirely solve the employee turnover problem. The vendor determined that the solution needed was training for managers on how to interview and screen potential employees. The problem was poor selection of new employees — not just more training for the clerks.

The winning vendor recommended training for both the managers and the clerks. The vendor did not totally dismiss the need for training clerks because the executives were so convinced that the clerks needed training. In fact, they would not accept any proposal that did not include some type of clerk training. The winning vendor identified the client's training needs and addressed them in the proposal but also redefined the need in a manner favorable to the vendor's solution. The winning vendor included the need for Web-based manager training when no other vendor even mentioned it.

As another example, a large consulting firm requested that an online role-play be developed to train new associates. Rather than frame the problem as one of training, the winning vendor framed it as one of communication and as a need to easily and quickly exchange ideas with more seasoned consultants. Rather than simply develop static e-learning modules, the vendor proposed an online bulletin board, a virtual chat feature, and a repository of seasoned consultants' "war stories." The vendor proposed the creation of a "community of practice" where seasoned and new consultants could share information within and outside of the online training environment. The approach worked.

Merely mimicking the words of the client does not show that you understand the "real" problem. It suggests that you are too lazy, uninformed, or do not care about the client's need. At the absolute minimum, you must describe the client's need in your own words and even that is not enough [1]. Mimicking the words of the RFP proves you understand the client's "words" but not the actual problem or need.

To demonstrate a clear understanding of the client's problem, you must capture the fundamental need of the client. Strip away all the trivia and excess demands and get to the business need driving the RFP. This is not to say that you should ignore the other requirements listed within the RFP. A simple clarification of the need helps you develop a clear and concise definition of the client's e-learning problem. Example 11.2 illustrates a vendor clarifying the needs of the client by dividing those needs into different sections.

DEFINING THE CLIENT'S E-LEARNING NEED

The first thing you want to do when clarifying the fundamental need of the client is to focus on the one thing that will have an order of magnitude impact on the client's organization. This is usually the business need underlying the RFP. The ability to identify the fundamental need of the client provides clear evidence that you understand the client and the client's basic needs [1].

While identifying the fundamental need, attempt to uncover hidden or not-so-obvious needs. Uncovering these needs is even better evidence that you understand the problem [1]. The convenience store example illustrates how the identification of a need, not even known by the client, led to an insightful and effective approach to solving the problem. It also led to a victory for that e-learning vendor.

Provides an overview of the solution.

Breaks problem into discrete sections which mak it easy to understand.

Section 2.0 Understanding of Scope

2.1 Synopsis of the Requests in the Project Scope

Marshall National High School plans to change from a paper-based learning institution to a web-based learning environment for high school students. Intelligent Multimedia Solutions (IMS) would be the ideal partner as well as a catalyst to enable this transition to occur as effectively, rapidly and smoothly as possible. To design and implement the web site for Marshall National High School, IMS will focus on meeting the needs of our client and the needs of your clients—the future enrollees of the "Virtual High School."

To accomplish this transition, IMS has identified the following primary areas:

- The design and development of a web site and homepage that will serve as the electronic interface for Marshall National High School and the general public, including the access point for student enrollees, their parents, and staff members. Web pages with links to all related sites will be designed and developed for each of the functions and activities that are planned for the students, staff, and parents. A login process will provide access to restricted areas for students, parents, and staff.
- An instructional analysis review of the present courses taught by Marshall. Emphasis will be placed on identifying the domains of learning for each instructional objective, then developing learning strategies that will provide interactivity, embedded assessment and quizzes with feedback. Marshall has requested that the instructional design process utilize the content of the courses presently offered by Marshall. IMS' Complete Quality Model (CQM) of instructional analysis will be used for the instructional design and development process. CQM is used to adapt instruction and learning activities to enable the lessons to be delivered effectively via the web.
- The present courses will be adapted to a module format. The modules will be designed to incorporate the present study guides as requested by Marshall. A curriculum review will compare and contrast the content and the objectives of Marshall's courses and study guides to other states' recommended curriculum for all subjects that are required for graduation. Additional content and instructional objectives may be recommended based on the results of the curriculum analysis.
- A customized database designed to effectively and efficiently meet the needs of both the on-line high school and the administrative requirements necessary for that function. These include but are not limited to the following: enrollment of students; secure sign-in access and tracking of student use of courses; book store; deliver and permit updates of course content; maintenance of records; test administration, scoring, and record keeping; provision for test-bank options; a means to link course achievement, grade reporting, and transcript functions; e-commerce capabilities for the student store and payment of fees via the Internet. All of this must be designed as an absolutely safe environment with three levels of access: students, faculty and administrative personnel.

#

Example 11.2 This is an example of how a vendor clarified the needs of the client by dividing the needs into different sections under the heading of *Understanding of Scope.*

Uncovering hidden needs can be accomplished in a number of ways. The first is to look beyond the client organization and into the client's industry. Identify the drivers of the client's industry. They could be low cost, quality service, time to market, or other factors that separate winners from average performers in that industry.

Another effective technique is to read between the lines of the RFP. What is the client not revealing in the definition of the problem? What key issues are going to impact the client when the desired solution is implemented? Does this client have problems or needs that have nothing to do with a training solution? Can you leverage part of your solution to fit into a more strategic need of the client?

These types of questions and considerations will help you to identify needs that are above and beyond anything written within the RFP. Worksheet 11.1 provides assistance in defining the client's need and developing an appropriate solution. Use this worksheet to generate ideas and to consider what elements of the client's need you can use to frame the client's e-learning problem in a manner favorable to your firm's capabilities.

THE BOTTOM LINE

For many reasons clients may be confused about their actual e-learning need. Cut through the confusion and provide a clear, concise explanation of the client's e-learning problem. Do not mimic the words of the client. Frame the client's e-learning problem in a manner that favors your firm. Think strategically, not just at a tactical level. You need to be the only firm to see the client's e-learning problem in a unique way. Provide a solution to the actual client problem, the problem the client does not even know exists. Do not be afraid to think outside the box for your description of the client's problem.

Understanding the Problem/Overview of the Solution Worksheet
(Solution Definition)

Statement of Client Need: What did the client say they needed to solve the problem?

Real Need: What does the client actually need to solve the problem?

Industry Needs: What types of problems do companies within this industry frequently encounter? How do other companies solve those problems?

Redefinition of the Problem: How can you frame the problem presented in the RFP in such a manner that it would be advantageous to your firm?

Worksheet 11.1 Use the *Understanding of the Problem/Overview of the Solution Worksheet* to write your description and interpretation of the client's e-learning problem.

12

SOLUTIONS

INTRODUCTION

The heart of your proposal is the description of your solution. This is where your capture strategy and proposal theme combine to convince the client of the value and credibility of your solution. It is here where your innovative ideas, unique approach, and technical acumen become evident to the client. Clients want to know how you propose to solve their e-learning problem. The *Solutions* section is where you explain it to them.

WHY THIS SECTION IS NEEDED

It is one thing for you to promise to solve the client's e-learning problem; it is another to describe, in detail, how you will do it. In this section you describe your instructional and technical solutions in simple terms while providing enough detail for clients to understand what you will be doing for them. Provide clients with confidence in your firm's ability to create an effective solution for their e-learning problem. You want to paint a picture of what the completed solution will encompass and what it will do for clients.

WHAT SHOULD BE IN THIS SECTION

A well-written *Solutions* section typically consists of two parts. The first is a description of the instructional solution and the second is a description of the technical solution. Both solutions must support each other and work together to meet the client's need. The combination of these two solutions is the core of your e-learning proposal.

In some cases, when only an LMS is desired, the technical portion of the proposal will be larger than the instructional section. However, this entire field is about learning, and even if only a technical solution is desired in the RFP, a savvy vendor will include information about how the LMS facilitates effective instruction and employee learning. Ignoring the learning aspects of any e-learning solution is not conducive to winning. The entire purpose of any e-learning venture should be to support and facilitate learning.

The instructional and technical aspects of your solution need to be explained clearly and simply to the prospective client. Most clients have little understanding of instructional design (ID) and even less understanding of the technological aspects of an e-learning solution. Use this section of the proposal to educate your client on the need to follow an ID process and on the various technical aspects of your solution.

INSTRUCTIONAL SOLUTION

The instructional solution section describes how you will employ the instructional systems design (ISD) process to solve the client's instructional need [1]. You describe your use of instructional strategies and why it is important that you follow a defined process for developing e-learning. You also establish why instructional strategies are important to the client and why following the ISD process is valuable to the client.

When you describe the instructional strategies, there is little point in going into the complex instructional theories behind those strategies. Many managers reading the proposal will be unfamiliar with instructional theorists such as Robert Gagné or Smith and Regan. Few know the difference between constructivism, cognitivism, and behavioralism. Instead, these managers want to know that the instruction will work and that you have a plan for making it work.

So instead of talking about Gagné's Nine Events of Instruction, simply list them and describe how they will be used to ensure learning. Rather than describe the merits of one ID model over another, simply describe your instructional development process and how the client benefits from that process. Many clients will not understand the benefits of a certain instructional approach unless you tell them the benefits of that approach. Link the instructional approach to the business need you identified when you analyzed the RFP.

Another important element in this section is a statement of the assumptions you are making about any existing instructional material. For example, you may be assuming that the materials to be placed online are already instructionally sound and that you do not need to rewrite objectives or make changes to the content. If that is what you are assuming, make that statement. Otherwise you will get into a situation where you end up rewriting the objectives for "free" because the client assumed you knew the objectives were not instructionally sound.

In this section of your solution, you want to describe, in general terms, how you are going to apply your solution to the client's e-learning problem. You do not need to provide a detailed outline of how you are going to develop every single lesson or module. Instead, provide a general sense of how the instructional development process will take place.

In the instructional solution section, you need to answer potential client questions such as the following:

- How do we know the training will be effective?
- Will the e-learning be high quality?
- What type of learner interactions will occur during the e-learning?
- Will the instruction meet my immediate needs?
- Will the e-learning be educationally sound?
- Will the trainees like the e-learning?
- Will the trainees take the e-learning once it is made available?

This is where you flesh out the solution that you preliminarily developed during the *Conceptualizing the Solution* (Chapter 5) phase of the E-BAP. You explain what steps you would take to solve the client's problem from an instructional perspective.

■ ■ ■

EXPLAINING INSTRUCTIONAL DESIGN METHODOLOGIES TO A CLIENT

Lisa Verge, Learning Products Manager, EduNeering, Inc.

Clients researching an e-learning solution are savvier than ever. CEOs, CFOs, and everyone in between now utter the term "instructional design," which was once only known in the training industry. The reason? Online or computer-based training is no longer looked at as the cutting edge where you must validate your reasons for taking the plunge. The benefits of online training vs. traditional classroom training are well documented, mostly from a cost and convenience perspective — which makes a CEO or CFO stand up and take notice. RFPs used to be most interested in the financial bottom line only.

Now, in addition, they also mention ID either directly or indirectly. Companies are realizing that getting something that works will not only provide them with the results they want, it will save money in the long run. In essence, if they are going to require their employees to use e-learning, how will they know that they will learn from it? ID is the answer. Now comes the hard part — convincing the client that your company is the right one for the job.

ID has its roots firmly planted in the field of education. In short, it is the process by which you create effective instruction. There are many learning theories that identify what types of tasks are learned best by which approach. For instance, does one learn a procedure by reading it or practicing it? Questions of this type are really what ID is all about — setting up the right structure so that learners will succeed by accomplishing the objectives of the training.

The term "instructional design" is no longer foreign, but the question is, "Do clients really understand what they are getting?" Can any vendor spout off some ID terminology and convince the decision-makers that they deserve the business? The trend in today's business is "no." It is no longer sufficient to create a "bells and whistles" type of learning product without good instruction behind it. The buyer has become more educated, and the differences between vendors have become less distinguishable. Every vendor in today's online marketplace has an ID process — the trick is convincing the client that you use it and it works. Therein lies the challenge.

So what differentiates one ID process from another? Is a five-step process better than a four- or six-step process? There is no magic combination and, frankly, clients do not care. What is important is that you can explain why your process works and clients believe it. Do you have a proven track record? Do not underestimate the power of successful cases or testimonials. Usually, a client who is happy with the process and the product is willing to sing the praises of the vendor responsible. Likewise, if the product received has gotten such poor results that it is no longer used, others will get an earful of why they should not go with that vendor. In the end, you will find yourself trying to explain why your ID process and your course development process are one step above the others. Here are some general things to keep in mind when explaining the benefits of your process in an RFP.

Know what the client wants — Before you cut and paste your "canned" RFP response, take the time to identify what it is the client is really looking for. Often if basic questions are not answered, your response will go in the "no" pile pretty quickly — even if it is the best option. It is important to make the client feel understood. And although it seems early in the process, chances are that if a client feels you do not understand what they are looking for, you will not get a chance to prove it.

Expect the unexpected — You have examined and responded to eight RFPs this month and they are all the same, right? Wrong. Just when you think you've got the song and dance down, the tune will change. This may be due to the specifics of the project, or maybe it is due to a savvy client. Does the client refer to some learning theory that you have never heard of? Investigate it. You do not want to find yourself agreeing with something that has no validity. In the same sense, you do not want to trash a valid learning theory just because it is not in the book you read in school.

Don't muddy the waters with jargon — Clients are becoming more aware of why a good ID process is necessary. Do not push that too far by throwing out specific theorists, statistics, and other jargon that tend to give decision-makers a glazed look. Keep it simple. A clear process with documented results will take you a long way. If you feel you need to mention a name to provide validity, fine. Just don't mention it in every paragraph. Clients are not looking for a theory; they are looking for a vendor.

Know the buzzwords — While you should not cloud things with jargon, it is important to know the current buzzwords and what they mean. Clients generally know enough jargon to make them dangerous. For instance, saying content is SCORM™ compliant has nothing to do with the ID process; it is more the technology behind the content. But clients might mention it as an ID requirement. Buzzwords will appear in the RFP; don't ignore them. Make sure your answers will satisfy any questions — remember your proposal usually has to stand on its own two feet. By not addressing concerns, you are risking the chance that it will get tossed aside. However, stay away from putting too many buzzwords of your own in your response. If you have to explain too many, it will seem as though you are talking down to the client.

Have an acronym — It may sound silly, but if your company has a design process called "Design of Content," think about calling it DOC — maybe even get it trademarked. It adds validity to your process and it is catchy when written in a proposal as opposed to writing "our design of content process" over and over.

Make it meaningful — Using a process in the abstract has little value. Making a process, especially an ID process, connect with the client's content is extremely powerful. It shows the client that you understand the need and it gives the client concrete examples. This may take a little research on your end, but it usually pays off. You will have to evaluate this for each RFP based upon your firm's confidence in winning and the estimated size of the award. You may invest the time to develop storyboards for a $100,000 project, but for a $1,000,000 project you might create a prototype demonstration that will knock the client's socks off.

Give examples of success stories — Just saying your process works is not enough. Provide case studies, testimonials, etc. to show the potential client that your process does work. Make those examples as relevant to the client as possible. For instance, if you are responding to an RFP from a trucking company and you have an existing trucking or railroad client, try to use that client as an example. Relevance goes a long way, especially when you consider that companies in the same business usually come across the same types of challenges. Make sure to get permission first; some companies will not want their names given, especially to a competitor.

■ ■ ■

ADDIE MODEL

The ADDIE model is one of the most common ISD models. It consists of the elements of analysis, design, development, implementation, and evaluation. Sometimes it even contains the concept of management, which changes it to the MADDIE model [2]. It is this model, or some variation thereof, that you will explain to the client.

You must be careful not to explain the model in terms that are too academic or contain too much jargon. The idea is to explain how the ADDIE model will be used to address this client's specific e-learning need. While many clients may have a basic understanding of the ADDIE model, many more will not. You need to explain the model and how it will impact the client in simple, easy-to-understand language. A brief summary of each of the aspects of the ADDIE model follows.

Analysis — While the RFP typically has some analysis and discussion of the needs of the client, good vendors always recommend that they be allotted time to conduct their own analysis. This is critical to the success of the e-learning project.

For many reasons a client can misread its own situation and provide an analysis that is faulty or biased. If you do not conduct a careful analysis of the learning environment, the actual learning need, and the learner characteristics yourself, problems could arise.

These problems might include developing instruction that does not match the needs of the learners, designing instruction that is not really needed, reconfiguring poor stand-up materials as poor e-learning, or developing courses that do not run over the client's current network. None of these situations is favorable to you or the client and almost all of them lead to cost overruns and missed schedules.

On the other hand, if you do take the time to conduct a careful needs analysis, you can ensure that the instruction matches the learner needs, the e-learning works on the client's network, and the learners are learning in the most appropriate manner.

Design — This section involves the application of appropriate instructional strategies to the client's unique learning needs. Average vendors treat this part of the e-learning development process as the need to develop good navigational screens, good page layout, and good graphics.

Truly excellent vendors develop an effective instructional strategy for the design of the client's e-learning. This portion of the e-learning design process is the real “engine” that powers an effective solution. In this section, explain to the client how you will use proven instructional strategies to design training that works. One of the best methods of explaining how you are going to design effective instruction is to discuss an instructional framework for all of your course design.

An example of a framework to use for the design of almost any learning event is some variation of Robert Gagné’s Nine Events of Instruction. These events provide a framework for designing e-learning that makes an impact. They are as follows:

- Gaining attention
- Informing the learner of the objective
- Stimulating recall of prerequisite learning
- Presenting the stimulus material
- Providing learning guidance
- Eliciting the performance
- Providing feedback about performance correctness
- Assessing the performance
- Enhancing retention and transfer [3]

While this framework is good, it is not enough. You also need to explain your use of *instructional strategies*. While many instructional designers will know that an instructional strategy is a method of influencing a learner’s ability to understand and acquire information, other professionals reading the proposal may be unfamiliar with the concept [4].

You might want to include a simple example to help them understand instructional strategies. One such example is the use of a mnemonic device to help with memorization. In grade school, the name ROY G. BIV is used to help students remember the colors of the rainbow (red, orange, yellow, green, blue, indigo, and violet). This is an instructional strategy. While this is a simple example, it can help to make the point.

In your proposal, you might need to explain that for conceptual learning an effective strategy is to use examples and nonexamples to teach the concept. You may also explain that there are predictable mistakes learners make and that well-designed e-learning will fix those mistakes. For example, a common mistake in learning a new concept is that the learner will tend to overgeneralize.

You need to provide the client with examples of how you will apply instructional strategies to their content. Explain how you will teach memorization, attitudes, concepts, rules, procedures, and problem solving using the appropriate strategy for each type of learning Let the client know that the proper application of instructional strategies is critical to the success of e-learning and that you apply those strategies when you design your e-learning.

Development — When describing the development of the instruction, you need to describe the software you will be using, any templates that you have designed, and how your audio, video, and graphic elements will be developed. Let the client know if you will use royalty-free graphics or will be creating them or if you require the client to provide them. Describe if you are going to use professional actors for the video portion of the e-learning or if you will use client employees or even your own employees.

Explain the review process and how client feedback will be incorporated into the development of the e-learning. In this section you want to provide the client with a comfort level concerning your firm's ability to create e-learning. You may describe some of the measures you take to ensure that the instruction is compliant with industry standards as well as government regulations such as Section 508.

The goal of explaining the development process is to provide the client with evidence that you have developed instruction before and that you know what it takes to do it right. However, do not go into too much detail. Keep it fairly generalized; clients want a sense of the development process, not a blow-by-blow explanation.

Implementation — This is where you explain the process by which you will ensure that the e-learning will be up and running on the client's network without any problems. In the case of CD-ROM delivery, this is relatively easy. You simply take the CD-ROM to the computers on which it will be used and make sure it functions properly. However, if the client will be running a full-blown LCMS system over an intranet or the Internet, then the implementation becomes a little harder.

Provide enough nontechnical details to give the client a general sense of the implementation process and how it will function, but do not dive into the nitty-gritty. When you win the contract and develop a statement of work, you can get into more detail. In the RFP/proposal stage, you do not have enough details to provide an exact implementation plan.

Your implementation plan may need to include usability testing, network stress testing, and a variety of other tests to make sure your e-learning solution is compatible with the client's existing network and software configurations. The goal is to ensure that your technological solution works on the client's network when it is implemented. If it does not, the quality of your instructional solution really does not matter.

At the implementation stage, it is a good idea to get the client's IT staff involved. This is true even if the client does not mention them in the RFP. With today's complex e-learning systems competing for bandwidth alongside the client's mission critical applications, you need to make sure that IT is involved and understands the demands that will be placed on the network.

Evaluation — In the formal ID literature, the topics of formative and summative evaluation are discussed under the heading of *Evaluation*. However, most clients are not familiar with those terms. Instead, they are more comfortable with the concepts of quality assurance and quality control.

Regardless of the terminology, the concept is the same. You want to explain how you are going to ensure the delivery of an instructionally sound, bug-free product. One method of ensuring a high-quality product is, of course, to follow the ISD process. Other steps involve usability testing, verifying the technological aspects of the instruction, and perhaps working with outside groups like the Advanced Distributed Learning Co-Lab or a Web site like www.bobby.com.

You want to ensure quality on three levels. The first is technical. The delivery of the LMS/LCMS or e-learning module needs to be bug-free. Technical problems are the most obvious to the client. The second level of quality is usability. Clients need to be able to easily navigate through the software and find what they need. The third level of quality is learning. This is important because the e-learning needs to be instructionally sound in order to be effective.

However, many clients are not interested in evaluating the effectiveness of the e-learning. They simply do not have the budget to evaluate already developed e-learning. While clients will pay for the development of the instruction and demand a quality development process, they tend not to go the extra mile to pay for an evaluation once the e-learning is online and being used. Be careful about allocating time (read *money*) to the evaluation of the e-learning once it is online and functioning. For those of you who are traditional instructional designers, focus on the formative evaluation and not the summative.

The explanation of the ISD process using the ADDIE model (or any other ISD model) is important for the overall success of your proposal. Clients need to have the e-learning development process explained in simple, easy-to-understand language. The explanation of your ID process should instill in the client a high level of confidence in your firm's ability to develop instructionally sound e-learning.

As you apply the ISD process to the development of the instruction, do not forget that often a blended approach of instructor-led and e-learning delivery can be a successful solution. Both types of instruction can be developed using the ISD process. When proposing the blending of different deliveries of instruction, provide visuals of how the two types will interact, along with an explanation of how each delivery method complements the other.

The time and effort placed into the development of the proper instructional strategy is worth it. The instructional strategy drives the e-learning proposal. The elements of budget, timeline, and even who is assigned to the project are driven by the chosen e-learning approach. Take the time to develop a learner-centric solution and the rest of the proposal will fall into place.

Example 12.1 is from the ID section of a proposal. Notice how the proposal describes, in some detail, the instructional elements that will be contained within each lesson. The proposal carefully outlines Gagné's Nine Events of Instruction

Response to Truckco's Request for Proposal

Instructional Solution

Describes the basic Instructional Design Model without referring to any specific theory or individual.

Instructional Design Process

The instructional design model that Workforce Interactive uses is based on four main steps: Determine, Design, Develop, Deliver. In addition, the phases of Evaluation and Revision are essential parts of instructional design, and used throughout the entire process. The following describes Workforce Interactive's instructional design process with the framework and strategies proposed to create all seven courses in the *Truckco Online* Training Center. For the purpose of this proposal, we will be using the "Securing the Load" course as an example to present our process and prototype.

Describes what the project team will do to develop the e-learning.

Determine

We assume that Truckco's course content is up-to-date and complete.

The first step will be determining the nature of the task and requirements to be learned. The project team will:

- Conduct a needs analysis to determine the need by observing Truckco's current learning situation and to compile a list of tasks to be completed.
- Create and/or reuse course content by reviewing existing material to apply to the new training using our Learning Management System. Workforce Interactive is working closely with IMS Global Learning Consortium, Inc. (IMS) to integrate content management standards into our LMS.
- Conduct analysis of learner characteristics and the environment to examine the potential learners that will be participating in the training, as well as the possible environments in which the training will take place.

Design

Provides a general overview of the design process.

In this phase, Workforce Interactive will design the content for *Truckco Online's* courses. This will include the creation of objectives, the test items, the strategies to deliver the instruction, and the flowcharts used to sequence the instruction. When a course is created using the LMS, the course content is segmented into reusable learning objects. These objects can be pulled out for future courses and/or be updated easily at any time, thus allowing us to keep courses current with the laws and rules governing the trucking industry. All of the *Truckco Online* courses will contain the framework and strategies below:

These are the elements of Gagné's Nine Events of Instruction.

Gain Attention

The training will gain the attention of the learners by presenting a compelling image of a truck damaged due to a load that was not secured properly. In addition, the material will include a motivating "What's in it for me?" (WIIFM) statement that will remind the learners of the benefits and importance of taking the course.

Confidential 2

Example 12.1 Description of an *Instructional Solution* portion of an e-learning proposal.

Response to Truckco's Request for Proposal

Recall Prior Knowledge
The course will recall the learners' prior knowledge on the lesson topic in the form of a simple pretest. The learners will be informed that, based on their performance on the pretest, the training will be modified to fit their prior knowledge.

Inform Learner of Objectives
Informing learners of the outcomes, or objectives, will help them understand what they are to learn during the course. Simple graphics and diagrams will be used to demonstrate the pieces of instruction that will be presented to learners to help them visually conceptualize what they will be learning.

Describes, briefly, how different types of information will be taught differently.

Present Information
Workforce Interactive's goal is to create effective and efficient instruction that meets the learners' needs and is meaningful and pertinent to their profession each time it is presented. The following are strategies that will be used to best present information for each type of learning:

- o Fact - organize into "chunks" to provide the learner with practice.
- o Concept - show the concept name, definition, and best example that will illustrate the category for the concept. Presenting additional examples as well as non-examples of the concept will break down the category even further.
- o Procedural Rule - break down the correct order of steps in the procedure and then present the procedure as a whole. In addition, steps in a procedure can be demonstrated using animations.
- o Problem Solving - list the rules that are required to solve the problem.

Lets the client know that they understand how to develop different types of training for different types of content.

Provide Guided Practice
Our instructional design team will use the following practice strategies for each type of information:

- o Fact - use rehearsal activities that will require the learners to answer questions related to the fact, and mnemonic exercises that will help recall facts.
- o Concept - present examples and non-examples of a concept and require learners to identify them as such.
- o Procedural Rule - list or describe steps of the procedure, then virtually perform the procedure in its entirety.
- o Problem Solving - apply correct rules that will address and solve a problem.

Confidential 3

Example 12.1 (continued).

Not only is the design team focusing on designing good instruction but they are also going to include strategies to motivate the learner. Always a good consideration in an e-learning environment.

Describes how they will summarize key points from each lesson.

Describes how the LMS will interact with the courses that are developed.

Provides information on how they will add retention and transfer of knowledge.

Incorporate Motivational Strategies

Because of time constraints and busy schedules that the truck drivers face every day, we realize that it will be essential to motivate them and keep them actively involved in the instruction. To do this, the team will implement various techniques based on the following four principles:

- o Keep the attention of the learner throughout all of the *Truckco Online* courses.
- o Show relevance of how the new training is related to the trucker's current job and establish the current value of the instruction.
- o Promote learner confidence when practicing.
- o Base learning on the theory that positive consequences are natural when learning is successful.

Provide Feedback

Constructive feedback will be given after each embedded question and following practice provided during the instruction. In addition, constructive feedback will be given after the completion of the final test so that the learner will have full understanding of which questions they answered incorrectly and to confirm questions they answered correctly.

Summarize

A summary of the key points will be provided at the conclusion of each lesson to review the information that was presented.

The LMS allows for question randomization, question pools, timed response, question retry, and immediate constructive feedback associated with questions. Question types will include true/false, multiple choice, and fill-in-the-blank.

Promote Retention and Transfer

Associations will be made between the learners' existing knowledge and the new knowledge gained in the training. The associations aid learners in retaining the new knowledge and applying it on the job.

Development

In the development phase, content will be converted into actual instructional courseware. Our LMS allows for quick initial design and development of courseware. This is done through the use of an authoring system and is based on instructional design principles that provide designers and developers the ability to create multiple methods of training materials. The team will:

Example 12.1 (continued).

Uses bullets to make the proposal easier to read and to provide more white space.

- o Create storyboards to design user interface and to choose course layout.
- o Transfer the storyboards into the desired delivery method. The LMS will create course structure based on the designer's requirements, and will build all navigation and page links automatically based on customizable templates.
- o Create prototypes of *Truckco Online.*
- o Test and validate the instruction to ensure it accomplishes all goals and objectives. In addition, Workforce Interactive will perform testing prior to final delivery to ensure a bug-free solution.
- o Publish courses from a single location and to selected delivery medium using the LMS, once courses are approved and ready for implementation.
- o Utilize XML to publish our course content into multiple formats such as CD-ROM, Internet, WML, and instructor-led documents.

This is a discussion of the implementation of the solution.

<u>Delivery</u>

At this point, the training will be implemented using actual learners. Once the development of the instruction is complete, the modules will be placed on the server. The courses will then be accessible from the portal once it is launched.

Describes the evaluation and revision process of the material. Identifies two types of evaluations and how the revisions process will work.

<u>Evaluation and Revision</u>

To achieve training goals, evaluation and revision will occur throughout the entire instructional design process. Tasks will include:

- o Internal evaluations - Workforce Interactive will conduct ongoing evaluations.
- o External evaluations - Truck drivers will go through the course to test for usability so that the course is truly designed with the learner in mind.
- o Revisions based on evaluation feedback - Workforce Interactive will make the proper adjustments within the program using the LMS. Revisions will be reviewed and approved by the senior instructional designer assigned to the project.

Example 12.1 (continued).

without burdening the client with an explanation of theories and concepts behind their application.

TECHNICAL SOLUTION

The second part of the *Solutions* section of the proposal is the technical solution. First and foremost, your technical solution must support your instructional solution. Too often proposal writers get caught up in the technical aspects of a solution and fail to pay attention to the instructional aspects. You must remember that technology is a supporting character in most e-learning implementations and not the star. Failure to keep this in mind results in the HAL Syndrome.

HAL was the on-board mission computer in the 1960 Stanley Krubrick movie *2001: A Space Odyssey*. In the movie, HAL's original purpose was to support the astronauts and help them successfully complete their mission. Unfortunately for the astronauts, HAL started taking over the mission and killed several astronauts in the process. HAL was no longer supporting the mission, he was subverting it. The focus then turned to HAL and not the original mission of the astronauts.

If you allow the technical aspects of your e-learning solution to overwhelm the learning aspects, you fall victim to the HAL Syndrome. This must be avoided. Focus on the instructional solution and allow the technical solution to support the instructional goals. It should not be the other way around.

This does not mean that the technology aspects of the solution should be ignored; instead, it means that technology should be carefully explained and integrated into the overall solution and not become *the* solution at the expense of good instruction.

The vast majority of clients reading e-learning proposals are not technical experts. They may have basic knowledge of databases, HTML editors, authoring tools, and networks, but they are not in the position to understand intricate details. The technical solution must speak to these professionals in a simple, straightforward manner, providing just enough detail for them to get a general idea of the technology behind the e-learning. If you feel compelled to include more detail, it should go into one of the appendices.

While the general tone of the technical solution should be conversational, it should also be accurate and correct. Because most managers making the decision of whether or not to choose a particular e-learning solution will not have a high degree of technical knowledge, they will need the assistance of their IT staff. It is likely that one or more IT professionals will be asked to review your proposal. This means there must not be any technical mistakes or incompatibility issues in your explanation of the technical aspects of your solution. If there are mistakes, the IT staff reading the proposal will find them and perhaps eliminate you as a possible vendor.

■ ■ ■

UNDERSTANDING THE STAKEHOLDER'S TECHNICAL CONCERNS

Chip Peters, Senior Education Consultant, Aetna

While e-learning initiatives vary greatly in size and scope, cost and complexity, form and function, they all share one unifying characteristic — they are all technology based. Yet despite its proliferation, the "e" in e-learning continues to be a concept few organizations clearly understand and fewer still comfortably embrace.

The following examines the technological considerations critical to an organization's decision-making process when evaluating e-learning proposals, in the context of the common roles, responsibilities, priorities/requirements, and challenges that impact it.

THE CLIENT ORGANIZATION: ROLES, RESPONSIBILITIES, AND PRIORITIES/REQUIREMENTS

Since a variety of functional areas contribute to setting the stage for organizational e-learning, let's begin by introducing the common internal players. In addition to the training function, vendors should also recognize the following contributors — some are obvious, others less so, but all are central to most e-learning initiatives:

- Finance/legal and/or procurement
- Executive management
- Core business areas (CBAs) (i.e., underwriting, manufacturing, sales, customer service, etc.)
- IT

All are considered *stakeholders* — each remaining more or less actively involved throughout the initiative, each with a vested interest in the outcome, and, important to the topic at hand, each may, to a lesser or greater extent, exert influence over the initiative and its outcome.

Depending on functional responsibility, the finance, legal and/or procurement area's involvement is critical but narrow — primarily serving as the client organization's contracting agent by identifying possible suppliers; contributing to, reviewing, and approving the request documentation; and negotiating financially favorable/cost-effective supplier contracts. The finance function may also have additional financial, legal, or procurement-related responsibilities based on the organizational structure.

Executive management and, to a lesser extent, the CBAs are commonly referred to as the initiative's sponsors: they provide the necessary financial resources/

funding for the project, and their constituents (customers, employees, etc.) are most often the direct/visible/tangible recipients/beneficiaries/targets/users of the output/deliverable. In a recent E-Learning Guild survey, targeting e-learning vendor and nonvendor practitioners, 39% of all nonvendor respondents identified executive management as the entity ultimately responsible for setting their organization's e-learning budget, followed by training at 27%, customer at 15%, and sponsoring business unit at a distant 8.6% [5].

While the CBAs are often engaged in initial needs assessment efforts, they tend to be less actively involved in the subsequent, mainly operational, stages of a project. In fact, the sponsors' involvement rarely extends beyond the fiscal responsibilities of the initiative. According to the same E-Learning Guild study, a full 56% of all nonvendor respondents receive their strategic direction from the training function, compared to executive management at 19% and the sponsoring business unit at 12%.

To paraphrase George Orwell, while all stakeholders are influential, some are apparently more influential than others: in most organizations, e-learning efforts are primarily initiated and managed by the client organization's training function, which typically defines the performance improvement strategy and executes both the high-level strategic and specific tactical plans.

However, that may be changing. Sponsor-level stakeholders are increasingly mandating stricter alignment to the organization's overall strategic plan and goals, and are instituting bottom line accountability, which is forcing a gradual redefinition of e-learning.

The operational responsibilities of IT include maintaining and safeguarding office productivity software, mission critical business systems and data, desktop/client hardware, and the overall infrastructure (software/hardware associated with servers, LAN, WAN, external connectivity), as well as maintaining and preferably staying ahead of the pace of emerging technology. As an e-learning stakeholder, however, IT has been content to play a relatively reactive consulting role, allowing others, most notably the training function, to peripherally encroach on its competency, in large part due to the fairly insignificant and therefore harmless nature of e-learning initiatives throughout the 1990s.

However, the emergence of the learning discipline as a strategic asset in the organizational value chain is resulting in the transformation of e-learning into an enterprisewide technology, traditionally a core domain of the organization's IT function. That, coupled with the increased complexity of new and rapidly expanding technology, is forcing the IT function to subject e-learning initiatives to the same guidelines and operating principles governing the practice as a whole.

This team, or some variation, is likely to expand on business needs and requirements. All enter the effort with a slightly different set of expectations (priorities/requirements), which must be managed. Table 12.1 shows a breakdown of the priorities and requirements of each stakeholder.

Table 12.1 Breakdown of Functional E-Learning Priorities/Requirements by Stakeholder

Stakeholder	Priorities/Requirements
Finance/legal/procurement	Cost effective, legally defensible
Executive management/CBAs (sponsor)	Cost effective, organizationally relevant/strategic, measurable
Training	Performance improvement/enhancement
IT	Maintainable/supportable/sustainable, configurable, scalable, function/interoperable (usability and technical performance), robust, secure

Understanding the various players within a client organization will help you to target your e-learning solution and presentation to meet these various needs. At all times, it is important to know which players will be in presentations or reading your proposal so you will know how to target your technical solution.

■ ■ ■

FIVE ELEMENTS OF THE TECHNOLOGY SOLUTION

Your proposal must address five elements when explaining the technological aspects of your e-learning solution. In reality, many of the elements overlap. For example, if your e-learning software is relatively easy to maintain (maintainability), then it is probably also easy to use (usability). However, looking at the five aspects individually will help ensure that you include all five in your proposal.

Maintainability — This is the ability of the client to maintain, over the long term, your solution. No client wants to be at the mercy of a vendor for maintenance, changes, and alterations to their e-learning modules. This means you need to show or explain to the client how easy it is to administer your technical solution and how simple it will be for the client to perform maintenance and updating of the e-learning.

You want to explain to the client how easy it is to update course content using your preexisting templates. This is where you may emphasize that you are separating content from structure so the client can update the e-learning modules without accidentally deleting critical navigational or menu items. This is a chance to discuss the built-in help system that "walks the client through" the update process.

Remember, the client wants assurance that if you, the vendor, go away, they will still be able to use and modify the e-learning. Tell the client that you are using open standards that are accepted within the industry. Name the well-known software you use in the development process. Your goal is to make the client

Table 12.2 International Organizations Working Toward E-Learning Standards

Organization	Web Site
Airline Industry CBT Committee (AICC)	www.aicc.org
EDUCAUSE Instructional Management Systems Project (IMS)	www.imsproject.org
Alliance of Remote Instructional Authoring and Distribution Networks for Europe (ARIADNE)	www.ariadne.unil.ch
IEEE Learning Technology Standards Committee (IEEE LTSC)	www.ieee.org
Advanced Distributed Learning Sharable Content Object Reference Model (ADL SCORM)	www.adlnet.org

comfortable with the fact that they can easily and quickly update your system without having to have you there all the time.

Compatibility — Clients look to see if your solution is compatible with other e-learning solutions on the market. The client wants to know that your e-learning modules are compatible with e-learning modules offered by other vendors or with the leading LMS or LCMS. In fact, I saw a proposal recently that asked for the e-learning to be "compatible with every known LMS on the market." While that request may be currently impossible to achieve, you can offer some level of assurance of compatibility by complying with e-learning industry standards.

Since many writers of e-learning RFPs do not understand all the technical nuances of getting e-learning modules to share information with an LMS, they look to industry standards for an assurance of compatibility. Clients view adherence to standards as an insurance policy of interoperability. The client's reasoning is that if your e-learning software is compliant with a certain standard and another vendor is also compliant with the same standard, then the two software systems will be able to effortlessly share data.

Even though this is not completely accurate, many clients believe adherence to standards is essential in choosing an e-learning vendor. The maddening part is that there are different standards and levels of compliance. Several groups are all vying for the right to claim to have *the standard* in e-learning. Your organization needs to determine which standards are most relevant for your target market and which standards are required by this particular client. Table 12.2 provides a quick reference list of some of the most well-recognized standards organizations in the e-learning industry.

The client may even not understand all of the ramifications of the standards they are requesting. However, clients still want to know that your solution is AICC (Airline Industry CBT Committee), or SCORM™ (Sharable Content Object Reference Model), or IEEE (Institute of Electrical and Electronics Engineers) compliant, even if they do not understand how that compliance will affect their e-learning efforts.

Since most clients only have a vague notion of standards and compliance, it is usually worth the effort to provide a brief explanation of the standards to which you are adhering for this project and your firm's level of compliance with those standards. Your short explanation may educate the client enough to choose your solution.

The basic idea behind e-learning standards is to allow one vendor's e-learning modules to share information with another vendor's module. Standards allow e-learning modules to easily share information with LCMS or LMS systems. If all vendors adhere to the same standards, a learning module or learning object can be used interchangeably in multiple LMS or LCMS systems.

■ ■ ■

A SCORM™ PRIMER (6)

Stacey Smith, Instructional Designer, Concurrent Technologies Corporation

As e-learning vendors, it is important to know about the SCORM initiative because many clients want to know that the content you deliver or the LMS/LCMS you have designed is SCORM conformant. The entire SCORM project is constantly evolving toward a general standard. To understand this emerging industry standard, it is important to know about the evolution of SCORM and where it is heading.

The SCORM e-learning standards are under the direction of the Advanced Distributed Learning (ADL) initiative. The ADL initiative is a collaborative effort between government, industry, and academia to establish a new, distributed learning environment that permits the interoperability of learning tools and course content on a global scale. As a result of a unique partnership between the Office of the Secretary of Defense, the Department of Labor, and the National Guard Bureau, the ADL Co-Labs have been established to serve as public and private sector forums for cooperative research, development, and assessment of new learning technology prototypes, guidelines, and specifications. ADL's vision is to provide access to the highest quality education and training, tailored to individual needs, delivered cost-effectively anywhere, anytime.

One of the most visible results of that effort is the development of the SCORM. SCORM defines a Web-based learning "Content Aggregation Model" and "Run-Time Environment" (RTE) for learning objects. The SCORM is a collection of specifications adapted from multiple sources to provide a comprehensive suite of e-learning capabilities that enable interoperability, accessibility, and reuse of Web-based learning content. The work of the ADL initiative to develop the SCORM is also a process to knit together similar groups and interests. This reference model aims to coordinate emerging technologies and commercial and public implementations.

SCORM applies current technology developments to a specific content model by producing recommendations for consistent implementations by the vendor community. The SCORM is built upon the work of the Airline Industry Computer-Based Training Committee (AICC), the IMS Global Learning Consortium, the IEEE, the Alliance of Remote Instructional Authoring and Distribution Networks for Europe (ARIADNE), and others to create one unified "reference model" of interrelated technical specifications and guidelines that meet Department of Defense (DoD) high-level requirements for Web-based learning content.

The SCORM includes aspects that affect learning systems and content authoring tool vendors, instructional designers and learning content developers, training providers, and others.

SCORM VERSIONS

VERSION 1.0

Released in January 2000, SCORM 1.0 was the inaugural release of specifications and guidelines to meet the DoD's requirements. SCORM 1.0 is comprised of three major elements:

1. **Course Structure Format:** An Extensible Markup Language (XML)–based representation of a course structure that can be used to define all of the course elements, structure and external references necessary to move a course from one LMS environment to another. *This was designed to support the interoperability requirement for allowing a simple course to move between heterogeneous systems.*
2. **RTE:** A definition of RTE that includes a specific launch protocol to initiate Web-based content, a common content-to-LMS Application Program Interface (API), and a data model defining the information elements that are exchanged between an LMS environment and executable content at run time. *This supports the interoperability requirement of allowing courses from many different sources to run in any one LMS and allows reusability in different systems.*
3. **Meta-data:** A mapping and recommended usage of IEEE meta-data elements for each of the following SCORM categories:
   - **Course Meta-data:** A definition for external meta-data that describes a course package for the purposes of searching (enabling discoverability) within a courseware repository and providing descriptive information about the course.
   - **Content Meta-data:** A definition of meta-data applied to Web-based content "chunks" that provide descriptive information about the content independent of a particular course. This meta-data is used to facilitate reuse and discoverability of such content within, for example, a content repository.

- **Raw Media Meta-data:** A definition of meta-data that can be applied to so-called "raw media" assets, such as illustrations, documents, or media streams, that provide descriptive information about the raw media independent of courseware content. This meta-data is used to facilitate reuse and discoverability of such media elements within, for example, a media repository.

It should be noted that Sharable *Courseware* Object Reference Model (SCORM) was changed to Sharable *Content* Object Reference Model (SCORM) for all versions after 1.0.

VERSION 1.1

Released in January 2001, SCORM 1.1 incorporated several changes from its predecessor. Corrections and improvements were based on feedback received from the SCORM Version 1.0 release.

Changing Sharable *Courseware* Object Reference Model to Sharable *Content* Object Reference Model is the most noticeable change. This was done to better show that the SCORM applies to various levels of content. Aligning with this shift, *Course* Structure Format was also changed to *Content* Structure Format to show that collections of learning content smaller and larger than an entire course could be represented through SCORM.

Changes to the SCORM resulting in Version 1.1 fall into three categories:

1. Improved Documentation
   - Consolidation of information to help describe the SCORM Run-Time Data Model in a more precise manner. A new table has been added to help clarify various aspects of the SCORM Run-Time Data Model.
   - Clarification on the use of Run-Time Environment API error codes
   - Clarification of problems found with the Content Structure Format (CSF)
   - Clarification of meta-data elements
   - General cleanup of all sections of the SCORM
2. Functional Changes and Fixes
   - Changes to the Run-Time Environment API
   - SCORM will now reference the AICC CMI001 Guidelines for Interoperability Revision 3.4
   - SCORM is using version 1.1 of the IMS Learning Resource Meta-data Specification, including a version of the XML DTD
   - Changes to Content Structure Format DTD
3. Deprecations
   - Data elements were deprecated in two ways:
     1. Permanently removed
     2. Remove and review

VERSION 1.2

The SCORM 1.2 release added the ability to package instructional material and meta-data for import and export. These XML-based specifications provided a crucial link between learning content repositories and learning management systems. This version of SCORM incorporates the IMS Global Learning Consortium's Content Packaging Specification and expands it to include additional course structure capabilities.

- SCORM 1.2 is now a multipart document composed of three separate books:
  1. The SCORM Overview
  2. The SCORM Content Aggregation Model
  3. The SCORM RTE
- The IMS Content Packaging Specification Version 1.1.2 is now included and adapted for the SCORM through an application profile.

The Content Aggregation Model is updated to reflect the merger of the CSF into Content Packaging. The stand-alone CSF specification has been deprecated. This means that it will not be supported in a future version. For instance, when stuff is deprecated in Java, that means that the next version of Java released may support it, but there is no guarantee and it will eventually be removed.

- The SCORM Meta-data specification is updated to reference the IMS Learning Resource Meta-data Version 1.2.1.
- Cleanup and clarification of the following:
  1. SCORM RTE Data Model
  2. Run-time behaviors (affects both content developers and LMS vendors)

VERSION 1.3

The scope of changes being introduced for Version 1.3 is defined as follows:

1. Introduction of changes required for the utilization of the IEEE 1484.12.1-2002 (IEEE Learning Object Meta-data [LOM] Standard)
2. Introduction to changes required for the utilization of IEEE P1484.11.1 Draft Standard for Data Model for Content Object Communication
3. Introduction to changes required for the utilization of IEEE P1484.11.2 Draft Standard for ECMAScript API for Content to Runtime Services Communication
4. Introduction to the IMS Simple Sequencing Specification
5. Require LMSs to support all data model elements

Candidate changes to the SCORM will be released for preview as Draft Application Profiles. These profiles will be made available to the ADL Community on ADLNet.org for review and comment prior to the refinement and release of SCORM 1.3.

Although the scope of SCORM 1.3 has been defined above, there are still issues to be resolved by the ADL Technical Team. For the latest development updates, visit ADLNet's Web site at http://www.adlnet.org.

COMPLIANCE

The ADL initiative wishes to support the widespread adoption of the SCORM™ specifications. ADL has developed criteria, a test suite, and procedures for SCORM 1.2 compliance. ADL is actively looking to support, through a compliance program, communities of interest (i.e., "third-party" organizations) that currently use SCORM conformance testing software to perform compliance testing.

A draft Certification Memorandum of Agreement (MOA) outlining the expectations ADL has for the Certifying Organizations (CO) has been developed and submitted for review. The MOA will be made available to those requesting a copy once approved.

The MOA is considered by ADL to be a necessary first step toward widespread adoption of a certification program. ADL envisions a global certification process that will eventually include many organizations becoming certification centers. These organizations will also be responsible for their certification program's associated liability.

■ ■ ■

Usability — The customer wants to be assured that the e-learning solution will be simple and easy to use. This is important because if technology is seen as cumbersome or difficult to navigate, the potential learners will never use it.

Too many training departments have old CD-ROM training disks lying around that were too hard to use. These departments do not want a repeat. To help convince the client that your software is easy to use, include screen shots of the solution, tutorials, and help screens. Also include a discussion in the proposal about the navigation of the e-learning software and how it functions. The more the client sees the e-learning or LMS software, the more confidence they will gain in terms of being able to use it to achieve their goals (unless, of course, your software is cumbersome and difficult to navigate).

Modularity — E-learning solutions can now be developed as small interchangeable knowledge objects. A knowledge object or learning object is a small piece of self-contained information that can be reused as necessary to meet the instructional needs of the learner. Learning objects "provide a means of developing small bits of instruction which may be used for one distance learning application, then reused for a completely different application, substantially decreasing development time" [7].

The analogy most often used for learning objects is one of Lego blocks. Lego blocks can be snapped together, unsnapped, and rearranged in different configurations regardless of their size or color. They are all essentially interchangeable. Each learning object is self-contained but can easily be added to or subtracted from similar pieces just like Lego blocks.

Another good analogy is video games. There are many video game formats such as XBOX, Sega, Playstation2, and Nintendo. One game cannot be played in another console because the formats are incompatible. If there was a learning object plug-in for video games, you could play any game in any console. The use of learning objects is facilitated by the development of e-learning standards. The interchangeability of learning objects is heavily dependent upon industry standards such as SCORM and AICC.

Many clients are seeking to reuse learning objects to reduce their e-learning development time and to provide standardized content across their organization. Depending upon the needs stated in the RFP, you should discuss how your solution supports the learning object concept.

Accessibility — This can cover two areas. The first area is where the e-learning program is accessible to all individuals regardless of physical obstacles. This may mean that your e-learning program conforms to the Americans with Disabilities Act (ADA) and Section 508 standards. This can be required when you are doing work for the federal government.

The second area of accessibility is more common and has to do with technology. You have to make sure that the technology you are proposing is available to all users within your client's organization. For example, if the client's IT department does not support the latest Macromedia Flash plug-in, then the learners will not see your brilliant simulation using Flash. If the table structure you use is for a 5.0 browser and your clients have a 4.0 browser, they will not be able to access the information.

Managers want to know that their staff can gain access to the e-learning without any technical obstacles. Your solution needs to be checked in the browsers that are going to be used by the learners. You need to check several scenarios to ensure that the e-learning works on various platforms. You need to indicate to the client that you will do some testing on the client's system to ensure accessibility and that you will need to meet with the client's IT staff. A meeting early on with the IT staff can avoid complications later and help you to understand the process for enabling e-learning within the client's network.

■ ■ ■

A SECTION 508 PRIMER

Kevin Schmohl, Operations Manager, Universal Systems and Technology

On August 7, 1998, a federal law was put into place that fell under Section 504 of the Rehabilitation Act. This was the Workforce Investment Act of 1998. In this act was Section 508, Electronic and Information Technology, which impacts any e-learning work that is used or funded by a federal agency.

The purpose of Section 508 is to have the electronic and information technology used by federal agencies accessible to people with disabilities. The act states that information available to people with disabilities must be comparable to information available to people without disabilities. Confused?

Simply remember this: whatever training you develop for people without disabilities you must also provide to people with disabilities without losing any of the original training value. You can complete this task by developing the e-learning to meet needs of the disabled and nondisabled or by developing separate e-learning modules, one for those with disabilities and one for those without. Therefore, you may end up with multiple versions of the same e-learning, some with sound, some with large letters, some with no animation, etc.

Now that you know what Section 508 means and what you should do to meet the requirements, you are ready to begin. What was that? You are not ready to begin; you want to know: "What are the specific standards that must be met for 508 compliance?" Well, that is simple. There are none. If you are looking for a checklist defining rules or items to mark off or some explicit guidelines, there are none. I suggest you go to http://www.section508.gov for the latest happenings, but in the meantime, let me explain where things are now. Section 508 compliance must be met by all federal agencies' electronic and information technology unless "undue burden" would be imposed on the agency.

The following is the government's definition of "undue burden." Undue burden means significant difficulty or expense. In determining whether an action would result in an undue burden, an agency shall consider all agency resources available to the program or component for which the product is being developed, procured, maintained, or used. Now, everything is 100% crystal clear, right? If you said "yes" then you are not stopping to think about all the implications of this policy.

When looking through the undue burden definition do you see any defining scale, any percentage quota, or any measurement that defines what undue burden really is? No. All this definition gives you is a vague idea of what undue burden could be. Depending on who is interpreting the definition, the meaning can be turned and twisted according to the needs of the agency or vendor.

Now, if you fall into the undue burden category, it states only that you need alternative means of access to allow an individual to use the information and data. For example, if you have some interactive Web-based training created for the Army on how to drive a tank, this might fall under "undue burden" in trying to make the training 508 compliant because of the cost and the actual use that training would receive by persons with a disability. What can be argued is that you must meet certain physical criteria to drive a tank (being able to see, hear, etc.), but keep in mind that under 508 you still need to provide this training in an alternative format.

Now you should be asking, "What is an alternative format?" Alternative format can mean many different things. One way to solve this problem and be compliant is to have a paper-based course on driving the tank if it is ever needed for someone with disabilities. This may seem silly, but trust me, you do not want to go back and transcribe an e-learning with heavy animation into a paper-based course that is 508 compliant when you have a lawsuit breathing down your neck.

What many people are doing when creating computer/Web-based training is writing "treatments." A treatment is a paper-based version of the course being developed. Think of it as a storyboard in a written format. You list the title page, text, audio, graphic designs, graphic alt tags, developers' notes, and so on. By designing your course this way, not only can you give the client something to review before production, but you also have an alternative method for delivering the training. This allows you to save costs by using the treatment as a storyboard and as a remedy to 508 compliance for the course you are developing.

If for some reason your application must meet 508 compliance but does not fall under the undue burden clause, what should you do? If you know your application must meet 508 compliance, then you need to start at the beginning and work the requirements into your e-learning development process.

First, you need to look at how you will be delivering the instruction. Will the training be all Web-based? Will some items need to be printed out and filled in? Is there going to be audio dialogue? Any or all of these factors will help to determine the design and development of the training application because each one must be addressed to determine how it will meet the 508 compliance. Keep in mind that the application you develop must be able to be read by a screen reader and comply with a comprehensive Web accessibility software program designed to help expose Web pages that have a 508 compliance conflict. Some different applications for screen readers are Jaws, Window-Eyes, and Hal. Some different Web accessibility software includes SSB Technologies InSight/InFocus, Bobby, and A-Prompt.

What is the standard checklist that must be met? What is the standard screen reader to be used? This is not defined by 508 and probably never will be because it is very hard for the government to settle on just one product. This would show "favoritism" toward one company. Each agency has its "preference" as to what is used; therefore, make sure you ask what helper applications should be used in association with the training piece. Of course, this will only work with training being used internally. If the application is going to be used by the public, then you must develop the training application to meet client specifications and provide a list of the helper applications that work best with the training.

Another good option when developing e-learning to meet 508 compliance is to have someone from the federal agency you are doing the work for test the training being developed. Or, better yet, sit with a person using a screen reader. You can really learn a lot watching how the individual interacts with the screen reader. I cannot emphasize enough how important this is, even if you are not a developer. The experience gives you great insight into how your application is being used and where it can be improved.

From my experience, I learned that the screen reader I had used to test the training had more options than I was aware of. Most screen readers can be set to read a certain number of words per minute, which can be adjusted according to individual preference. One thing learned from this experience was that if a screen reader is set to read too fast, necessary directions can be missed. Is this an instructional issue or a user error? I'll let you think about this one and draw your own conclusions.

When you start a federally funded project, be sure to define the client's 508 expectations up front. If you do not, you may incur increased costs for retrofitting the e-learning once you are halfway through. Failure to reach an agreement on the 508 expectations can double your development costs if you are not careful.

Complete a contract that both you and the client can sign, designating what will satisfy 508 compliance. I suggest that the contract state that the user can navigate the application using a screen reader, that it meets a Web accessibility test to the best of your abilities, and has been approved by the 508 Compliance Coordinator if possible. Due to the law being so vague, it can be difficult to get someone to sign off on a project stating it meets 508 compliance.

Section 508 may be starting to trickle down to the state level. This has not been made official, but on the government Web site http://www.section508.gov/ in section "508 and You – State Agency" it states: "Section 508 applies to the federal government but there may be implications for employees and others at the state level." For additional information on state Section 508 requirements, please see National Institute on Disability and Rehabilitation Research (NIDRR) (http://www.ed.gov/offices/OSERS/NIDRR/).

Whether you are writing a proposal for a federal or state agency, it seems that Section 508 is something you should be well aware of because it will impact your time and cost when producing e-learning.

■ ■ ■

USE TECHNICAL ILLUSTRATIONS

It is one thing to explain all the technical aspects of your solution to the client; it is another to actually show the client. You should include a diagram of your technical solution in this section of the proposal. Many complex technical ideas can be explained simply through a diagram.

Use a diagram to show what the network will look like or to show how the server will be protected by a firewall. Use a comparison chart to show the relative value of one technical solution over another. Use screen captures to show the login process or to show a sample learning path. Do not just tell clients about the ease of navigation; include a screen shot to show them. The technical portion of your solution is the ideal location for diagrams, charts, and figures. Incorporate the ideas from Chapter 7 into your technical solution. Example 12.2 shows a technical solution from the Truckco proposal using graphical elements in the form of tables to help illustrate key points.

THE BOTTOM LINE

Clients want to know how you are going to solve their e-learning problem. Describe to them in simple terms how you intend to address both the instructional and the technological needs of the project. Make sure you avoid discussing theories or abstract concepts. Also, avoid the HAL Syndrome; do not let the technological aspects of your e-learning solution overwhelm the instructional elements. E-learning is first and foremost about learning. Tell your clients how you will build and implement a unique and effective solution to fit their needs.

Describes various aspects of the technical solution.

Response to Truckco's Request for Proposal

Technical Solution

Technical Solution

Our technical solution is based on the assumption that Truckco is interested in minimizing the costs associated with implementation of the portal, and that they currently do not have a technical infrastructure or personnel. Workforce Interactive also assumes that the minimum number of users of 8,000 is expected to increase as this portal expands to other states.

There are many technical issues that Workforce Interactive will address according to Truckco's requirements in the RFP.

Provides details about the user interface.

User Interface

Workforce Interactive will construct *Truckco Online's* interface with the following in mind: ease of navigation, simplicity of graphics, and common look and feel. Ease of navigation and a help screen, available to the learner at all times, will assure that the user will not "get lost" within the site. We will emphasize relevant information by using simple non-distracting graphics. A common look and feel will let the user know that they are in *Truckco Online* at all times.

Addresses client concerns about administration and maintenance.

Administration and Maintenance

We understand that Truckco requested all source code and graphics to retain maintenance flexibility. However, due to the fact that Truckco does not have any instructional designers or technology personnel, it is our recommendation that Workforce Interactive maintain the portal. If Truckco decides to acquire technology personnel, then Workforce Interactive will provide the requested materials. All created materials will become property of Truckco. To state ownership, we will place the words "All Rights Reserved" at the bottom of every web page in *Truckco Online.*

Describes the LMS to be used.

Learning Management System

We will use our Learning Management System to design and develop the *Truckco Online* Training Center. Our LMS runs on a Windows NT 4.0 platform with IBM's DB2 Universal Database and WebSphere Application Server. In addition to the development component described in the Instructional Solution, our LMS will also allow administrative access to employers, such as test tracking and user profiling, including the date the driver completes each course. The LMS provides a learner component that will allow the user to register for courses, create user profiles, and receive course content based on user profiles and pretests. It provides learner progress by using tracking, bookmarking, and glossaries.

Confidential 6

Example 12.2 Description of the *Technical Solution* portion of an e-learning proposal.

Response to Truckco's Request for Proposal

Portal Builder Software

Describes software used by vendor.

To design and develop the *Truckco Online* Information and Shopping Centers, Workforce Interactive will use Portal Builder, software that provides framework, information application, and e-commerce solutions. Because Portal Builder is based on industry standards, it leverages XML to communicate between all components of our information technology infrastructure, allowing new technology and systems to be integrated quickly and efficiently. Web developers will use Portal Builder to create the various components of the Information and Shopping Centers by integrating relevant and useful information for display on the portal through dynamic page generation with customizable templates.

Portal Payment Solution

Provides software recommendation.

We recommend using CyberCash, Inc., the e-commerce leader in payment solutions, for all financial transactions on *Truckco Online*. CashRegister, offered by CyberCash, Inc., provides the e-commerce community with high-speed, secure, and reliable online payment processing.

Uses language to help the reader visualize the solution.

To make payments in *Truckco Online* for the subscription service, Shopping Center, and/or training courses, users will use a "check-out" system. To do this, users will select items they wish to purchase, enter a credit card number, and click the submit button. Once they click the submit button, CyberCash is alerted. CyberCash will encrypt the transaction and scramble it to make it secure so that no one else can retrieve the information. To use this secure transaction system, Truckco will pay CyberCash for the setup, and for monthly and transaction fees. Truckco will be responsible for choosing a bank of choice for payment solutions.

Delivery Environment

Kiosk

Describes "current state" of most truck stops.

Many truck stops are already equipped with Internet kiosks. In order to incur a minimal cost and, thus, save Truckco the expense of purchasing and installing Internet kiosks, the maintenance and servicing fees, and the subsequent overhead required, Workforce Interactive recommends Truckco take advantage of existing technology.

We propose that Truckco develop a strategic partnership with an existing kiosk provider. Partnerships currently exist between kiosk manufacturers, kiosk management software companies, communication companies, transportation technology organizations, and truck stop owners. *Truckco Online* will be added to Internet kiosks currently located throughout Pennsylvania.

Confidential 7

Example 12.2 (continued).

Suggests a strategic partnership.

Some kiosk providers that may be willing to partner are TIMM Communications/Ambest/DRIVER Net and NetTrans/AT&T/NetNearU/Petro. There are several advantages to forming a partnership with one of the aforementioned kiosk companies:

- o Incurring minimal cost reduces expense of purchasing, maintaining, and servicing kiosks.
- o Inclusion of diagnostic and maintenance software indicates the need for servicing and troubleshooting repairs.
- o Remote monitoring and management of Internet-based terminal networks provides back-up data to Truckco regarding kiosk users.
- o Meeting federal regulations according to handicapped accessibility assures compliance.

The figure below illustrates the difference between the two kiosk options.

Provides a comparison chart for the client to review and make objective comparison.

Figure 1. Comparison of New Kiosk Setup Versus Existing Kiosk

	New Kiosk Setup	**Existing Kiosk Setup**
Cost of kiosk (sit-down model) o **Enclosure** o **Touch screen** o **Keyboard, touch pad trackball** o **Printer** o **Credit card reader**	$5,000 - 10,000	$0
Service calls	$100 - 200 per 1 hr visit	$0
Maintenance fees	$25 per 1 hr visit	$0
Cost of Internet connection	$40 per month	$20 per month per kiosk
Percentage of kiosk revenue given to truck stop owner	25 - 40% depending on net revenue generated by kiosk	$0

As a value-add, provides client strategies to increase visibility.

To maximize the visibility of *Truckco Online* within the existing kiosks, we suggest the following two high-visibility strategies:

- o Place an advertising banner on the outside of the kiosk enclosure. This will allow high visibility of *Truckco Online* to passersby.
- o Become a static link on the existing kiosk interface, so *Truckco Online* will be easily accessible and highly visible to the user at all times.

In order to meet the kiosk technical requirements outlined in the proposal, Figure 2 describes the typical specifications of existing kiosks.

Example 12.2 (continued).

Includes necessary hardware specifications for the kiosk.

Figure 2. Existing Kiosk Specifications

Delivery Hardware	Intel Celeron 400 or above
Browser	Internet Explorer 4.0 or greater or Netscape 4.0 or greater
Dialup	56K or Ethernet
Display	15" touch screen
Audio	Built-in speakers with headphone accessibility
Print	Yes
Active X Controls/plug-ins	No
Other Software	Tracking software
Other Hardware	Touch-pad mouse or trackball
	Cash or credit card payment options

Desktop/Laptop Computer
Workforce Interactive realizes that many truck drivers will be accessing training from their home, company, and laptop computers. Truck drivers that have Internet availability from their home computers will be able to access *Truckco Online* through its URL. Truck stops in 41 of the 50 states have Internet access. This will provide drivers who have laptops the opportunity to visit the portal. The minimum requirements to access *Truckco Online* from a personal computer will be a 28,800 bps Internet connection with a minimum version of Internet Explorer 4.0 or Netscape Navigator 4.0 or greater.

Explains why a suggestion within the RFP was not really feasible.

Wireless Devices
Workforce Interactive understands Truckco's suggestion to use wireless devices such as cellular telephones and personal digital assistants (PDAs) as a delivery method for *Truckco Online* because of their convenience when sending and receiving information. However, we do not recommend using this delivery method at this time for a number of reasons:

- Screen size too small.
- Processing too slow.
- Storage capacities limited.
- Navigation poor.
- Security issues.

We will recommend delivering *Truckco Online* through the existing kiosks and personal home computers and laptops. However, we will remain current on improvements that are made within wireless technology to re-evaluate this option at a later date.

Example 12.2 (continued).

Builds a case for why vendor should house the server.

Response to Truckco's Request for Proposal

Server and Backup

Workforce Interactive is an Application Service Provider (ASP). We understand the requirement stated in the proposal to recommend a server size. However, we recommend that Workforce Interactive host *Truckco Online* on a dedicated server in an ASP arrangement. Studies have indicated that ASP customers save between 33% and 53% using an ASP over purchasing and managing the hardware and software for the application themselves. Following is a list of other advantages to this approach:

- Workforce Interactive already has the equipment, applications, and expertise to handle security and backup.
- Truckco does not need technology personnel and infrastructure.
- Truckco can focus its resources on core business function.
- No capital expenditure is necessary for software, hardware, and technology personnel.

Describes value-added services.

As Truckco's ASP, Workforce Interactive will provide:

- Service for hardware failures.
- Server monitoring 24 hours a day, 7 days a week, 52 weeks a year.
- Uninterruptible power management system.
- Space on our backup server.

Provides specifications of the server that will house the clients materials.

Server Specifications

The server we use is the IBM S/390 Parallel Enterprise Server-Generation 5 with IBM HTTP Server. The server operates on Microsoft Windows NT Server 4.0.

Database

Workforce Interactive uses ODBC compliant IBM's DB2 Universal Database Enterprise Edition with WebSphere Application Server V3.02 Enterprise Edition for OS/390. We will use one database to handle the Information and Shopping Centers, and a separate database to store Training Center information. Because Truckco has indicated the potential for expansion of courses and users, we feel that DB2's reliability and scalability will allow us to meet these needs.

Bandwidth Considerations

Workforce Interactive is aware that bandwidth is an important consideration in choosing an ASP, so we will use the IBM HTTP Server that has high bandwidth Asynchronous Transfer Mode (ATM) connectivity. In the RFP, Truckco specifies that we should design 56K minimum connection. With the number of users currently predicted at 8,000, we feel that this connection speed will be sufficient.

Addresses security issues.

Security

Workforce Interactive will provide a secure environment in the Training Center and Information Tollway by requiring a user ID and password. The server that we use is fully integrated with SecureWay firewall technologies and security via System Secure Sockets Layer (SSL) protocols. SecureWay Firewall enables safe, secure business by controlling all communications to and from the Internet. For added security, the portal will have a ten-minute time-out feature.

Confidential 10

Example 12.2 (continued).

13

PROJECT MANAGEMENT AND SCHEDULE

INTRODUCTION

Managing and scheduling an e-learning project is difficult. It requires an understanding of ID, a dose of insight, and a great deal of tenacity. Well-managed projects require the right balance between technical and staff issues and good client/vendor communications. E-learning project management requires adherence to established procedures and, most importantly, good project management requires a good plan. The *Project Management and Schedule* section of the proposal is where you describe your firm's plan for tracking, monitoring, and completing the client's e-learning project.

This discussion of how your firm manages projects must instill confidence in clients, convincing them that your firm knows what it is doing. The *Project Management and Schedule* section of the proposal conveys your understanding of what needs to be done and in what order. It demonstrates that you are capable of successfully completing the client's e-learning project.

WHY THIS SECTION IS NEEDED

E-learning projects are expensive. Clients do not want to waste money on cost overruns, missed deadlines, or e-learning that does not work. In many cases, clients are not sure how to manage an e-learning project. They are not familiar with the technology, the team aspects of ID, or even the use of instructional strategies. The client is relying on you to describe how the project will be initiated, monitored, and completed. The client wants assurances that your organization is capable of successfully implementing your solution in their organization.

Clients want to know what will be expected of them during the development of the e-learning. In many cases, clients are unsure as to what the working relationship will be between your firm and their organization. They are looking for an easy-to-follow explanation of the different steps or phases of the e-learning development process and how they fit into the process. You need to provide this information at a level of detail that helps the client to understand their role and responsibilities within the process. Your job is to explain the development process so the client understands that it is systematic, repeatable, easily monitored, and effective.

Avoid the misconception that an e-learning developer meets with the client once, goes off to create an e-learning masterpiece, and then presents only the finished product. This client misconception could cause you to lose the proposal if another vendor presents a project plan carefully describing how the client will be consulted throughout the entire development cycle.

While everyone knows that elements and details of a project plan often change throughout the course of a project, a good plan is the foundation of a successful e-learning product. Clients want to know that you have created a strong foundation upon which you will build their e-learning.

■ ■ ■

EDUCATING THE CLIENT'S PROJECT MANAGER

Kathleen Ergott, Team Leader, E-Learning Development Group, Siemens Health Services

You have won the e-learning business from the client only to find out that they have not managed an e-learning project before. Not only are you going to be required to provide a quality e-learning product at the end of the contract, but you must also educate your client on how to manage an e-learning project. Your client is extremely nervous and does not want to fail in the management of this project.

Your client has good reason to be nervous. Software development projects have a high failure rate. The Standish Group, an IT research firm, periodically conducts surveys and releases reports on IT project success. The Standish Group defines a successful project as one that was completed on time, on budget, and contains the originally specified feature/function set. Using this definition, only 26% of projects are completed successfully. That means that nearly 75% are unsuccessful [1].

As you can see, you have reason to proceed carefully with your client. Helping your client to make effective use of good proven management techniques will greatly increase the chance of success for this e-learning project and hopefully lead to follow-up work with the client. You need to explain to the client that there are three phases to managing a project: (1) planning, (2) organizing, and (3) communicating. While the bulk of the work will be done by your firm, the client project manager has a number of important responsibilities.

PHASE 1: PLAN

Your first task is to help your client understand the business need that the project will address (hopefully this was done prior to the RFP being issued but that is not always the case). Sometimes the client's project manager was not even involved in the RFP process.

The client project manager must also understand the project goals that need to be met and the metrics that the project will be measured against. These metrics are important because ultimately you, the vendor, will be measured against them as well.

It is vital that your client understand the underlying business issues and the criteria by which the decision to issue the RFP and award the contract has been made. Staying true to the project goals when decisions need to be made will be key to success for both your organization and the client. Here is an example of a scenario and the associated business need:

> At present, 90% of the client's training is instructor-led and 10% is delivered over a corporate local area network (LAN). The project goal is to have 50% of all education delivered over an Internet site, with 50% remaining instructor-led. The Internet site requested in the RFP must use a Learning Management System (LMS) to track employee education. An LMS automates many of the administrative tasks typically required of training events including student registration, data recording and tracking, reporting, and launching of online courses.

Although not stated, the business need in this case is to lower the cost of delivering education within the client organization. The client's company wants to reduce costs by lowering the amount of instructor-led training and increasing the amount of available e-learning. Both you and the client project manager need to know the underlying business need and make decisions related to that business need.

Next, you and the client need to determine the project players. Typically projects have an executive sponsor, who is funding the work, and stakeholders. Stakeholders are individuals or groups who are affected in any way by the project.

Stakeholder groups could include the client's customers, administrators (who may use the product), and support resources (who will support the product, should questions or problems arise). You should encourage your client contact to meet with the executive sponsor and stakeholders early in the project to understand the executive sponsor's needs and assumptions about how e-learning will meet those needs. If possible, attend a meeting with the executive sponsor as well.

Encourage your client project manager to form a stakeholder core team that will review the e-learning product in its various phases to make sure it is meeting the needs of the organization. Make sure your client sets clear expectations about what the project will and will not accomplish. Otherwise, you will be stuck in endless rounds of revisions with constantly changing client contacts and stakeholders.

> In this example, the executive sponsor is the vice president of sales, whose team requires the majority of corporate training. The stakeholders include employees, an administrator responsible for producing education reports, and the IT support organization that will install and support the finished site.

Make sure the scope of work is very specifically defined in the proposal and that the client project manager understands what is written in the proposal and what is scheduled to be accomplished. You and the client project manager need to agree on all finished deliverables and the amount of work to be accomplished. Encourage your client contact to meet with the executive sponsor so he or she is also made aware of the agreement. If this does not happen, the executive sponsor might come in at the end of the project and demand unreasonable and costly changes. The agreement of the scope of work should also include standards for quality and time to deliver.

> In this example, the scope of work includes soliciting input, creating requirements, finding and purchasing an LMS that meets the requirements, and managing the installation of the Internet site and LMS with the help of an internal IT group. The project is scheduled for six months and a $250,000 budget.

Inform the client project manager that the e-learning development team will mostly be professionals from your organization but that you will also need some people from his or her organization because the project team should consist of client representatives such as SMEs and IT staff. Project team members from both the client and the vendor should be chosen because of the particular expertise or viewpoint they bring to the project.

When discussing the project with the client project manager, make sure you discuss potential risks (issues that could impact your project time or cost) and mitigation strategies (planned responses to your risks). Consider possible things that could go awry. Create contingency plans for each of these risks, so that if a problem should materialize (and it probably will), you and the client will lose less time because you have preplanned for just such a situation. These discussions also help keep the novice project manager from panicking when problems arise.

> In this case, the team consists of the following people from the vendor's organization: an instructional designer, graphic artist, and three developers with expertise in Web development. The client organization has contributed two SMEs and a member of the IT department to deal with integration and testing issues within the client's environment.

PHASE 2: ORGANIZE

Sometimes clients will want to forego the kickoff meeting, but do not let this happen. Insist on a kickoff meeting. The kickoff meeting is an assembly of the client and vendor project team, executive sponsor, and stakeholders. This meeting provides a timely forum to make introductions, explain roles and responsibilities, set expectations, reveal the work plan, and address any underlying assumptions.

The goals of the meeting should be to align expectations, explain the work process, and set the ground rules for working together. The phases of the development process should be reviewed and phase sign-off points explained. Requiring the stakeholders and the client's executive sponsor to sign off on the work completed within a phase encourages them to take responsibility for reviewing and accepting the work and relieves some burden from the client project manager. Enact change control procedures. If a scope or deliverable change is needed, document the change and the cause for the change, risks, and costs, and modify the schedule before it is approved and signed off on by the client project manager.

Once the project begins, it is important that the client project manager hold regularly scheduled project meetings to discuss the current status of the work, address and resolve problems, and discuss upcoming issues. Make sure the client project manager always creates and distributes an agenda prior to the meeting. The client project manager should post or distribute meeting minutes to all appropriate parties following the meeting. This includes the stakeholders, the executive sponsor, and the vendor. If meeting notes are exchanged between the client project manager and the vendor only, others within the client organization may not be aware of the progress of the project and may be blindsided by unexpected delays.

Periodic meetings provide an opportunity for the client project manager to gauge the work effort and organize internal resources to meet any upcoming needs. Periodic meetings also provide a place to anticipate and deal with issues before they become full-blown problems. The risk planning completed at the front end of a project helps with this, as the vendor and client have already assessed potential problem areas and considered solutions.

Encourage your client project manager to remain vigilant to that perennial project problem — scope creep. Should changes to the scope of work be requested, they should be handled as planned for in the change control process. The client project manager needs to understand that process and be able to explain it to internal stakeholders.

The goal of your client project manager remains unchanged — bring the project in on time, within budget, and containing the originally specified feature/function set. However, if change is required, the client must understand that you have instituted a mechanism to deal with it.

PHASE 3: COMMUNICATE

Communication is the lifeblood of any team and any e-learning project. It sets the tone of the project. It can motivate and encourage the team or discourage and deflate it. Communication can be guarded and politically motivated or it can be straightforward and professional. Open communication leads to trust among team members, executive sponsors, and stakeholders and between the client and vendor. If the client hides bad news, that will not make it go away. Acknowledging issues early will help team members face them and work through them before they become major problems. Your client contact needs to communicate openly with you and with his or her stakeholders.

Encourage your client project manager to communicate freely and often. Part of the client project manager's job is to facilitate free communication between team members, especially internal members within the client organization. Team members also need to be kept informed of issues concerning the executive sponsor and stakeholders. These should be discussed and documented at project meetings.

Typically, the client project manager is also the communication liaison for the executive sponsor and the stakeholders. The client project manager should be the most knowledgeable about all aspects of the project, and must freely share pertinent information with all appropriate parties. The stakeholders and executive sponsor need to be kept up to date on the project. Ask the client project manager to consider sending status updates to all parties to keep them informed on progress and to share potential issues. These updates should include items such as project progress, sign-offs, accomplishments, issues, decisions, setbacks, and changes.

As a vendor working with a project manager who has not worked with e-learning projects before, you have your job cut out for you. Educating a client while managing an e-learning project can be difficult. Although there are many technical aspects the client project manager must coordinate, the people side of the project holds an even greater challenge. Proper planning, careful organization, and open communication significantly increase the project's odds of success. Take the time to educate the client in the following three areas:

Planning tips

- Understand the project's underlying business need, goals, and metrics by which project success will be measured.
- Meet and understand the issues of the executive sponsor and stakeholders.
- Form a stakeholder core team to review deliverables.
- Specifically define the project requirements.
- Use the project team's input to create the project plan and work schedule.
- Use the project team's input to create a risk and mitigation plan.
- Set clear expectations with everyone involved.

Organization tips

- Hold a kickoff meeting to align expectations, explain the work process, and set the ground rules for working together.
- Hold weekly meetings to organize work effort, address and resolve problems, and discuss upcoming issues.
- Prepare and distribute meeting agendas and meeting minutes.
- Control the project through the use of phase sign-offs and a change control process.

Communication tips

- Communicate openly with the project team, stakeholders, executive sponsor, and vendor.
- Communicate freely and often.
- Discuss executive sponsor and stakeholder concerns with the project team at project meetings.
- Send status updates to the executive sponsor and stakeholders to share project progress, sign-offs, accomplishments, issues, decisions, setbacks, and changes.

If the client follows the rules of good planning, organization, and communication tips, he or she will quickly learn how to be an effective e-learning project manager.

■ ■ ■

WHAT SHOULD BE IN THIS SECTION

When writing the *Project Management and Schedule* section of the proposal, you are required to cover several areas:

- The working relationship you will have with the client
- Assumptions you are making about the project
- Elements of project management that support your capture strategy
- Overview of the plan you will use to develop the e-learning

Each of these elements works together. When combined, they present the client with an understanding of your process for developing and implementing e-learning within its organization.

WORKING RELATIONSHIP

The working relationship between a development firm and a client can range from nothing more than a simple transaction where the client pays for a few off-the-shelf e-learning classes to a full-fledged partnership where the two organizations work in concert to develop and market an e-learning product, sharing in revenues. Most likely the arrangement is something in-between.

It is always good to articulate the intended working relationship so both organizations have an understanding of what is expected and what their level of commitment should be. This section describes how the development firm intends to interact with the client. It will answer questions such as:

- Will the client's employees be on the development team?
- Will a partnership arrangement be used?
- Is the client to supply storyboards and course material?
- Will the client have a designated contact? How many?
- How will SMEs be contacted?
- Will the development firm have a project manager?
- Will the project manager interface with the client's project team?
- Is this just a one-time fee-for-service project or is a long-term relationship being established?

This discussion of the working relationship lets the client know how the two organizations will work together to share information and expertise during the e-learning development process. The paragraph below provides an example of how a working arrangement can be explained within a proposal.

> The Web-Training Company (WTC) will work directly with the AZME Corporation's SMEs to discuss all aspects of the project. The project

manager will meet with AZME's representatives on a weekly basis to discuss the project status and ascertain any changes deemed necessary in mutual agreement. The meetings can be conducted via teleconferencing, with the exception of the milestone meetings, which must be face-to-face. Milestone meetings will be held to receive the agreed upon sign-offs for each deliverable in accordance with the mutually agreed upon Milestone Schedule. AZME will provide contact information for all SMEs at the first meeting. WTC will provide status reports and graphical project plans on our secure project management Web site for AZME personnel to access whenever they would like.

PROJECT ASSUMPTIONS

The next part of the *Project Management and Schedule* section is a discussion of assumptions related to the project. An assumption is something that the e-learning development firm believes to be true but has no verification. For example, when converting stand-up instruction to Web-based instruction, most clients claim to have already existing, measurable objectives developed for the stand-up training. Therefore, one assumption that an e-learning development firm can make is that the objectives will not need to be rewritten to be measurable. The client already stated that they were measurable and so the price and management of the project go forward under the assumption that measurable objectives already exist.

If the assumption is correct, then the project proceeds as outlined. However, if the assumption is incorrect and the objectives are not measurable (they contain verbs such as *know* and *understand*), then the e-learning firm must take time to rewrite the objectives. If the objectives need to be rewritten, the development time for the e-learning project will probably increase, as will the cost. Because the vendor stated the assumption up front, it is now "on the table" and the client is responsible for making the objectives measurable and for covering the related costs. If the assumption was not stated in the proposal, the client can state: "We assumed that rewriting the objectives was part of your proposal."

If the assumption is stated up front ("We assume that the existing objectives are written in a format that is measurable.") and the objectives are found not to be measurable, then the development firm can state: "We wrote that we assumed the objectives were measurable, you told us they were measurable, and now we find that they are not. You need to pay for the rewriting of the objectives." While this is an issue you may not want to deal with before a contract is even signed, if you do not address it now, it will come back to haunt you.

In reality, you may not even charge the client for the rewrite because of your relationship with the client or the size of the rewrite; however, without a stated assumption you have no room to negotiate. If you have stated an assumption and it turns out not to be true, you can at least negotiate with the client about a possible increase in fee or a movement of a deadline.

Stating assumptions will help the project to avoid scope creep. Scope creep is when the project gets larger and larger without a corresponding increase in budget or time. One of the biggest issues most vendors deal with is controlling the scope of the project. Well-stated assumptions help control the scope.

Stating assumptions in the proposal may help in other ways. Stating assumptions is important because the client then knows what you based your decisions and recommendations on. For example, a client might disagree with some of the recommendations in your proposal only because the assumptions you made underlying those recommendations were incorrect. If you list your assumptions in the proposal, the client will know that the assumptions you made were wrong (although you should check as many assumptions as possible).

If the assumptions are written, the client might give you the benefit of the doubt because they can see that the assumptions underlying your recommendations are wrong. The client may believe that if you had all the facts and made the correct assumptions, you would then make the correct recommendation. If no assumptions are listed, the client will not know that your recommendations were made based on false assumptions and may discount you and your firm because your assumptions were never stated and the client does not like the resulting recommendations. If you do not state your assumptions, the client cannot correct you or help lead you to correct information. Examples of assumptions are stated below:

- All existing course materials will be provided in electronic format.
- All applicable Standard Operating Procedures (SOPs) will be provided to the development firm.
- It is the responsibility of the client to ensure that all content material is accurate, up-to-date, and complete with respect to your policies and procedures.
- The client will review the content outline, storyboards, and prototype, and will provide feedback within two weeks.
- The client will provide an employee test group possessing diverse levels of computer literacy and subject matter proficiency to assist in evaluating the instruction.
- The client will coordinate testing of the LMS internally with the IT staff.

HIGHLIGHT ELEMENTS OF YOUR CAPTURE STRATEGY

As mentioned in Chapter 5, there are ten elements of e-learning project management. These elements are the management of scope, quality, instructional design, time, cost, human resources, technology, communication, risk, and wow factor.

Usually one or more of these aspects of project management are going to be part of your capture strategy.

In this section of the proposal you want to select one or two of these elements to highlight. The idea is to support your capture strategy through the description of how you will manage the e-learning project. If your strategy revolves around constant communication with the client, highlight how the project plan emphasizes communication. Then describe how your firm has a development Web site containing the latest updates to the project and how it is accessible to the client via the Internet through a secure password.

In addition to including elements of project management that support your capture strategy, sometimes the client will request specific details on an element of project management through a statement in the RFP such as "Explain what you will do to mitigate the risk of working with content that is subject to frequent change."

In this case, the client is asking you to explain your risk mitigation procedures and policies. You might want to explain how you handle change orders from the client and how you separate content from course architecture to allow frequent changes with minimal disruption to the structure of the program. The goal is to provide the information the client requires in enough detail to satisfy the client's concerns.

Highlighting elements of your capture strategy and a specific area of project management required by the client will help you build a persuasive case. It will highlight your strengths as you attempt to sell your solution.

OVERVIEW OF THE DEVELOPMENT PROCESS

Once the proposal outlines the working relationship with the client and the assumptions underlying the project plan, the next step is to describe how you are going to develop the e-learning. An effective method of describing the e-learning development process is to break it into phases. These phases or steps usually follow the instructional design process but can be based on each major deliverable, sign-offs, or some other division of the project into manageable chunks.

Breaking down the process into discrete phases (even if there is some overlap) allows you to explain the e-learning development process in an easy, methodical manner. The idea is to explain how the process will be applied to this particular e-learning project without a lot of jargon or technical explanation. Describe the development in enough detail so the client understands what you will be doing but not in so much detail that you confuse the client. Example 13.1 is a proposal describing three steps of an e-learning development process.

Another effective method of explaining the e-learning development process is to depict it in a diagram or flow chart. A visualization of the different phases helps the client to understand the sequence of the e-learning development pro-

Three-Phased Approach

Phase One: Analysis

The first phase is to analyze the information contained within the two manuals and to develop a navigational paradigm for the e-learning module. This involves determining a "theme" and a "look and feel" for the module. The theme and look and feel involve the development of appropriate icons, the selection of the correct colors, and an overall look. This will be accomplished by developing a course map and three visual prototypes. AZME personnel will be able to choose examples and navigational formats from three different visual prototypes. The prototypes will be established on-line so AZME personnel can log into the site while it is being developed and make comments and critique the information.

Phase Two: Information Placement

The second phase will be placing the information into the framework of the module and developing the interactive exercises. Studies reveal that the more interactive the learning experience, the more students remember and retain what they have learned. The goal is to develop interactive activities that will hold the trainees' attention and allow them to learn what they need to learn to properly complete their job. This phase will involve the programming and the development of tools for communicating between the student and the training staff of AZME. This phase will also be a chance for AZME personnel to review the exercises and make comments on the layout and content of the e-learning module. We will not release any exercises or content without review from AZME personnel.

Phase Three: Quality Control

The final phase will involve quality control and sign-off by AZME. WTC will conduct quality testing for navigation, functionality of the links and exercises while AZME will check for content accuracy. This is the final phase prior to the implementation of the e-learning module onto AZME's server.

Example 13.1 Description of a three-phased approach for describing the process of developing e-learning to a client.

cess. The diagram should provide the client with a sense of how one phase of the project flows into the next. Figure 13.1 is an image of a project plan model. The diagram does not need to be complex. It simply needs to provide a general description of the flow of the project.

Another effective method of displaying the project plan, client/vendor responsibility, and due dates is to include the information in a table. The table should list the major elements of the project, which can include milestones and deliverables, a brief description of each deliverable and what is needed to complete this step in the project, responsibility for the item (usually this column will list the names of the organizations involved [i.e., WBT and AZME]), and the amount of time it

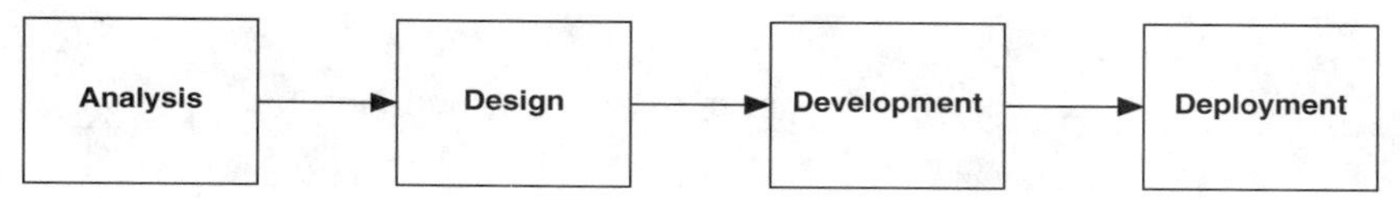

Figure 13.1 Graphical representation of the movement from one stage of e-learning development to another.

will take to complete this task or actual due dates for each milestone. An example of a table is shown in Example 13.2.

Another popular technique for displaying information related to a project is to create a project plan Gantt chart. This requires some type of project management software. The software allows the user to enter a list of tasks, dates the tasks must be completed, amount of time needed to complete the task, and the resources that may be applied to the task. A nice feature of project management software is that the resources can be associated with a cost. After you have entered each task, assigned a time for the tasks, and assigned resources to the task, the software calculates a budget. Example 13.3 shows a Gantt chart. One problem with using Gantt charts in the proposal is that they usually include hard-to-read print and can sometimes be confusing to potential clients.

An even more confusing display of a project timeline for many managers is the use of a project network diagram showing the critical path. A project network diagram is defined as a "schematic display of the logical relationships of project activities…drawn from left to right to reflect project chronology" [2]. The critical path is the "series of activities that determine the duration of the project. It is the longest path through the project." In Example 13.4, the critical path is through the middle.

While both the Gantt chart and the project network diagram are excellent project management tools, a common mistake is that proposal writers usually provide too much detail in these charts. In addition, these tools may be beyond the understanding of some of the individuals reading the proposal. The goal of the e-learning proposal is not to plan the entire project down to each and every task; it is to sell the client on your basic plan for developing the e-learning or implementing the LMS.

If the client is too confused or misunderstands your project management methods or uses PERT (Program Evaluation and Review Technique) to manage its internal projects when you use Gantt charts, your chances of winning become diminished. Save the technical, in-depth project management tool discussions for internal meetings or until after the project starts. You certainly want to mention that you do use some type of project management tool and you can show a simplified Gantt chart with only the milestones or a few tasks. However, a chart showing milestones, tasks, and responsibilities is usually enough detail at this point in the E-BAP.

AZME Territory Manager E-Learning Development Project Plan and Timeline			
Milestones	**Description**	**Responsibility**	**Est. Time**
Kickoff Meeting	This meeting determines client expectations, allows design team to meet with key client personnel.	**Client/ Vendor**	1 day
Agree on Training Manual Content/ Receive Digital Images	Copy of final manual is provided to vendor. Content cannot change after this point. Client provides photographs digitized on CD-ROM or other digital artwork to use in manual and requested forms.	**Client**	1 week after kickoff
Prototype Review	Vendor reviews material and makes final recommendation on "look and feel" and navigation based on three prototypes. Client chooses prototype.	**Vendor**	4 weeks after kickoff
Revise Prototype	Make changes to prototype based on input from client personnel.	**Vendor**	1 week after prototype review
Approval Final Manual Design	Approve the navigation and "look and feel" of site.	**Client**	1 week after revised prototype
Storyboards Developed for Content Display	Client personnel review the storyboards for approval of interactive components and display of information.	**Vendor**	1 week after final design approval
Program Web Site and Interactive Exercises	Information is placed into the web site. Interactive web exercises are developed. Client personnel can review on the on-line web development web site.	**Vendor**	4-week development process
Review Site	Client personnel review the site for content and general navigability.	**Vendor**	throughout development process
Final Review of Site	Final changes are agreed upon and decided upon by client and vendor.	**Client/ Vendor**	1 week after development process
Completion of Training/Manual Conversion to WBT	Vendor completes on-line training incorporating comments from final review by client.	**Vendor**	1 week after final review
Creation of Master CD-ROM	Master disk containing all the web files and folders delivered to client. Final sign-off on completed project.	**Vendor**	1 week after completion of manual

Example 13.2 Chart format for describing the project development phases to a client in a simple, easy-to-read format.

ID	Task Name	Start	Finish	Duration
1	**Kickoff Meeting**	**2/12/2002**	**12/13/2002**	**.4w**
2	Agree on Training Manual Contents	12/12/2002	12/12/2002	.2w
3	Prototype Review	12/13/2002	12/13/2002	.2w
4	Revise Prototype	12/16/2002	12/17/2002	.3w
5	Approval of Manual Design	12/18/2002	12/18/2002	0w
6	Begin Storyboard Development	12/18/2002	12/19/2002	.4w

Dec 1 2002: 5 6 7 | Dec 8 2002: 8 9 10 11 12 13 14 | Dec 15 2002: 15 16 17 18

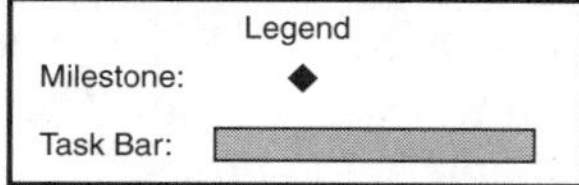

Example 13.3 Gantt chart for describing the development of a project.

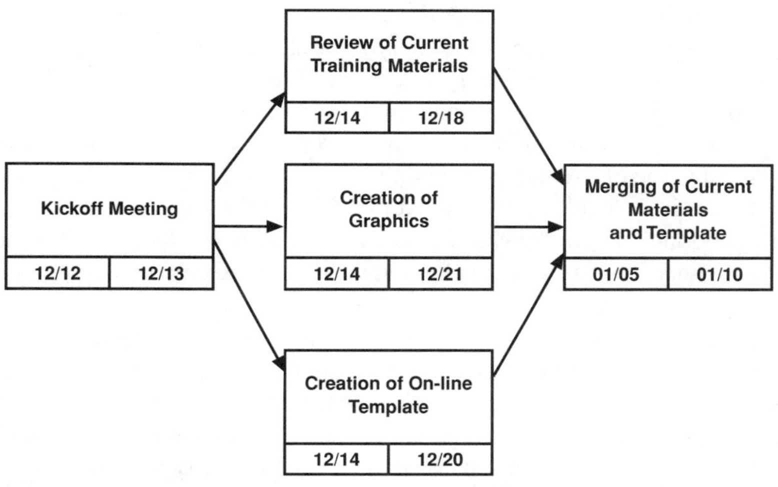

Example 13.4 Network diagram for graphically showing the development of an e-learning project.

PROJECT TIMELINE ESTIMATION

"How long will it take?" is, perhaps, one of the most frequently asked questions in the realm of e-learning development [3]. Managers, executives, clients, and anxious learners all want to know how long it takes to develop e-learning.

Unfortunately, the answers are not always simple or clear-cut. The amount of time it takes to develop a quality e-learning solution depends upon a number of variables. The variables include the complexity of the material, the experience of the designers, the amount of communication between the client and the vendor, the level of quality desired, and the e-learning experience of the client.

Typically, a client will provide you with an end date. You must then schedule your work to be completed by that end date. Usually clients are in a hurry to choose a vendor for their e-learning project and are in an even bigger hurry to have the project completed. As an indicator of the urgency of the project, the client usually picks an overly aggressive start date. Unfortunately, once the contract is awarded and before development can begin delays occur.

Most often the delay has to do with the two organizations hammering out contract details. This usually takes a while and even when the start date of the e-learning project slips, the due date usually does not. This can cause problems because you must make adjustments to accommodate the new start date. Therefore, care must be taken to develop an accurate estimation of the project's time requirements. However, you must understand that estimating e-learning development times is a fluid process and even the best estimates do not always hold up.

What you want to do is provide an accurate and fair estimate to the client and include enough assumptions and caveats so that when circumstances change, you can fairly and honestly charge the client for the changes (this is always easier said than done). You must make every effort to ensure that the amount of effort required to successfully complete the project is correctly estimated. The results of poorly estimated e-learning projects can be disastrous for both the vendor who miscalculated the effort and the client. For the vendor, a miscalculation means a possible loss in revenue, employee overtime (even if unpaid this is expensive in terms of morale and employee burnout), and inability to allocate the needed resources to other projects. For the client, it means missed deadlines, quality issues, and delays.

A correct estimate is essential for completing an e-learning project on time and within budget. Unfortunately, determining the amount of time needed to develop one hour of Web-based instruction can be a tricky process. Many variables must be considered in the development of the time estimate. These variables include complexity of the proposed instruction, amount and type of media elements, level of interactivity, experience of the development team, and the number and type of revisions requested by the client.

During the life of a Web-based development project, many variables are unknown, subject to change, and in a constant state of movement. The job of the proposal writing team is to present a realistic estimate of the project but not an exact number. Many e-learning projects are doomed from the start because of poor estimates. Your estimation needs to be accurate but not precise.

AMOUNT OF WORK EFFORT VS. CALENDAR TIME

When making an estimate, you must consider two forms of time. The first is *amount of effort*. This is the calculation of how many work hours are required to complete a project. This is sometimes called *man hours* or *person hours*. For example, you might estimate that programming 100 screens of e-learning will take 120 hours. The 120 hours is the amount of person hours or effort required to create 100 screens. If one person worked 120 hours straight, the 100 screens would be finished. Of course, no one can work 120 hours straight so *calendar time* must also be taken into account.

We might estimate that it would take one person 3 weeks (40 hours a week) to program 100 screens. Realistically, no one works 40 solid hours a week so, more likely, this phase of the project would take approximately 4 weeks. However, if we put three people on the project (each working approximately 40 hours a week), it could be completed in a little over a week (accounting for the fact that not everyone works a solid 40 hours a week on the programming).

Therefore, when estimating a project, you need to determine the amount of work required to complete the project as well as the calendar time. When working with the calendar, you must realize that not every person will work a solid 40 hours a week because of meetings, phone calls, and other interruptions. Also realize that people should not be scheduled to work holidays and weekends. You do not want to send a message to your client that the success of the project requires your people to work through major holidays. If a client sees your people working on holidays or weekends, they may assume that their people may also be required to work on holidays or weekends to keep the project on time.

Another advantage of not scheduling holidays or weekends as part of your regular project schedule is that if the time does get tight, you can use those days as a backup and work them in if they are needed. This is not advisable but does come in handy when the deadline is looming and not all the work is completed.

Another consideration that must be made when estimating completion times is that adding more people does not necessarily shorten the development timeline. Sometimes there are dependencies built into a series of tasks. For example, programming 100 screens cannot begin until the objectives for each lesson are written and the storyboards developed. These dependencies will elongate the effort regardless of the number of people you are able to "throw" at the project. Programming cannot begin until objectives and storyboards are ready. There is no value in working on the programming when the objectives are not even written. You need to keep dependencies in mind when creating an estimated completion date for the project.

You also need to consider that clients need about two weeks turnaround time to sign off on material. Clients are notoriously late returning material that is needed to continue the project. When estimating client sign-offs, it is a good idea to estimate at least two weeks. You can try to estimate less than two weeks but, typically, the client is late returning material but still expects you to meet your deadlines. Be generous with client turnaround times.

There is one last item to consider when developing your e-learning estimate.

When converting classroom instruction to e-learning, you can usually reduce the delivery time by as much as 40 to 60% [4, 5]. This means that ten hours of classroom instruction can be decreased to as little as four hours of online instruction. This is due to the fact that e-learning has more time-on-task than classroom instruction.

In many classroom environments, the instructional time is spent on noninstructional tasks. These noninstructional tasks include facilities orientation, review of the day's agenda, adjustment of furniture for the right level of comfort, students returning late from a break, the instructor helping a "lost" student while the others wait, and many other distractions.

With e-learning, these types of interruptions do not occur. This lack of distraction helps to dramatically reduce the time needed for e-learning. In addition, most e-learning is developed using a sound instructional design methodology which only teaches the learner what he or she needs to know. Sometimes in a classroom environment, instructional elements are put into a class just because it is an eight-hour class and it needs to last eight hours whether the learners need eight hours of instruction or not. When estimating development time, keep in mind the time reduction when you convert classroom instruction to e-learning. This can have a big impact on your estimation.

In summary, when estimating the amount of time to complete an e-learning project, remember these items:

- Clients want to see aggressive but realistically developed estimations for the amount of effort needed to complete the project.
- Clients want a realistic completion date for the project.
- More resources do not necessarily mean the project will be completed faster.
- Keep holidays, individual employee schedules, and vacations in mind when developing an estimated calendar completion date.
- Clients need as much turnaround time as possible regardless of what they tell you about their ability to turn material around quickly.
- Placing instructor-led training online reduces the instructional time 40 to 60%.

METHODS OF ESTIMATION

There are four methods for determining the amount of effort it will take to develop e-learning. From there, you can determine the calendar time. While none of these methods is flawless, each contains some strength in terms of developing an accurate estimation of the amount of work that needs to be completed. The real trick is to pick a standard method and to utilize that method and refine it until your organization can accurately predict the amount of effort a project will take.

Let us take a look at each method to see when one may be more appropriate than another. The four methods are:

- Similar projects
- Formulas
- Industry standards
- Bottom up

SIMILAR PROJECTS

One method of "timing" a project is to compare it to past projects — Project X had ten objectives and took 200 hours to develop and Project Y has five objectives so it should take only 100 hours to develop. In project management jargon this is known as *analogous estimating* and is one method of determining the amount of effort needed to complete an e-learning project [6].

The underlying premise is that *this* project is analogous to *that* project. Since we know how long that project took, we can estimate how long this project will take. Analogous estimating means that you use the actual time frame from a previous, similar project as the basis for estimating the time frame for the current project [6]. Analogous estimating is used when not a lot of information is known about the current project or when two projects appear to be similar. Of course, if they appear to be similar but, in fact, are not, the estimates will be inaccurate. Analogous estimation is good for ballpark figures but it is not very good for actually estimating the project.

The problem with this method is that rarely is one e-learning project exactly like a previous project. Even if the projects are similar, the clients are not. Since much time is spent working with clients, attempting to understand content, and determining how the client organization functions and communicates, it is difficult to use analogous estimating to develop accurate estimates. The best time to use this type of estimation is with a different project from the same client or when you need a quick "guestimation" of how long a project might take.

USING A FORMULA

One method many e-learning firms use to determine the time required to complete an e-learning project is formulaic. The official term for this is *parametric modeling* [7]. This method involves using variables from the project description in a mathematical formula to develop an estimate.

Formulas are most effective when certain variables of the e-learning project are known. For example, if you know the number of screens that will be involved and you know how long it takes for your developers to create one screen of instruction, you can estimate the amount of time it takes to create the e-learning. If it takes your developers 10 minutes per screen and you have 1000 screens, then it will take 10,000 minutes, which is 167 hours or a little over 4 weeks for development. From there, you can determine the calendar time.

In the book *Project Management for Trainers,* Lou Russell provides some numbers for formulas to determine the work effort for certain types of training projects [8]. First Russell identifies three variables that must be considered when estimating a project. They are:

- Expertise
- Project-related work
- Environmental factors

Each factor is assigned a weight. Then the weighted numbers are multiplied together to determine an estimation of the amount of effort needed to complete the task. The first step in the process is to determine how long you think a particular task will take to be completed. You might think that creating an interactive lesson for an e-learning module on machine safety might take, on average, 27 hours. Once you have that estimate, you add on certain variables until you arrive at an actual project time.

For the *expertise* variable Russell has created two factors: an instructional design expertise factor and a content knowledge factor [8]. For the instructional design expertise factor, a weighted percent of between 0.5 and 1.5 is assigned. If the person performing the work is an expert, he or she receives a percentage of 0.5; if he or she is not an expert, the percentage is closer to 1.5. The more experienced the developer, the less time needs to be added onto the estimate.

For the content knowledge expertise factor, a value between 0.75 and 4.0 is assigned, with 0.75 being assigned to someone with a lot of content knowledge and 4.0 being assigned to a person with little content knowledge. If you have less knowledge of the content, it will take longer to develop the instruction. If your developer has no knowledge of machine safety, he or she may get a content matter expertise factor of 4.0. If he or she has worked a few years in a factory and understands something about machine safety, he or she might get a factor of 3.0. If your developer wrote a book on machine safety, he or she would get a factor of 0.75.

Russell's formula calls for first applying the instructional design expertise factor by multiplying the estimated time for an activity by a number between 0.5 and 1.5 and then multiplying that number by the content expertise factor, which is between 0.75 and 4.0. The result would work as follows:

Estimated time for activity	27 hours
Instructional design expertise factor (0.5 to 1.5)	1.2
Subtotal	32.4 hours
Content expertise factor (0.75 to 4.0)	3.0
Total time based on expertise factors	97.2 hours

When you provide an estimate to a client, round up to the nearest whole number. You are estimating the amount of effort, not giving an exact number. Therefore, the number presented to the client in the previous case would be 97 hours, not 97.2. The 0.2 is a mathematical result and not really a true estimate of 12 minutes needed to complete the task.

The next factor is that of *project-related work*. This is the amount of time added to an activity to take into account the number of people working on the project and the time it takes for them to accurately communicate with one another to successfully complete the task. When more people work on a task, the level of difficulty becomes higher. Russell's numbers range from a factor of 0.10 for a few people to a factor of 0.20 for more people [8].

Time based on expertise factors	97.2 hours
Project-related factor (0.1 to 0.2) (in this case two people)	0.16
Number of additional project-related factor hours	15.5 hours
Total time based on project-related factors	112.7 hours

The final factor mentioned by Russell is the *environmental factor*. This factor is for nonproject activities such as checking e-mail, answering phone calls, attending meetings, breaks, and other nonvalue-added tasks [8]. It also takes into account illnesses and other nonscheduled events. The environmental factor can range from a low of 0.25 to a high of 0.35 depending upon the type of work environment. The more chaotic the work environment, the higher the number.

Time based on project-related factors	112.7 hours
Environmental factor (0.25 to 0.35)	0.3
Number of additional environmental factor hours	33.8 hours
Total time based on project-related factors	146.5 hours

Another factor often included in parametric modeling for e-learning is the amount of interactivity. Although Russell does not include a factor of *interactivity*, it is essential for e-learning. Interactivity is the number and types of interactions the program has with the learner. This factor can range from a low of 1.0 to a high of 4.0. The 1.0 level would be for e-learning that is not very interactive; 4.0 is for a highly interactive simulation.

Time based on environmental factor	146.5 hours
Interactivity factor (1.0 to 4.0)	3.0
Total time based on interactivity factors	439.5 hours

Parametric modeling for estimating time for e-learning projects provides an effective method of determining the amount of work effort needed for a project; however, it does give a false sense of precision. The method still requires a great deal of guessing. The multiplication factors are a guess (perhaps educated but still a guess). When these numbers are used, you need to keep in mind that some of the underlying factors may not be 100% accurate. For example, what is the difference between a 2.0 and a 3.0 content knowledge expertise factor? How is this difference measured? Is an experienced instructional designer with no expertise in a subject area given a higher or lower factor than an average instructional designer with superior knowledge of a subject area?

Another problem with this method is that it relies on analogous estimation. It assumes that this hour of e-learning is the same as an hour that was created before, and that is almost never the case. Another shortcoming is that it is almost impossible to predict every single variable that impacts the development of an hour of instruction. It is difficult to accurately predict the level of interactivity, the level of developer experience, and the level of effort needed to extract the necessary knowledge from the SMEs. It is also easy to get too carried away with variables. You could create a variable to indicate whether or not a client company has had experience with e-learning, a variable for the number of animations required, a variable for the number of people on the project, and a variable for the number of delivery platforms. It can become very easy to have too many variables.

To make sense of all the possible variables, choose the ones that are meaningful and that accurately predict the amount of work effort within your organization. To do this, you must track the amount of effort it takes you to actually complete e-learning projects. Once those numbers are collected, you can use them to help determine what variables you should use and what factors are appropriate in your estimation formulas. Worksheet 13.1 provides an example of how e-learning factors can be used to help estimate the amount of work effort for a project. The first row is filled in as an example.

BOTTOM UP

Another type of estimation is a bottom-up estimation or what is sometimes referred to as a Work Breakdown Structure (WBS). Bottom-up estimating is a process by which the major deliverables of the project are broken down into smaller tasks until each task can be easily assigned a time value. The idea is that if you can break down every activity into a definable task and then assign an estimated time to each task, you can then roll up all the tasks to determine the total amount of effort it will take for the entire project.

Following is an example of a preliminary bottom-up estimation for a project involving a needs analysis and the subsequent development of a 15-minute e-learning piece in HTML. The topic is "Successful Initial Customer Contact." Using the bottom-up approach, a list of each task that needs to be completed, along with an estimated time for each task, was developed.

E-Learning Formula Estimation Sheet

Use this worksheet to determine the amount of time it will take to complete an e-learning project. Fill in the first column with the name of the task that needs to be completed. In the next column, fill in the number of hours it will take to complete the task. Use the next five columns to indicate the amount of each factor that should be used as a multiplier (note that not all activities will require all factors). The final column indicates the total number of hours needed for each task. When you have completed calculating each activity, you will have the total number of hours required to complete the e-learning project.

		E Learning Factors					
E-Learning Project Activity	**# of Hours**	**Instructional Design (0.5 to 1.5)**	**Content Matter (0.75 to 4.0)**	**Project-Related (0.1 to 0.2)**	**Environmental (0.25 to 0.35)**	**Interactivity (1.0 to 4.0)**	**Total # of hours**
Write Objectives	10	(0.5) x 15 hrs	(3.0) x 45 hrs	(0.2) x 54 hrs	(0.25) x 67.5 hrs	None	68
Total number of hours							

Worksheet 13.1 Use the *E-Learning Formula Estimation Worksheet* to determine how long it will take you to complete an e-learning project.

Kickoff meeting with three stakeholders (1 hour)
Development of needs analysis questionnaire (2 hours)
Meeting with SME (1 hour)
Phone call to SME (0.5 hour)
Recording notes from SME phone call (0.25 hour)
Administering the questionnaire (4 hours)
Collating data from questionnaire results (3 hours)

Developing objectives for the instruction (2 hours)
Gather material needed for the lesson (1 hour)
Chunk gathered material into parts of the lesson based on objectives (2 hours)
Development of the template in HTML (2 hours)
Placing chunked material into HTML template (3 hours)
Have client review lesson and chunked materials (2 hours)
Test lesson to make sure it functions properly (1 hour)
Client implements lesson onto their internal server (1 hour)
Client tests lesson in their environment (1 hour)
Total time for development (26.75 hours)

The process of determining the smaller tasks of a project is known as "decomposition." Decomposition "involves subdividing the major project deliverables...into smaller, more manageable components" [9]. These smaller components (tasks) can then be given time estimations more easily and accurately than larger chunks of tasks. It is easier to estimate how long it will take to create a template in HTML than to estimate how long it will take to create an entire e-learning lesson. The smaller and more tangible a task, the easier it is to create an accurate estimate. This decomposition process uses the following steps:

1. Identify the major deliverables of the project (i.e., development of an e-learning lesson).
2. Identify the tasks that must be completed to make the deliverable possible (i.e., writing objectives, storyboarding the screens, etc.).
3. Break down the subtasks into smaller tasks to a point where they can be accurately estimated.
4. Do not forget items such as project management and client communication.
5. Verify the estimation with others to make sure nothing is missed.

The bottom-up calculation is the most accurate for forecasting time requirements but, as you can see, it is time consuming itself. One shortcut you can take with this method is to determine an estimate for one lesson and then use that estimate as a multiplier for the total number of lessons you need to develop. If you estimated that one lesson will take 100 hours to develop, you can multiply the number of lessons you need to develop by 100 to determine the total number of hours for all the lessons.

While this method can be effective, it is not perfect. Often a project team will forget to include certain tasks or will severely over- or underestimate a task. Once that task is incorrectly estimated, it can impact the entire project. The project team also needs to take into account the fact that some of the tasks can be done in parallel. So, the actual completed calendar time for the project needs to be examined to ensure that any parallel processes are accurately reflected in the final delivery date.

Table 13.1 Time to Develop One Hour of Instruction Based on Industry Averages

Type of Training per 1 Hour	Low Hours per Hour of Instruction	High Hours per Hour of Instruction
Stand-up training	20	70
Self-instructional print	80	125
Instructor-led, web-based training delivery (using software like Centra or InterWise—two way live audio)	30	80
Web-based developed from scratch		
Web-based training: text only, limited interactivity	100	150
Web-based training: text and graphics	150	200
Web-based training: text, graphics, and animation, moderate interactivity	250	400
Web-based, fully interactive, text, graphics, and animation but not a simulation, full interactivity	400	600
Web-based, fully interactive virtual reality simulation, full interactivity	600	1000
Web-based developed within a template		
Web-based training: text only, limited interactivity	40	100
Web-based training: text and graphics	100	150
Web-based training: text, graphics, and animation, moderate interactivity	150	200
Use of learning objects using dynamic Web page development (after site structure is already developed) depends on element (video is more time consuming than text)	60	300
Populating an online help system (like RoboHelp)	3	10

INDUSTRY STANDARDS

Another method of e-learning project estimation is to get some type of benchmark within the industry for the amount of development effort required per hour of instruction. For example, if you know that most organizations take 100 hours to develop 1 hour of e-learning, you then know approximately how long your firm should estimate to develop 1 hour of e-learning — 100 hours. Unfortunately, the e-learning industry does not have a universally agreed upon set of standards for predicting the number of hours it takes to develop one hour of e-learning.

While a single standard has not been agreed upon by an international standards group, the ratios in Table 13.1 do provide some degree of standardization concerning development times. These estimations are based on interviews with several e-learning development firms and internal e-learning developers, and a careful review of literature concerning the topic. The numbers are displayed as a range to account for the variability within the industry concerning e-learning development times. The amount of work effort for many e-learning projects will comfortably fit within these ranges; however, there will also be projects that, for whatever reason, will not fit within the ranges. Use these numbers as a frame of reference and strive to develop a similar set of numbers for your own internal development efforts.

SUMMARY OF ESTIMATION EFFORTS

The methods of estimating a project are varied and each has advantages and disadvantages. Your goal as an e-learning firm is to track your own projects and use a combination of the methods described above to determine the best estimation practice for your organization. Each client and each project is different. You need to carefully weigh key variables to determine as accurate an estimation as you possibly can. You will then use that estimation to determine the completion date of the project and the price of the project. For determining the price, you will multiply the amount of hours for the project by the price per hour. This will be discussed in more detail in the next chapter.

Example 13.5 shows a *Project Management and Schedule* section from a proposal. Notice how it includes key information to provide the client with a high level of comfort concerning the development of various e-learning elements.

THE BOTTOM LINE

Good project management is essential to the success of e-learning. You must present a process by which you are going to manage the project in a straightforward, easy-to-understand manner. You want to convey to the client that you are capable of completing the project on time. You also want to make sure that elements of your capture strategy related to project management are highlighted. Every section of the proposal must sell your solution.

Response to Truckco's Request for Proposal

Project Management and Schedule

Working Relationship

Stating the assumption up front helps avoid problems later.

We assume that the seven courses are currently being offered as instructor-led and that Truckco will provide all available resources, such as content and materials from these courses. In addition, we assume Truckco will provide a subject matter expert and usability testers who will be available throughout the entire scope of the project.

Describes the resources that will be assigned to the team and the working relationship they will have with the client.

Workforce Interactive will hand select each member of the core project team to work with Truckco. The resources that this team provides are detailed in the Corporate Capabilities section of this document. The subject matter expert that will be provided by Truckco will, in essence, become a member of our core team. We will utilize the expertise of this individual to ensure that we are meeting all of Truckco's needs. In addition, Truckco's usability testers will assure the portal is functional and user friendly.

The core project team will be responsible for creating a positive working relationship with Truckco and the subject matter expert. Workforce Interactive's project manager will keep Truckco informed throughout the entire project. Contact will be made through the use of telephone conversations, conference calls, e-mail, faxes, overnight delivery service, and scheduled face-to-face meetings.

Scheduling

Divides the project into phases based on the desired deliverables.

Upon being awarded the contract, a kick-off meeting will be held. This project will be broken into four phases:

- o Phase I: Information Center
- o Phase II: Training Center
- o Phase III: Shopping Center
- o Phase IV: Delivery of the final product

This proposal used a Gantt chart that was not in the body of the proposal but contained in the appendix.

Following the kick-off meeting, Workforce Interactive will begin analyzing the design and development of each of the three centers. (Refer to the Appendix for Project Timeline.)

Describes, at a very high level, the phases of project.

Prior to prototype development for any center, the core team members will devise a requirements document. This document will outline fonts, colors, graphics, etc. to be used to create a common look and feel for the entire portal. Each center will have a prototype developed to allow Truckco the opportunity to see different variations of the proposed portal. After a prototype is approved, team members will design and develop the Information Center and Shopping Center at the same time. Concurrently, the courseware will be created for the Training Center. As the courses are completed, they will be added to the portal. The entire portal will be evaluated, revised, and tested prior to delivery.

Confidential 11

Example 13.5 *Project Management and Schedule* section of a proposal.

Response to Truckco's Request for Proposal

Project Management and Schedule

Describes the quality aspect of the proposal's capture strategy

Quality Assurance

Quality Assurance is an integral part of Workforce Interactive's design and development process. Team members have been formally trained in quality assurance procedures and conduct initial checks. The Quality Assurance Specialist will perform the steps below before delivering the product to Truckco for review and sign-off.

Provides a high level of detail concerning the quality assurance process.

Quality Assurance Checklist

1. Content
   - o accurate spelling, grammar, and mechanics
   - o inclusion of all critical information
   - o accurate titles, headers, and navigation
2. Documentation
3. Media and visual design
   - o quality images
   - o quick download time
   - o effective screen layout
   - o accurate color
4. Browser compatibility
   - o compatible on many platforms
   - o compatible on many browsers
5. User preference compatibility
   - o font size
   - o link colors and underlining
   - o window size
   - o plug-ins
6. Usability testing
   - o link functionality
   - o user friendly navigation

Divides the project into phases based on the desired deliverables.

Workforce Interactive's quality assurance plan will follow a schedule where time is given for suggested changes by Truckco. A sign-off policy will be used at the end of each deliverable. This schedule will guarantee Truckco's satisfaction with each phase of the project, while keeping the project moving forward.

Discusses how the quality process incorporates special software and how long the warranty period will be.

We will use WebLoad software for testing and analyzing the performance of Web applications. Based on the data returned from the server, WebLoad ensures applications function properly and according to requirements, and provides a detailed breakdown of every component file of every failed operation. Also as part of our quality assurance plan, Workforce Interactive offers a ninety-day product performance guarantee. If Truckco finds any performance problems during this period, we will provide prompt technical diagnosis and repair free of charge. After this ninety-day period, Workforce Interactive will provide quality service at a reasonable cost.

Confidential 12

Example 13.5 (continued).

14

BUDGET

INTRODUCTION

The budget is usually the first item looked at by a potential client. Everyone always asks the question "How much is this going to cost?" Clients sometimes get nervous about the price of e-learning. In fact, according to a *U.S. News & World Report* article, creating one customized e-learning course can cost anywhere from $25,000 to $50,000 [1]. However, the cost of an LMS can range from $250,000 to $700,000 per year, depending on the size of the enterprise, amount of integration with other enterprisewide systems, and the degree of customization [2]. If clients decide to have a vendor host the LMS, vendors can charge as much as $30,000 per year for between 2000 and 3000 seats, plus any customization and integration costs [2]. Many vendors sell their LMS on a per-seat basis of anywhere from $30 to $50 per user. The pricing of e-learning can seem expensive and confusing to a potential client. This confusion can make it difficult for you to sell your e-learning solution.

So, the secret to a good budget is presentation. Present the budget in an easy-to-understand, straightforward manner emphasizing the value of your solution. Present the budget in a manner that eliminates any possible client frustration. If you present an overly complex budget with hidden costs and other potentially misleading items, the client may throw away the entire proposal without ever looking at the remainder of the document. Or worse, the client may feel that you are trying to cheat him or her.

WHY THIS SECTION IS NEEDED

If it is correctly presented, the budget section of the document will sell your solution. The main thrust of your budget presentation should not be the *cost* to the client; it should be the *value* your solution brings to the client.

Your budget must be high enough to cover your costs plus profit but low enough to appeal to your client. Any final number you present is a combination of a profit margin and the cost to develop the e-learning.

The costs need to include all of your overhead expenses as well as personnel costs. Overhead costs consist of supplies, insurance, rent, equipment, phone expenses, Internet access, and other expenses that cannot be directly billed to the client.

You can determine the price to charge the client by using the same methods as for determining the amount of time needed to develop the e-learning. One of the easiest methods of determining the price is to multiply the estimated project completion time by the costs and profit margin. If you have estimated the time correctly and have a good sense of your costs and desired profit margin, determining the price the client will pay for your services becomes relatively easy.

However, you will also need to factor other items into your budget such as:

- Software to run the e-learning (LCMS or LMS)
- Hardware for housing the e-learning software
- Associated training for the client
- Specialized programming for connecting e-learning software to existing human resource systems
- Any additional services or products you provide

When you determine your budget, you need to take into account labor hours as well as hardware, software, travel, etc.

■ ■ ■

CREATING AN E-LEARNING BUDGET

Hank Bailey, Founder, CEO, Bailey Interactive, Inc.

INTRODUCTION

A budget is defined as the total sum of money allocated for a particular purpose or time period. Budgets include labor expenses, overhead of the organization, and the organization's desired profit.

It is important to distinguish between "cost" and "price." Labor and overhead are defined as "costs" to an organization. "Profit" is the money that remains after all expenses are paid. Since all projects are intended to be profitable, the "final bid price" includes the cost and the profit. The total estimated expenditure of personnel time, materials, overhead, and profit becomes the bid price for the project, depicted by the following formula:

$$\text{Price} = \text{Cost} + \text{Profit}$$

TYPES OF PROJECT BID PRICES

There are several ways to bid projects, each of which is defined and explained below.

- **Time and material** — A mutually agreeable hourly rate for personnel is established and billed accordingly as the project continues. Expended materials and supplies are added to personnel charges. This approach is most desirable when a detailed scope of work cannot be defined or if the scope of work is likely to change often during the life span of the project. While this approach appears to be the fairest for conducting business, it is not widely used for large projects. Most clients prefer to control project costs and opt for setting a "fixed fee" or "not to exceed" price.
- **Fixed fee** — A project price is bid based upon an understanding of the scope of work required. It becomes the vendor's responsibility to determine and to specify a detailed scope of work, then price the project accordingly. This approach allows clients to control project budgets, assuming the scope of work does not deviate from what was initially agreed upon. Alterations in scope open opportunities for negotiating a revised project price.
- **Not to exceed** — A maximum price is set for a project, but this price may be reduced if the project takes less than the allotted time to complete. As with the "time and material" approach, accurate records are maintained to track personnel time that is dedicated to the project.

Regardless of the type of bid price, there are two reasons why it is important to estimate accurately: (1) businesses must cover costs and (2) businesses must make a profit.

DETERMINING THE PROJECT SCOPE

Budgeting is built on project scope, especially when the bid price is "fixed fee" or "not to exceed." There are several factors that can affect project scope. Some factors that various vendors have used include:

- **Number and type of lesson objectives** — The assumption is that more objectives suggest more work and that instructional lessons for higher level objectives as categorized by Gagné and Bloom are more time consuming to prepare than lower level objectives. In this case, vendors have established fees for each type of objective based upon previous experience.
- **Number and types of interactions** — Linear electronic page-turners are more easily constructed than lessons with abundant branching options.

- **Assessment requirements** — The inclusion or exclusion of pretest, post-test, and embedded questions affects the complexity of a project. Also, true/false and multiple choice items are easier to create than drag/drop interactions.
- **Expected length of program** — Often the project price is based upon a unit price per hour of instruction. The hourly rate varies depending upon the type of lesson requested. For example, a one-hour lesson dealing with learning facts and basic knowledge may price out at $5000, whereas a one-hour lesson dealing with a simulation of a complicated company process may be priced at $11,000.
- **Level of media integration** — The type and amount of media used in a lesson affect the project price. Basic text is the least expensive; motion video is the most expensive. Animations are more expensive than static graphics, but static graphics are usually more expensive than clip art. The use of sound such as audio narration and special sound effects influences the project bid price.
- **Technical challenge** — The technical requirements such as the authoring/programming tools to be used, the delivery system, and any special requests certainly affect the personnel resources needed for a project. Sometimes the technical complexity of a project may exceed the expertise of the vendor, in which case expensive consultation services may be the only recourse.

None of the above-mentioned factors contribute solely to a project bid price. The most successful vendor will develop and implement a plan or tool that includes most or all of these factors when determining an accurate methodology for pricing projects.

DETERMINING PROJECT ESTIMATES

One approach for determining project estimates is to follow the basic steps of an instructional systems approach.

Step 1: Create a list of all major phases required to complete the project and the personnel required for each phase. For example, examine the steps from the ADDIE model.

- Analysis: project manager, instructional designer
- Design: instructional designer, SME
- Development: graphic artist, media integrator, programmer
- Implementation: any team member
- Evaluation: quality assurance specialist

Step 2: Break down all phases into small tasks. Examine the different tasks in each phase of the ADDIE model.

- Analysis: needs assessment, audience analysis, lesson goals, content acquisition
- Design: lesson objectives, instruction treatment, storyboards, flowcharts
- Development: graphics, media integration, programming, supporting manuals
- Implementation: formative evaluation: alpha test, beta test
- Evaluation: summative evaluation

Step 3: Assign a time and price to each task.

Step 4: Total the time and price for all tasks.

When determining project estimates, make sure to include all project personnel, travel time and expenses for all meetings, any materials that are not included in overhead, and extra services such as printing and postage.

AN EXAMPLE

An RFP seeking the creation of a small electronic performance support tool for a process containing eight steps is received. User input is to generate automatic calculations. Built-in training and help are desired. The total program will contain approximately 30 help screens. Determine the project price.

The positions required for this project include:

- A project manager to oversee the project
- An instructional designer for analysis and the preparation of training screens
- An artist for the graphic user interface
- A programmer for calculations, navigation, and program execution
- A quality assurance person for testing

Table 14.1 illustrates the final solution for the sample problem, with the assumption that the vendor charges an average, blended rate of $600 per day.

DETERMINING PERSONNEL LABOR PRICES

The previous example used an average blended rate of $600 per day. How is this rate determined? The answer begins with finding the hourly rate for each member of the team and then summing these values.

One approach to finding a person's hourly rate is to multiply the person's hourly salary by company overhead and desired profit. For example, if an

Table 14.1 Time Required for Each Task

Time	Task
2 days	1. Designer analyzes
1 day	2. Designer creates flow chart and storyboards
2 days	3. Artist creates graphic user interface
14 days	4. Programmer creates interactions and screens
1.5 days	5. Quality assurance person tests the software
0.5 day	6. Programmer makes final changes and packages for delivery
3 days	7. Project manager oversees project

employee's salary is $41,600 a year, the cost to the employer for general overhead which includes taxes, insurance, rent, equipment purchases, etc. (usually called General and Administrative [G&A] costs) combined with the cost of employee benefits (medical coverage, dental visits, eye care) is probably about 80% ($33,280), for a total personnel cost of $74,880 per year for the employee. Since there are 2080 working hours in a year (this includes time off for vacations and holidays), then the cost per hour of that employee to the e-learning firm is about $36.

The employee cannot be billed at $36 because the firm also needs to make some type of profit. If the company wants to make a profit, it needs to add a profit margin. Profit margins in the e-learning industry range from 15 to 40%. In this case, we will add a 40% profit margin. The total billable hourly rate then becomes $50.40. This number will probably be rounded to $50. When you have decimal numbers as part of the total, the best thing to do is to round up. It provides a false sense of precision when you include numbers past the decimal point.

$$\$20 \times 1.40 \times 1.80 = \$50.40$$

The $50 is the price the client will pay per hour of e-learning development. Now all you need to do to determine the overall budget is to multiply $50 by the number of hours that the employee (or employee position) will work on the project.

A second approach for finding a person's hourly rate is to multiply by a predetermined constant instead of using company overhead and desired profit. Assuming the predetermined constant is 3.5 and the hourly rate of the employee is $20, the new hourly rate for the same person is $70 ($20 × 3.5). Also note that the desired profit increases from 40% to 94.4% (the person's cost to the company is the hourly wage multiplied by company overhead = $20 × 1.80 = $36).

$$(\text{Price} - \text{Cost})/\text{Cost} = (\$70 - \$36)/\$36 = 0.944 \times 100 = 94.4\%$$

Table 14.2 Individual Rates of Team Members

Development Team Member	Hourly Rate ($)
Project manager	160
Senior instructional designer	140
Senior Web designer	145
Graphic artist	90
Audio specialist	120
Technical specialist	95
Instructional designer	100
Programmer	105

A third approach is to know the hourly rates of the competitors and charge a lower rate. For example, suppose the lowest rate of the competition is $85 per hour. Then, by selecting a rate of $75, the bid remains below the competition and the profit margin is raised to 108.3%: ($75 – $36)/$36.

SUBMITTING THE BUDGET SECTION OF THE PROPOSAL

The budget section of the proposal will consist of several tables that summarize and support various components that affect your final bid price. Described below are sample tables that might be appropriate for inclusion, depending upon the demands of the RFP.

Development team price per hour — Sometimes the RFP will request individual hourly rates for all personnel charged to the project. Provide information as suggested in Table 14.2 only if requested. Make sure all hourly rates are personnel prices, not costs; that is, they should include overhead and profit.

If the client does not specifically ask for a different rate for each employee, you may want to use what is known as a *blended rate*. The blended rate is simply an average rate for all employees working on the project. For the example above, the blended rate would be an average of all of the hourly rates. The blended rate works out to $119.38 ($955/8) but it is usually rounded to the next highest number. In this case, it works out to $120, as shown in Table 14.3.

Price breakdown by project phases — It is often informative to separate the project price into phases as illustrated in Table 14.4. Here, one can analyze and view quickly how the budget is distributed throughout the project. Figure 7.6 in Chapter 7 illustrates how the same information can be displayed graphically in a pie chart.

Travel expenses — You may want to itemize all anticipated travel expenses. These costs can be listed separately in the budget section or included in the ap-

Table 14.3 Blended Rate Calculation

Project manager	$160
Senior instructional designer	$140
Senior Web designer	$145
Graphic artist	$90
Audio specialist	$120
Technical specialist	$95
Instructional designer	$100
Programmer	$105
Total	**$955**
Divided by 8	$119.38
Blended rate	**$120**

Table 14.4 Price Breakdown by Project Phases

Components	% of Time	Phase Price
Project management	10	$34,320
Evaluation/quality assurance	8	$13,000
Analysis	10	$29,248
Design	20	$71,044
Instructional methodology	5	$20,444
Assessment features	8	$16,330
Graphics	10	$18,500
Audio	14	$36,133
Technical issues	5	$7,063
Programming	10	$22,140

pendix of the document because they are only paid if used. Example 14.1 shows how travel expenses can be included in the budget section of your proposal.

SUMMARY

You have submitted your response to the RFP, including the budget section. What happens next? The award is made based upon one of the following criteria:

- **Lowest price** — Some clients must award the project to the lowest bidder because of specific regulatory conditions. The value of the remainder of your proposal is inconsequential. This criterion for decision may seem unfair, but it does exist. If you should have the lowest bid, congratulations, your RFP is a winner. If you do not have the lowest bid, try again with another RFP.

The section starts with a statement of total costs, nothing hidden. Other tables in this section break down the costs.

This client wanted to see expenses broken out; this proposal breaks expenses out in great detail.

Workforce is using a blended rate for pricing the proposal.

Not only is travel discussed in this section, but it is discussed in the context of the project. This is a good technique.

Response to Truckco's Request for Proposal

Project Budget

Introduction
Workforce Interactive estimates that the total price for the development of *Truckco Online* will be $452,118. This includes the development team cost for the portal, travel expenses, software, the *Truckco Online* link on existing kiosks, and Workforce Interactive's quarterly fees for the first year.

Figure 7, Travel Expense Chart, breaks expenses down by meeting, and includes travel, meals, and lodging. Total project price breakdown, Figure 8, specifies all startup costs to be incurred by Truckco. A description of the ongoing fees that Truckco will be responsible for on a monthly basis has also been included. The payment schedule, Figure 9, details all deliverables and the amount due for each. The final chart shows how Truckco can break even with this investment.

Development Team Price
Our development team price is calculated by using a blended rate of $105.00 per hour. The total number of hours for this project will be 3,863. Based on the time and resources used within Phase II, the price per hour of instruction is estimated at $27,930.

Travel Expenses
Figure 7 depicts the travel expenses for eight face-to-face meetings with Truckco in Bloomsburg, PA. At the beginning of the project, an initial trip will be scheduled. Meeting 1, the kick-off meeting, will be used for Workforce Interactive to gain a better understanding of the project and its specifications. We will also conduct small group and one-on-one meetings with truckers provided by Truckco to better understand the needs of the learner. Meeting 2 will be used to review all content for courses 1-4. A prototype will also be presented for review. This prototype will encompass lesson one, as well as the overall look and feel of the portal. Meeting 3 will be a review of content for courses 4-7. At Meetings 4 and 5, team members will review all storyboards with Truckco. These meetings will allow Truckco to see exactly what is going to be put on each page of the portal. At meetings 6 and 7 we will deliver the programming for courses 1-4 and 5-7 respectively. At this point in time, Workforce Interactive will conduct formative evaluations. The final meeting will be for final signoff and delivery of the entire portal.

Confidential 13

Example 14.1 Budget section of a proposal.

This may be more detail for travel than what is needed. This level of detail should probably go into the appendices if included at all.

However, it does also provide a nice breakdown of the development process that will be undertaken by Workforce Interactive.

Figure 7. Workforce Interactive Travel Expense Chart

	No. of People		*Travel*	*Meals*	*Lodging*	
Meeting 1 **Kick-off Meeting** **Needs Analysis/Learner Characteristics** **Small Group Meetings/ One-on-Ones**	**3**	**3 nights 4 days**	**Rental Car $188**	**$360**	**$540**	**$1,000**
Meeting 2 **SME Meeting** **Task Inventory (Courses 2-4)** **Review of prototype**	**2**	**1 night 2 days**	**Rental Car $94**	**$120**	**$120**	**$334**
Meeting 3 **SME Meeting** **Task Inventory Courses 5-7**	**2**	**1 day**	**Rental Car $47**	**$60**	**NA**	**$197**
Meeting 4 **Delivery of storyboards for courses 2-4**	**3**	**1 night 2 days**	**Rental Car $94**	**$180**	**$180**	**$454**
Meeting 5 **Delivery of storyboards for courses 5-7**	**3**	**1 night 2 days**	**Rental Car $94**	**$180**	**$180**	**$454**
Meeting 6 **Delivery of programming for courses 2-4** **Evaluation/Testing**	**3**	**4 nights 5 days**	**Rental Car $235**	**$450**	**$720**	**$1,405**
Meeting 7 **Delivery of programming for courses 5-7** **Evaluation/Testing**	**3**	**4 nights 5 days**	**Rental Car $235**	**$450**	**$720**	**$1,405**
Meeting 8 **Final sign-off and delivery of *Truckco Online***	**1**	**1 day**	**Rental Car $47**	**$30**	**NA**	**$47**
Total						**$5,294**

Project Price Breakdown
Figure 8, the Project Price Breakdown, indicates all costs to Truckco for the design and development of *Truckco Online*. Also included in this section are all ongoing costs that Truckco will be responsible for on a quarterly basis, Figure 9. In this chart, per transaction fee refers to the amount of money that will be charged to Truckco with every transaction within the Shopping Center.

Example 14.1 (continued).

This chart provides a concise breakdown of the project.

This is a nice feature providing a breakdown of ongoing quarterly costs.

It is always good to provide a payment schedule so the client understands how much they need to pay and when.

Notice there is an initial payment to start the project. Usually this is due upon signing of the contract.

Figure 8. Project Price Breakdown

Development Team Total	$405,615
Travel Expense Total	$5,294
Software **CyberCash Bundle Pack** o CashRegister o Internet Merchant Account	 $249
TOTAL	**$411,158**

Figure 9. Ongoing Quarterly Fees

Truckco Online Link on Kiosk	$2,000 (for 25 kiosks)
CyberCash o Service Fee o Monthly Statement o Per Transaction Fee	 $200 $40 $0.30*
ASP Maintenance & Hosting Fee	$8,000
TOTAL	**$10,240**

**Not included in total.*

Payment Schedule

Figure 10 displays the requested payment schedule by Workforce Interactive. Payments will be made in three installments. An initial payment of 30% of the total project price is to be delivered on May 7 at the kick-off meeting. With the completion of each of the Information and Shopping Centers payment is estimated at 25% of the total. With delivery of *Truckco Online* on February 9, 2002, the remaining balance will be due. Payment should be made within 15 days of the delivery date.

Figure 10. Payment Schedule

Deliverable	Amount Due	Percentage Total	Delivery Date
Initial Payment	$135,635	30%	05/07/01
Completion of Phase I Information Center	$113,030	25%	11/05/01
Completion of Phase III Shopping Center	$113,030	25%	12/03/01
Completion of Phase II & IV Training Center & Final Product Delivery	$90,423	20%	02/09/02

Example 14.1 (continued).

- **Best value** — The budget section of the RFP was not the lowest bid, but your proposal won anyway because your company was considered the best value and the one most likely to complete the project satisfactorily, on time, and within budget. Congratulations, your RFP was a winner.
- **Prequalification** — The client was undecided between one or more proposals. You got your foot in the door, but the client will most likely want to negotiate with you to make a final decision. Congratulations are pending; the ball is in your court to win or lose the project.

Before writing your response to the RFP, any information you can receive in advance pertaining to that RFP and the company is to your advantage. For example, knowing in advance whether the project will be awarded to the lowest price bid, the bid with best value, or a bid that potentially qualifies you for another round of negotiations will affect how you prepare your response. At best, the entire process of responding to an RFP, including the budget, remains an arduous task with no guarantees for return on investment, but is one of the primary ways of obtaining new and repeat business.

■ ■ ■

VALUE VS. PRICE

The value of an e-learning project is the return it provides to the client regardless of the price. When you present your budget you want the client to understand that you are providing a high-value product for a fair price. Regardless of the amount of your budget, you want to focus on the value it will bring to the client, not how high it seems. Clients usually want to purchase products and services when they perceive value — your job is to present the budget in such a way that the client is convinced of the value of your solution.

You can show value to clients by pointing out the advantages of your solution as you describe what they will receive for their money. You want to explain cost savings, operating efficiencies, the costs of nonaction, and the multitude of advantages that your solution offers. If the perceived amount of benefit is high, the likelihood of your solution being chosen becomes higher. Do not assume that clients knows all of the potential benefits because they issued the RFP. You must take the time to remind them of the value of your solution to their e-learning problem.

A good way to show value is to compare your option with another, more expensive, option. The more expensive option could be the client's traditional method of providing the training or could be another e-learning method.

For example, you could include a chart comparing the cost of hosting the e-learning courses on the client's internal server vs. having you host the courses on your server and supplying the client with logons for all of the employees.

■ ■ ■

SUCCESSFULLY PRICING AN E-LEARNING SOLUTION

Maria Plano, Manager of E-Learning Solutions, Latitude360, a division of RWD Technologies

Successfully pricing an e-learning solution is a challenging task. The industry is young, the market is competitive, clients (and even some vendors) are sometimes uneducated about the effort required to do the job, and expectations of what the end product will be are often unclear. So can it be done? I have learned from pricing and managing many e-learning projects (and from working with some of the best minds in the business) that it can — even without a panic as the proposal goes out the door.

The goal is to identify a price that is fair to your client, profitable to your organization, and competitive enough to win the work. No rocket science there. But often the information needed to arrive at such a price (information such as requirements and design ideas) does not exist because clients hope to be able to work with their e-learning vendor to figure that out. Ideally, your pricing system will allow you to come to an accurate price quickly if you know the requirements, and to provide clients with a clear set of options and costs if you do not.

This vignette discusses one system that has worked for my company. This system is based on classifying an e-learning course on a scale that includes two major factors — the state of the content that will comprise the course and the level of multimedia and interactivity that will be required to accomplish the learning objectives. Each course is evaluated to determine where it falls on this scale and, therefore, the price range required for development.

First, the course is evaluated from an instructional design and content perspective. Courses fall into one of three categories:

- Low instructional design effort
- Moderate instructional design effort
- High instructional design effort

Where a course falls on this scale is based on several factors, including:

- Whether or not a course currently exists, including goals and objectives, instructional strategies, etc.
- Extent to which content — what an instructor would say when teaching (whether in a course or another format) — is documented

- Extent to which questions, interactions, and feedback have been designed and written
- Whether or not a reusable learning objects strategy will be employed

Clearly, evaluating into which category a potential course fits is not an exact science. However, the examples below provide a framework for the level of effort that would coincide with each category.

LOW/NO INSTRUCTIONAL DESIGN EFFORT

- Instructional objectives have been written
- A course outline has been created — chunking and sequencing of content is complete
- Text has been written as it should appear on the screen
- Instructional interactions and tests or other evaluation items, including feedback, have been designed and written

MODERATE INSTRUCTIONAL DESIGN EFFORT

- A course exists
- Course goals and objectives have been identified
- Instructional strategies for instructor-led training have been developed, but need to be modified for application in an e-learning environment
- Documentation that describes what an instructor would say when covering each topic can be provided
- Documentation is largely up-to-date, but needs to be tweaked in places

HIGH INSTRUCTIONAL DESIGN EFFORT

- No course or content exists in any form
- Course goals and objectives as well as evaluation and instructional strategies must be developed
- Course content must be captured via interviews with subject matter experts

Once the required level of instructional design has been determined, a similar evaluation is then completed from the perspective of multimedia and Web development. Within this area, the following factors should be considered:

- Complexity of interactions required to support and reinforce learning
- Frequency of interactions required to maintain learner interest and reinforce concepts
- Extent to which templates can be created for interactions and therefore reused throughout the instruction

- Level of media (animation, audio, video) required to communicate information and keep learners' attention
- Extent to which complex graphics need to be developed to illustrate concepts

Again, it is difficult to be exact. Multimedia and Web development effort is most easily defined using metrics, such as number of questions and interactions, minutes of audio, and number of pages. However, to avoid being too simplistic, these metrics should be used to give clients a general idea of what they will be getting and to protect against scope creep rather than count exactly. The examples below provide general guidelines for qualifying effort in this area.

LOW MULTIMEDIA/WEB DEVELOPMENT EFFORT

- Finished course will include pages of text and a navigation framework with very little interactivity (fewer than 8 interactions per hour per 40 pages of courseware)
- Interactions that are included are simple, such as rollovers, multiple choice questions, and pop-up boxes, and are based on a set of templates that will not be modified
- Feedback for questions is simple, including the answer and a text explanation
- Navigation through the courseware is linear
- No media, such as animation, audio, or video, is included
- Stock graphics can be used and custom graphics are not needed

MODERATE MULTIMEDIA/WEB DEVELOPMENT EFFORT

- Finished course will include pages of text and a navigation framework with a moderate level of interactivity (interactions every three to four pages)
- Interactions that will be included per hour per 40 pages of courseware are:
  - Ten basic interactions such as rollovers, pop-ups, and multiple choice questions that are developed from templates that will not be modified
  - Two to three complex, custom interactions such as matching, drag/drop, simulations, and games
- Navigation may be linear or exploratory
- Audio and animation are used at key points throughout the course, including narrated screens and a static character for introductions and summaries
- A few custom graphics are required

HIGH MULTIMEDIA/WEB DEVELOPMENT EFFORT

- Finished course will include pages of text and a navigation framework with a high level of interactivity (interactions every one to two pages)
- Interactions that will be included per hour per 40 pages of courseware are:
  - Fifteen basic interactions such as rollovers, pop-ups, and multiple choice questions that can be developed from templates, but may be modified as necessary
  - Three to four complex, custom interactions such as simulations and games
- Navigation may be linear or exploratory, including branching
- Audio, video, and animation will be used frequently throughout the course — potentially with narrated screens and video or a three-dimensional character for introductions, summaries, and explanations of complex concepts
- Several custom graphics will be developed

Determining the level of instructional design and Web/multimedia effort required to develop a particular course allows you to identify your costs, based on the various skill sets needed. These costs, along with the labor markups that your company deems appropriate, will comprise the bulk of your pricing. Table 14.5 is one way of summarizing the various levels that exist and the pricing that results.

A pricing matrix such as this one is useful both for identifying pricing to submit in a proposal and for explaining the elements that comprise pricing to clients. This version includes large ranges within each category, and is based on standard industry numbers. However, there are several factors that will push the price up or down within or outside the range for a particular vendor and/or project.

For a particular vendor, competitive advantages such as experienced project teams, strong project management, well-defined methodologies, and a well-developed code base can translate into a better value per hour for clients (not to mention profitable projects for the vendor). Specific price ranges within each category must be determined by individual vendors based on the effort hours and billable rates/labor markups with which they are comfortable.

Within a particular project, a vendor may want to include additional costs in a proposal if the project is the client's first foray into e-learning, a learning objects model is designed, there is an extremely tight schedule, integration with a new learning management system is required, or other complex technical requirements exist. Conversely, costs may be reduced if clients provide media such as video and graphics or other significant inputs to the project.

Any e-learning professional will tell you that many variables can impact the price of an e-learning solution, and that these variables can cause two qualified vendors to come to vastly different prices. The key is to find a pricing system that

Table 14.5 E-Learning Pricing Matrix

ISD Development Level		Web/Media Development Level: Low	Web/Media Development Level: Medium	Web/Media Development Level: High
	High	$30-35K	$35-40K	$40-60K
	Medium	$20-25K	$20-35K	$35-40K
	Low	$10-15K	$20-25K	$30-35K

works well for you and your organization by reliably generating projects that are priced competitively, yet profitably.

■ ■ ■

WHAT SHOULD BE IN THIS SECTION

The best method for presenting the budget has been argued about for years. Some people believe that you should not provide the client with a total — let the client add it up. The belief is that the number will seem smaller. Others believe that you should include one initial low price and then add on other items to slowly increase the price but still not show a grand total. The problem with both of these approaches is that the client feels deceived. Remember, the client is trying to eliminate possible vendors as well as choose a desired vendor. If you seem too sneaky, you will be eliminated.

It is far better to be honest with the client and give a variety of choices rather than try to win the proposal and then sneak in additional high-priced items. In today's business environment, you want to gain a client for life. It is far less expensive to obtain repeat business from a client than to try to get new clients. Also, the e-learning industry is not that big. If your firm gains a bad reputation, it may be unable to shake it.

Provide the client with a total for the project or, if you provide several options, give multiple totals. Do not make the client pull out a calculator to determine how much your solution is going to cost. Also, make sure you do not forget to mention any ongoing costs. Clients have been burned in the past because they

Table 14.6 Budget Showing Hardware and Software Prices Listed Separately

Item	Price
Hardware (server)	$10,000
Software	
▪ LMS ($45 per user × 5000 users)	$225,000
▪ Content development system (1)	$25,000
▪ SCORM plug-in	$50,000
Implementation/training	$60,000
Travel/lodging	$2,000
Total	**$372,000**

Table 14.7 Budget Showing Price by Deliverable

Deliverable	Date	Amount ($)
Needs assessment document	08/02/02	29,400
Course content outline	09/27/02	10,730
Flow chart and storyboards	10/18/02	37,890
E-learning prototype	11/01/02	70,000
Finished e-learning course delivered	11/29/02	90,000
Total		**238,020**

have forgotten to ask about ongoing costs and are shocked to see a bill arrive a year after they purchased the e-learning software. Be very clear about what ongoing costs are going to be and the likelihood of increases or changes in those costs. This includes ongoing licensing fees for any third-party software you may be proposing.

A good method of clearly explaining all of the costs to the client is to divide the budget into sections. You may want to have sections for hardware, software, licensing fees, product development, and implementation. Table 14.6 illustrates a breakdown of what the client is paying for each item.

An alternative to this method is to show the price by deliverable. This is traditionally done with a chart showing deliverables in one column, due date in another, and price in a third. This allows clients to see what they are paying, how much they must pay, and when payment is due (illustrated in Table 14.7).

The previously mentioned method is effective because it also provides a built-in payment schedule. Clients know how much they need to pay and when. Do not forget to include a payment schedule so clients know how to budget their money for the e-learning project. It is also good to let clients know the terms of payment for your firm (i.e., net 30 days).

Table 14.8 Budget with Options

Project Item	Solution with Kiosks	Solution without Kiosks
E-learning course development	$421,200	$448,200
Travel costs	$4,380	$5,093
Hardware/software	$195,000	$80,000
Total	**$620,580**	**$533,293**

Another effective method is to provide a couple of options and let the client decide which is most advantageous. This is sometimes called a *tiered pricing* approach. Since potential clients usually do not reveal their budget, a tiered pricing approach allows you to fit within their budget even if you have no idea of the size of their budget. If you provide a broad enough range, you can usually hit the client's budget. The more options you provide, the higher your chances of hitting the budget.

Table 14.8 shows two options, although you can show as many options as are needed. The multiple options technique is commonly used with support contracts as well as features for an LCMS. With this type of budget presentation, each option or added functionality is shown with its associated price increase. It allows the client to compare the price of different options.

A method of helping the client to see the value of your solution is to break down the budget and present the elements of the project in smaller chunks. For example, you can show the price per screen, client employee, hour of developed instruction, or objective. It is advantageous to explain that the price per employee is only $45 a year rather than concentrating on the price tag of $45,000 for training 1000 employees. Example 14.1 illustrates a sample budget.

ADHERENCE TO BUDGET

You may want to include a paragraph or two concerning efforts that you will use to maintain the integrity of the budget. Include wording that helps to clarify how changes in the project scope will impact the price to the client. An example paragraph follows.

> Adherence to the budget is the primary responsibility of Interactive Multimedia. We will do everything possible to ensure on-time delivery of product and adherence to the budget. If delays or rewrites occur because of ABC's requested changes outside of the scope of this proposal, ABC's project manager will be asked to prepare a Project Change Notice indicating the nature and the scope of the change. Then Inter-

active Multimedia will assign a price to that Project Change Notice. Once that price and change notice is approved, Interactive Multimedia will implement the change to the project. Interactive Multimedia will not proceed with any changes unless sign-off is received from ABC.

EXAMPLE OF INCOMPLETE BUDGET

Example 14.2 shows an inadequate budget for the project. Notice that the budget provides too little information for the busy executive who only turns to the budget page of the proposal. There really is no evidence at all of value-added or any type of description of how the development process correlates to the budget.

THE BOTTOM LINE

Clients want to know they are getting value for their money. Present a clear, crisp, concise budget that indicates the value of your solution. Let the client know that your solution is cost effective. Make sure the budget is tied to the rest of the project and that it supports your e-learning solution.

This book has free materials available for download from the Web Added Value™ Resource Center at www.jrosspub.com.

Often the budget section of the proposal will be called an "investment."

Inconsistent use of decimals in presenting the numbers.

Any number ten or less should be spelled out as a word.

No explanation of what will be done during customization is given with this budget. What is the project manager doing for 160 hours? Development is only 200 hours?

Reader has to figure out that the 15% is $12,750.

Gives LCMS maintenance charge as yearly fee and merchant service as monthly.

Investment Analysis

LCMS System License Pricing		
LCMS License	**$85,000 × 1**	**$85,000.00**
Development Seats	**$3600 × 2**	**$7,200.00**
Training on LCMS	**$2000 × 5**	**$10,000.00**
ECommerce Elements	**$5,000**	**5,000.00**
Subtotal		**$107, 200.00**

Notes:

1. *1 development seat is included with the LCMS license*
2. *2 Training is 5 days at our location.*
3. *ECommerce fee is Merchant set up fees. Refer to Appendix D for transaction charges.*

Professional Services Fees		
Site Customization and	**200 hours × $150/hr**	**$30,000.00**
Development	**200 hours × $150/hr**	**$30,000.00**
Chat Software	**$12,000**	**$12,000.00**
Project Management	**160 hours × $150**	**$24,000.00**
Subtotal		**$66,000.00**

Notes:

1. *Site customization beyond 200 hours would be in addition to project scope as quoted here.*
2. *Chat Software has real time chat rooms for 100 users with event moderation for instructor/student mentoring. Unlimited license for asynchronous classroom and message board is also included in this price.*

Grand Total **$173,200.00**

Special Notice 1: Annual LCMS software maintenance charge is 15% of license fee is required after year #1 for version upgrades and support.

Special Notice 2: Monthly Merchant Service Maintenance of $200 per month applies.

Example 14.2 Inadequately explained budget.

15

CALCULATING RETURN ON INVESTMENT

Nancy Vasta, CIGNA Corporation

INTRODUCTION

Business clients for e-learning initiatives are demanding return on investment (ROI) analysis. They want the vendor to provide a "business case" that they can then turn around and show to management. Clients want you to provide an ROI analysis based on whatever information they are able to provide.

The e-learning industry has responded with various ROI calculation methods that focus on delivery cost savings of e-learning vs. traditional instructor-led training. While this approach is adequate for a quick and dirty ROI, it ignores what clients are most interested in — the benefits of improving employee performance.

Popular measures such as reduced travel costs and participant time spent on training demonstrate that e-learning is a cost-effective method for delivery when compared to instructor-led training. But does the e-learning event result in increased employee performance? When writing a proposal, you want to focus on performance-related ROI and the methods for calculating the results if you can get the numbers from the client. Focusing on performance rather than cost avoidance creates a powerful business case for your e-learning solution as opposed to one centered totally on cost savings or avoidance.

WHY THIS SECTION IS NEEDED

When selling e-learning to clients, one effective method is to develop an ROI business case. Show clients how much money they would make with your solution in place. Traditionally, e-learning is sold as a method of cost avoidance or cost savings. Clients are told that if they buy e-learning, they will save thousands or millions in travel expenses. While that method is effective for showing costs savings, it is not really a return on an investment. To show a return, you need to show how e-learning can bring money to the bottom line of the client's organization.

If you can get good numbers from your potential client, you can make a strong case for e-learning when you can show impact on the bottom line. While an ROI section is typically not a requirement of an e-learning proposal, it is always a good idea to include a section like this to bolster your case for e-learning and to help sell your solution to your client. Positive numbers tend to encourage clients to invest in an e-learning solution.

ROI DEFINED

A review of common terms and calculations is needed prior to discussing ROI measurement for e-learning. ROI is defined as evaluating an initiative's benefit compared to the cost. Table 15.1 provides common formulas for calculating ROI. For example, assume that Project X costs $10 and yields a benefit of $100. The formulas in Table 15.1 can be used to provide ROI measurements for this scenario:

- **Net Benefit of $90** — The project yielded $90 in benefits after considering cost.
- **Benefit Cost Ratio of $10** — The project yielded $10 for every dollar invested.
- **900% ROI** — The project yielded $9 for every dollar invested when considering cost.

Unfortunately, measuring ROI for e-learning initiatives will not be so simple. Following is a list of considerations when calculating ROI for an e-learning initiative.

- **Understand the client's ROI methodology** — Ask the client how ROI has been measured for other projects of similar size and scope. Discuss how the client organization tracks costs and employee productivity relative to e-learning projects. Ensure that the ROI portion of the proposal is structured based on the client's needs and using the client's terminology.
- **Be practical** — Limited time and resources will require a practical approach to measuring ROI. Make assumptions and validate your assump-

Table 15.1 Common Formulas for Calculating ROI

ROI Formula	Calculation
Net Benefit Demonstrates the benefit after considering the cost	Net Benefit = Benefit – Cost
Benefit Cost Ratio (BCR) Demonstrates the return for every dollar invested	BCR = Benefits / Costs
ROI% Demonstrates the percentage of return for every dollar invested when considering cost	ROI% = (Net Benefits / Cost) × 100

tions with the client. In most cases, you will not have the time or extra resources to form control groups and isolate variables, especially during the E-BAP. Clients are looking for possible performance data based on your estimated impact of the e-learning initiative.

- **Be honest** — Will the e-learning initiative meet the client's need and will it be cost effective? If not, winning the contract and not delivering on the promise can be harmful for the client and your firm.

To demonstrate value to potential clients, you need to determine ROI for e-learning initiatives by determining costs, benefits, and improved employee performance and then calculating ROI. You also need to determine how best to structure the ROI information in your proposal.

WHAT SHOULD BE IN THIS SECTION

Measuring costs for any learning project is done by adding all of the direct and indirect costs associated with the project from the assessment through implementation. There is not a single formula to estimate costs for e-learning initiatives. Each organization and project is unique and the cost drivers will vary based on complexity and scope of the initiative.

Table 15.2 outlines common costs associated with e-learning initiatives. All items may not be applicable and additional items may be required for a specific client or e-learning project. The specific cost for each item is dependent on the vendor's proposed solution.

CALCULATING THE BENEFITS OF E-LEARNING INITIATIVES

The industry has overemphasized delivery benefits associated with e-learning and has almost completely ignored the primary goal of e-learning, which is to

Table 15.2 Common Costs Associated with E-Learning Initiatives

Vendor resources People resources provided by the vendor	■ Account/project manager ■ Instructional designer ■ Programmer/developer ■ Graphic artist ■ Quality assurance analyst ■ Flat rate (average hourly rate per resource) ■ LMS implementation resources
Client resources People resources to implement the project	■ Project manager and content expert(s) ■ IT representative(s)
Infrastructure Tools and technology to deliver e-learning	■ Personal computers ■ Software ■ Servers
Pricing model Pricing methodology on learner usage	■ Unlimited number of learners and usage ■ Per seat ■ Unlimited usage by learner ■ Per course ■ Pay as you go
Miscellaneous	■ Travel for team member meetings ■ Technical/services support

increase employee performance. Measuring benefits associated with e-learning efforts should focus on increased employee productivity.

The following scenario demonstrates how measuring e-learning ROI based on delivery cost saving does not address the primary needs of a client. Assume that a sales organization has sent an RFP to implement an e-learning initiative to improve the performance of sales representatives. Through a quick needs assessment you determine that lack of skill/knowledge is the cause of the poor performance and that a technology-based learning solution is appropriate. You recommend an e-learning solution and use cost saving in delivery as the criterion for demonstrating an ROI. By leveraging technology you can reduce travel costs, the need for trainers, and the amount of time the customer service representatives spend away from the job. Does this approach focus on the client's primary concern? No, reduced training delivery costs does not represent improved sales performance.

So how do you measure the impact of e-learning on employee performance? Performance metrics established by the client provide a tangible method for evaluating the e-learning initiative impact on actual performance. Performance metrics

Table 15.3 Question to Determine E-Learning Benefits

Benefit Type	Questions to Establish Performance Metrics
Improved employee productivity	■ How is employee performance measured? ■ What are the current performance levels for these measurements? ■ What are the performance measurement goals after the e-learning initiative? ■ How can the performance improvements be quantified into bottom line savings?
Improved quality	■ How is quality defined and measured? ■ What are the current quality levels and projected quality levels after the e-learning initiative? ■ How does improved quality relate to business results?
Improved customer satisfaction	■ How is customer satisfaction defined and measured? ■ What are the current customer satisfaction ratings and projected ratings after the e-learning initiative? ■ How does improved customer satisfaction relate to business results?

are measurements that quantify employee performance. It is vital to establish a core set of performance metrics that are objective and reported on regularly. By comparing the performance metrics before and after e-learning, you can calculate the impact learning has on actual performance.

Of course there are variables outside of the e-learning initiative that can impact the change in performance. In this case you will need to either make assumptions or conduct further research using a control group. The recommendation is to be practical and outline these assumptions with your client. Again, detailed research will require additional time and resources that are most likely not available. Table 15.3 outlines questions you can ask your clients to determine various types of benefits they may receive from your e-learning solution.

By asking your client these questions, you can determine the potential benefits of the project. You can then quantify those benefits and use them to calculate the ROI for your client's e-learning project.

EXAMPLE OF DETERMINING ROI FOR A CLIENT

A major call center sends an RFP for an e-learning solution to improve the performance of 8000 customer service representatives by consistently training the entire population on how to use the company's call tracking system.

A high-level needs assessment indicates that lack of skill/knowledge is the cause of poor performance and that a technology-based solution is appropriate. You estimate that the project will cost $1,400,000. The challenge is to perform an

ROI analysis based on productivity improvements measured through performance metrics.

How would you work with the client to establish performance metrics to measure productivity? The measurements may already exist or you may have to work with the client to generate new performance metrics to adequately measure the desired performance. You must work with your sponsor to establish a core set of performance metrics that are objective and reported on regularly.

The client indicates that call center representatives are evaluated on the following performance metrics:

- **Average time spent per call** — The average time it takes to answer a single call
- **Average hold time per caller** — Average time a caller spends on hold
- **First call resolution** — Frequency of caller issues being resolved during the first call
- **Customer satisfaction scores** — Caller satisfaction with service received

After selecting the appropriate performance metrics, you need to determine how the e-learning effort will improve performance by outlining the goals. Then you must calculate how the increased performance will have a direct impact on business. This will require access to hard data and well-educated assumptions.

DISPLAYING THE RESULTS

Here are the results of calculating ROI based on increased employee productivity measured through performance metrics. Tables 15.4, 15.5, and 15.6 outline the project cost, benefits associated with productivity improvements measured using performance metrics, and ROI calculations using the definitions discussed earlier. Table 15.4 shows the costs associated with the customer service e-learning initiative.

It is important to let the client know what types of metrics were used to determine the ROI and what the expected goals are after the e-learning. Table 15.5 provides an example of an effective layout for displaying that type of information. It is also important to note that some results are simply not quantifiable or the information is proprietary and not provided by the client in the RFP phase. However, it is a good idea to show clients how you developed the ROI so they can plug in their own numbers to do their own calculations.

Table 15.6 displays a good method of showing clients various ways of determining their ROI and the different formulas used. Clients may be unfamiliar with ROI calculations for e-learning programs and may need some education within the proposal. Showing calculations and formulas helps to educate the client on the ROI formulas you used to arrive at your ROI figures.

Table 15.4 Costs Associated with an E-Learning Initiative

E-Learning Cost		
Intervention	**Calculation Description**	**Total**
Call tracking system	Course development	700,000
	Hosting fees	75,000
	Per-seat fees	400,000
	Implementation support	50,000
	PC hardware upgrade	100,000
	Client resources	75,000
		TOTAL COST = $1,400,000

Table 15.5 E-Learning Benefits Based on Performance Metrics

Calculating Benefit Associated with Productivity Improvements Measured Using Performance Metrics			
Metric	**Current Performance**	**Performance Goals after E-Learning**	**Benefit Calculations with Assumptions**
Average time spent per call	300 sec	240 sec	20% increased productivity. Results in a minimal reduction in staff by 5% or 400 employees. Each employee earns an average of $25,000 per year. 400 × 25,000 = **$10,000,000**
Average hold time per call	20 sec	15 sec	Reduction in phone costs. Approximate phone fee of $1,500,000 reduced by 25%. $1,500,000 × 0.25 = **$375,000**
First call resolution	85%	90%	Reduce the number of repeat calls, resulting in improved customer satisfaction. **Nonquantifiable**
Customer satisfaction scores	75%	90%	Improved customer satisfaction while reducing staffing levels. **Nonquantifiable**
			Total Benefits from Increased Performance = $10,375,000

Table 15.6 ROI Formulas and Resulting Calculations

ROI Calculations		
Method	**Description and and Calculation**	**ROI**
Net Benefit (NB)	Compares benefits to cost of the initiative. NB = Benefit – Cost	10,375,000 – 1,400,000 = **$8,975,000 Net Benefit**
Benefit Cost Ratio (BCR)	Ratio for benefit returned for each dollar invested. BCR = Benefits / Costs	10,375,000 / 1,400,000 = **7.41 Benefit Cost Ratio**
ROI%	Percent in net benefits for every dollar invested. ROI% = (NB / Cost) × 100	(8,975,000 / 1,400,000) × 100 = **641% ROI**

PRESENTATION OF ROI IN THE PROPOSAL

Customize the ROI section of the proposal based on client-specific needs. Be sure to include each item outlined in the RFP and performance-based analysis. Also leverage additional insight learned through client discussions if possible.

If a client is asking for ROI measurements based solely on e-learning delivery savings (i.e., reduced travel, material duplication, etc.), be sure to include this information. Also include performance-based ROI measurements which can be leveraged as a competitive advantage by demonstrating greater returns and further differentiating your solution from other vendor proposals.

Use the tables presented in this chapter as a starting point and customize the formatting and verbiage based on client requirements outlined in the RFP.

THE BOTTOM LINE

This chapter demonstrated how to calculate ROI for e-learning initiatives based on increased employee productivity measured by performance metrics established by the client. This methodology addresses the client's primary goal of delivering learning solutions that improve business results.

Performance-focused ROI provides a tangible method to demonstrate significant returns. When estimating ROI for a proposal, remember to understand the client's ROI methodology, be practical and agree to ROI methods, and be honest. When designed and implemented appropriately, e-learning is a powerful tool that improves employee productivity. Effective ROI measurements can demonstrate the results.

16

CORPORATE CAPABILITIES

INTRODUCTION

It is one thing to provide a good plan and a good idea; it is quite another to execute the plan successfully. After reading the other sections of the proposal, clients want to know: "Can this firm really do this work, with this budget and this timeline? How are they going to staff this project? What work have they successfully completed that is similar to our e-learning project?" Few clients want to be a vendor's first e-learning project.

With literally hundreds of e-learning firms competing for business, clients want to know about your company's past performance, past clients, and relevant projects. You need to supply this information in the *Corporate Capabilities* section.

WHY THIS SECTION IS NEEDED

This section of the proposal provides the client with information regarding the stability of your company, its ability to perform the work, and the level of expertise it can bring to the project. The corporate capabilities section provides prospective clients with a certain degree of comfort and assurance. This section tells the client what your firm has done in the past and what it is capable of doing in the future. In short, this section tells the client you are reputable, stable, experienced, and capable of delivering what you promised in the proposal.

WHAT SHOULD BE IN THIS SECTION

A mistake many vendors make with this section is to use standardized material for every single proposal, called *boilerplate* material. To truly gain a competitive advantage, it is much better to tailor your corporate capabilities to match the needs of a particular client and to support your capture strategy rather than use boilerplate material. Corporations can be understood on a variety of levels and presented from a variety of perspectives. Take advantage of the perspective that best suits the particular client and proposal.

In some cases, you may want to highlight the history your firm has within a particular industry such as pharmaceuticals. Other times, it makes more sense to discuss the type of project work you have done in the past such as leadership training.

For clients concerned about stability, you may want to discuss your history as a vendor in the field of instructional design or your strong financial backing. If clients are interested in prestige, you may want to "name-drop" Fortune 500 clients for whom you have worked in the past.

Each of these different perspectives requires a slightly different slant on your corporate capabilities section and each can provide you with an advantage over vendors that simply use boilerplate materials in this section. Yes, it is easier to use boilerplate material but it is not as effective. If you really want to win the business, you need to make the effort to highlight the various aspects of your firm's capabilities as they relate to a specific client.

The corporate capabilities section can be laid out in a variety of formats with a variety of names. Each section detailing corporate capabilities should contain information on the following:

- Development team/staffing
- History of the organization
- Similar past/ongoing projects
- High-profile clients

DEVELOPMENT TEAM/STAFFING

This section contains a profile of the team that will be working on the project. It usually starts with an overview of the team and then continues with a brief summary of the number of years of experience the team has had working within the industry. Sample overview paragraphs follow.

> The core project team selected for this e-learning course development assignment has been working together for over three years. Each member of the core team will work through the entire length of the project. From time to time, additional personnel such as junior level instruc-

> tional designers, graphic designers, Web designers, database administrators, and quality assurance specialists will work with the core team to assure a top-quality product.
>
> SDI employs a competent staff of designers and programmers who utilize the most recent advances in their respective fields. The team selected to answer Truckco's challenge has created eight products for various transportation companies.

After the overall team composition and dynamics are discussed, a brief profile of each team member explaining what he or she will be doing for this particular project is presented. It is important to explain how each member contributes to this particular e-learning project. Provide a summary of the years of experience in projects related to the one in the proposal and the team's experience with similar content. Additional details about each person and his or her job history should be contained on the resumes in the appendix.

HISTORY OF THE ORGANIZATION

Clients want a good "story" behind an e-learning firm. They need to be able to identify with how the firm came into existence and why it is focused on e-learning. The corporate history section should provide a good story and information about the direction and vision of the firm.

The history section of the organization should be designed to show stability, future potential for growth, and a strong focus on clients. This can be accomplished by explaining when and how the company was founded and by highlighting major milestones in the life of the company. Take the opportunity to highlight major clients, special projects, and any products that have been developed along the way.

If there are mergers or acquisitions in the history of the firm, you need to explain the purpose of the merger or acquisition and how it has benefited the firm.

SIMILAR PAST/ONGOING PROJECTS

A particularly strong selling point is to present the fact that you have successfully completed similar e-learning projects. Some vendors simply attach a listing of every single project they have ever completed. This is not appropriate. If you do that you are forcing clients to wade through information to find what may be relevant to them and, during the process, they may find information they do not like. For instance, they may notice a large number of projects in a field that has nothing to do with their industry. Instead, provide a "select" list of projects that are relevant in scope, content, or functionality to the project you are currently proposing. Carefully explain to clients how the projects you have selected are relevant to them and their projects.

HIGH-PROFILE CLIENTS

Name-dropping works in social circles and it works in the field of e-learning. If you can land a big-name client, it helps to use that client's name in proposals. People like to know that some due diligence has gone into investigating your firm and assume that a big-name client means that you have been thoroughly investigated.

In most cases, big firms do not do more due diligence than small or medium firms, but the perception is that they do. Therefore, when a large client or many large clients are associated with your firm, it adds credibility. If you have some big names on your client list, do not be afraid to use them (unless, of course, they expressly forbid you to use their names).

You can even use clients that have big organizations but not big names. For instance, one company worked for the Pennsylvania Department of Public Welfare, which had over 8000 employees to train. While not everyone thinks of the Pennsylvania Department of Public Welfare as a major organization, its training needs are not very different from the needs of other large organizations. Example 16.1 illustrates a typical *Corporate Capabilities* document.

THE BOTTOM LINE

Clients want to know with whom they are dealing. They want a firm with a good reputation, strong experience in the industry, and the ability to successfully complete the project. To achieve these goals, your corporate capabilities section should accomplish the following:

- Establish your firm's credibility.
- Show the client that you have the expertise to complete the project on time and within budget.
- Highlight the talent in your organization and position it as unique.
- Provide information on similar projects you have done in the past or are currently developing.
- Show samples of past work efforts.
- Sell the client on your capabilities and e-learning acumen.

This book has free materials available for download from the Web Added Value™ Resource Center at www.jrosspub.com.

Provides information on how the firm was founded. Shows growth over time.

Response to Truckco's Request for Proposal

Corporate Capabilities

Founded by Jack McClain in 1988, Workforce Interactive has grown from a small office in Alexandria, VA, to a company employing over 75 people with sales associates throughout the U.S. During the 1980s, as Vice President of Human Resources at L&W Trucking, McClain saw a decline in the size of his training department due to downsizing and reorganization of the company. He realized the opportunity to become an external provider of a variety of training to the trucking industry. His next step was to open Workforce Interactive and provide multimedia training to the trucking industry.

Company History

1988 - Jack McClain started his company by providing various instructor-led training seminars for truck drivers.

Explains acquisitions and shows milestones in the life of the firm.

1992 - The company's services expanded to provide performance-based training solutions for all workers in the trucking industry, such as accounting, dispatcher training, and managerial skills training.

1995 - In 1995, Workforce Interactive acquired EduInteractive, a small multimedia-based training company located in Alexandria, VA, to meet the demands of the growing distance learning market.

1997 - Workforce Interactive developed *R-Express*, a customized training solution for Roadcarry Express in 1997. *R-Express* is an intranet-based training and orientation program covering key policies, procedures, and safety rules. The program replaced a half-day instructor-led seminar.

Mention the receipt of industry awards.

1998 - As a result of efforts with Roadcarry Express, Workforce Interactive was given the ***Distinguished Contribution to Workplace Learning and Performance Award*** by the American Society for Training and Development (ASTD).

2000 – Our Learning Management System was developed to create efficient and effective learner-focused instruction. Our first web portal was developed for Tewel Corporation.

2001 - McClain continues to lead the organization in developing learning solutions for the workforce. His Research & Development team in Alexandria is currently investigating a partnership with the National Private Truck Council (NPTC) to launch several online courses targeted at fleet managers.

Explains how project team works and is selected for the project. Also indicates the amount of time the team has spent working together.

Workforce Interactive's Project Team

The Vice President for Development, Jeffrey Waters, selects each team member and appoints a project manager for all design and development teams. Waters looks at participation in past projects as well as the dynamics of the team members. He strives to create a cohesive team that stimulates creativity and effective production.

The core project team selected for *Truckco Online* has been working together since 1995. Each member of the core team will work throughout the entire length of the project. From time to time, additional Workforce Interactive personnel, such as additional instructional designers, graphic designers, web designers, database administrators, and a quality assurance specialist, will join the core team.

Confidential 16

Example 16.1 *Corporate Capabilities* section of an e-learning proposal.

Each team member is introduced and his or her role is explained.

Response to Truckco's Request for Proposal

Key Project Members
(Refer to Appendix E for Core Project Team Member Résumés)

Beth Bridgette, Project Manager: Beth has worked in multimedia project management for 6 years and the instructional technology field for over 13 years. She is responsible for coordinating team members and acting as liaison between the designers, developers, multimedia specialists, technical specialists, and quality assurance teams. She manages daily development responsibilities and works with the client and Workforce Interactive team members to meet final deliverables. Beth is also responsible for development of budgets and deadlines schedules.

Nancy Kapp, Senior Instructional Designer: Nancy brings 10 years of experience to Workforce Interactive and leads our team of instructional designers who create high-quality and effective training materials. She is responsible for developing instructional strategies, doing skills and task analyses, and working with subject matter experts, course developers, and client representatives to produce customized training programs and related materials. She was also responsible for the implementation of our Learning Management System designed to create learner-focused, training in an effective and efficient manner.

Peter Jones, Senior Web Developer: Peter has 11 years of experience in developing and implementing the technical approach in the creation of custom computer- and web-based learning solutions. His expertise is in authoring and programming of high-level instructional code, models, templates, and engines. He also assists in the development, testing, and implementation of programming/authoring process improvements and quality standards.

Bridget Smith, Senior Multimedia Specialist: Bridget is responsible for recommending and brainstorming the creative approach on projects. She has 12 years experience in designing and developing computer-based and web-based screen interfaces, 2D and 3D computer illustrations and graphical elements, Internet/intranet web pages, and multimedia presentations.

Describes how long the members have been working for the company as well as describing work with past clients. Includes the names of large clients.

Related Experience
All members of this project team have been at Workforce Interactive since 1995. They have collaborated on numerous projects including the award-winning *R-Express* intranet-based training and orientation program. This team also created web-based training for truck drivers at Hone Trucking Company, located in Harrisburg, Pennsylvania. A trucking resource center was developed, which operates five truck stops across Ohio, Indiana, and Pennsylvania. The project was initially deployed in one kiosk at their Emlenton, Pennsylvania location and has since been successfully implemented in their other locations.

Workforce Interactive has successfully developed web-based learning solutions, CD-ROM training, instructor-led seminars, kiosk-based instruction, e-commerce portals, and standardized courseware for numerous companies. (See Appendix F for a detailed description of these related projects.)

Confidential 17

Example 16.1 (continued).

17

THE APPENDIX

INTRODUCTION

The body of the proposal should be easy to read, allowing the client to quickly move from section to section. Excessive detail slows the reader, causes confusion, and dilutes your point. On the other hand, detailed explanations of certain information could be essential to your winning the e-learning business. Often detailed information is necessary to support your capture strategy and verify your services. To balance the need for detail with the need for an easy-to-read document, detailed information should be placed at the end of your proposal in an *Appendix*.

WHY THIS SECTION IS NEEDED

This section of the proposal is a "catchall" for any miscellaneous details required for support of your solution. The appendix is where you can provide details about ROI information, project timeline breakdown, hardware or software specifications, corporate policies, press releases, storyboards, or sample screen captures. This is where you place the intricate details of your solution.

In addition, the appendix should support your capture strategy. If you are emphasizing quality, include copies of your quality control forms. If you are emphasizing innovation, include a list of innovation awards. If you are highlighting partnerships with other vendors, include supporting letters.

WHAT SHOULD BE IN THIS SECTION

While a variety of material can be contained within an appendix, typically it includes one or more of the following items: resumes of the project team, letters of recommendation from satisfied customers, letters of support from partners, quality control forms, corporate brochures, and other material to support your solution.

PROJECT TEAM RESUMES

One of the most frequently included items in the appendix is the resume of each project team member. The resumes are usually in addition to the short description of each team member in the corporate capabilities section of the proposal. The resumes should all be the same format because they are coming from the same company and they should highlight the work that the person has done while at this e-learning company. Resumes can be any standard format, although one format that works particularly well is to have a brief summary at the top of the resume and then provide details about the career history of the individual as shown in Example 17.1.

LETTERS

Two types of letters typically appear in the appendix of an e-learning proposal. One type is from satisfied clients indicating how pleased they are with your services. These testimonial letters (as shown in Example 17.2) are an effective method of selling your services. However, before you include a letter from a satisfied client, consider the possible relationship between the satisfied client and the client you are trying to convince to buy your e-learning. Are the two organizations competitors? Will a relationship with the new client cause a conflict of interest? Can you assure your new client that none of their information will be shared with the existing client? You want to make sure that you do not raise too many questions by including the letter, especially if it is from a direct competitor.

The letter should describe the ability of your firm to complete work on time and within budget. It should explain how easy and convenient it is to work with your firm and emphasize the client-driven nature of your organization.

If a client is pleased with your work and had a good experience with your firm, ask the person if he or she would put that sentiment in writing. The person writing the letter should also be willing to serve as a reference should a prospective client want to call or e-mail for additional details.

The other type of letter often contained within the appendix is a partnership letter. This is a letter from another vendor with whom you are partnering on this e-learning project. Clients like the idea of a one-stop shop for e-learning services;

Provides brief summary of overall qualifications as a developer.

Contains career history information emphasizing work within the field that is relevant to work performed at Workforce Interactive.

Indicates the educational level of this project team member.

Describes the computer software this individual has worked with before. Shows depth of experience.

Peter Jones
Senior Web Developer
Workforce Interactive

Skills Summary

Responsible for the web development process at Workforce Interactive. Possess excellent communication and programming skills. Able to coordinate the development of LMS systems using server-side scripting. Capable of leading fellow programmers to complete projects on time and within budget. Create database-driven dynamic Internet and intranet sites, interactive forms, user environments, and dynamic interfaces.

Professional Experience

Senior Web/Multimedia Developer 1998-Present
Workforce Interactive Alexandria, VA
Create and develop client and server-side programming for interactive e-learning web sites. Responsible for overseeing junior developers and for creating programming standards within the organization.

Multimedia Developer 1996-1998
Ardent Learning, Inc. Rochester, NY
Created and maintained corporate web site in a Windows NT environment. Implemented procedures for updating both infrastructure and content of web site. Coordinated web development team to create appropriate levels of interactivity on the web site.

Junior Database Programmer 1993-1996
Megasis Computer Corporation Pittsburgh, PA
Designed, implemented, and maintained databases in MS SQL. Wrote Visual Basic scripts, coordinated and taught computer training classes for new hires, developed procedures and policies for database population and maintenance.

Education

M.S. Bloomsburg University, Bloomsburg, PA Graduation: 1993
Degree in Computer Programming and Information Systems

B.S. Rochester Institute of Technology, Rochester, NY Graduation: 1991
Computer Science, Minor in Art

Software Skills

Authoring: Authorware, Flash, Director
Graphic Programs: PhotoShop, 3D Studio Max
Relational Databases: DB2, Oracle, SQl
Operating Systems: Windows, Linux, Unix
Web Technologies: HTML, XML, DHTML, Cold Fusion, Active Server Pages
Languages: Java, C++, JavaScript
Management Systems: Saba, Docent, Revolver

Example 17.1 Resume from an e-learning proposal.

Provides address of client. If possible, get the letter on letterhead.	1000 Cascade Building Corporate Headquarters Atlanta, GA
Date should be recent (within three months)	April 14, 2002
	Workforce Interactive c/o Jack McClain, President 1325 West King Street, Suite 105 Alexandria, VA 22313
	Dear Mr. McClain:
Shows that the vendor is capable of performing quality work.	I wanted to express a sincere "thank you" to you and your employees at Workforce Interactive for the excellent e-learning product they delivered to our organization. The project is on time and on budget. The quality of the training was excellent and our employees are still raving about the on-line instruction.
Provides quantitative data, reinforces how pleased client is with services	We have estimated that the training that you have provided has reduced the amount of errors in our client invoicing by over 10% in the first 7 months since the training was placed on-line. To say the least, we are very pleased. This reduction in error rate has allowed us to shift resources from the invoicing department to other areas of the company and has saved us a tremendous amount of money.
Indicates that they would work with the vendor again.	Once again, thank you for your good work and for your team's attention to detail. We found working with Workforce Interactive to be a pleasure and we look forward to working with you on future e-learning projects.
	Sincerely, *Michael Parker* Michael Parker Director of Training

Example 17.2 Testimonial letter.

however, it is extremely difficult for any one vendor to be an expert in every aspect of e-learning. So clients understand that partnerships are formed between e-learning firms to help solve problems. Clients usually do not have a problem with a partnership as long as it is clearly explained within the body of the proposal.

For example, your firm may be the best LCMS firm but may not have any

This letter shows a high level of commitment to the project by a third-party vendor.

BrightStar
409 N. Pacific Coast Hwy, Suite 400
Redondo Beach, CA 92077

NU Training Solutions
235 PPG Place
Pittsburgh, PA 15272

Dear Mrs. Unger,

Thank you for the opportunity to work with you again to complete an on-line course catalog for Trucko.

Based on the information that you provided, we are excited about the opportunity to work with you on this request. BrightStar will provide you with the support services and skills necessary to complete our portion of the project on time and within budget. As you know, we have successfully implemented over 24 different e-learning systems and are confident we can assist you in helping your client achieve a high-quality solution.

Our highly trained staff has been briefed on the project and we have assembled a number of knowledgeable system designers to help make this project a success. Many of individuals chosen for the project team have worked with your organization before and are looking forward to working with your staff again.

With our experience in this industry, dedicated team members and a strong commitment to our clients, we will provide you and Truckco a quality e-learning solution. We look forward to working with you again.

Best Regards,

Charles Roman

Charles Roman
President and CEO
BrightStar

Example 17.3 A partnership letter explaining how the two vendors will work together to meet the client's needs.

instructional designers on staff to develop material for the client. In that case, you may partner with an instructional design firm to write e-learning lessons that will fit into your LCMS.

If you do partner with another firm, it is usually a good idea to have a representative from the partnering firm write a letter to include in your proposal. The letter, as shown in Example 17.3, should indicate to the client that you and the

Client clearly knows what will be required if a change is instituted to the project.

Provides evidence of a well-thought-out plan for making changes to the project.

Clearly indicates to the client that sign-offs will be required.

PROJECT CHANGE ORDER REQUEST

Project Title:			Date:
Project No:	Task No:	Revision No:	Date Revised:

Description of Change:

Reason for Change:

Schedule Change Information (include affected milestones):

New Start Date: New End Date:

Estimated Cost:

APPROVALS:

Originator:	Date:
Client Project Manager:	Date:
Vendor Project Manager:	Date:
Task Owner:	Date:

Example 17.4 Sample change request form. Quality control and sign-off forms are good items to place in an appendix.

firm have a good working relationship. Clients want to know that the two vendors will work well together to solve any problems that may arise.

FORMS

In some cases, you may want to provide your client with sample sign-off forms or sample quality control forms so the client can gain some insight into the process you use to ensure a quality product. You may even want to include a sample change order form indicating how your firm handles changes to the project. A sample form is shown in Example 17.4.

SCREEN CAPTURES/STORYBOARDS

An extremely effective method of conveying what your solution will look like is to provide a screen capture or storyboard of your proposed solution. If you have an LCMS or LMS, it is a good idea to provide captures of your basic screens. The captures provide your client with an idea of the screen flow and how easy it is to use your product. Clients want to know what your product looks like as early as possible. If you have an impressive screen capture or functionality, you will set the standard for the other vendors.

If you are creating an e-learning program for your client from scratch, you will want to provide a storyboard of possible screens. You can even provide multiple storyboards to show what different versions might look like with different colors or different arrangements of the navigational convention. It is usually better to provide a storyboard in this situation as opposed to a screen capture because a storyboard implies that you are working on the e-learning while a screen capture implies a finished product, as shown in Figure 7.11 in Chapter 7.

PRESS RELEASES/NEWS ARTICLES

If any positive items have appeared in print regarding your organization, it is generally a good idea to include them in the proposal. An article or other news piece published in a trade journal represents a good "third-party" endorsement of your firm. Most clients will afford your firm a great deal of credibility if information about it has appeared in industry publications. It is one thing to advertise, it is another to actually have an article written about your firm.

If you do not have a recent article featuring your firm but want to convey some information to the client, you can include a press release. The press release should be written in a newspaper article format so that it can be picked up by a news agency for possible publication. The press release, while not as credible as an article, can provide useful information about your firm. A well-written press release can provide detailed information to support your capture strategy and to strengthen the case of why you should be chosen as a vendor for the project.

OTHER MATERIALS

Other items you may want to include in the appendix are a corporate brochure, detailed information about your ROI or price assumptions, descriptions of standards to which you adhere, and any appropriate corporate policies.

A corporate brochure is an effective tool for conveying your corporate image and corporate ideals to clients. Brochures should reinforce the statements and capabilities of your organization and not be a substitute for information you supply in the proposal. If you include a brochure, make sure it is firmly attached to the proposal so that it does not become separated. It needs to stay with your proposal.

In addition, you may want to include detailed assumptions and numbers related to any ROI, cost/benefit, or break-even analysis. The body of the proposal should contain the result of the calculation. The appendix should contain assumptions and numbers used to derive the final figure. Clients want to know how you arrived at financial numbers. It is always a good idea to provide this level of detail in the appendix.

Another good item to place in the appendix of the document is an explanation of any standards or regulations to which you adhere. Even though clients request that you follow certain standards, they may not know exactly what they mean. Remember, e-learning is about making information understandable. If you cannot do that within the proposal, the client may feel that you will not be able to do that when you develop the instruction.

You may also want to include any corporate policies that you follow that positively impact the relationship with the client and support your capture strategy. These might include quality control policies or risk management policies. Do not include any policies that may seem antagonistic or detrimental to the client such as late payment penalties, penalties for not signing off on storyboards, or legalese concerning ownership of intellectual capital. Set strict ground rules in the contract, not in the proposal. Remember, you are still selling your services.

Make sure to include a reference within the body of the proposal to each item in the appendix, such as *See Appendix A for additional detail* or *See page A5 in the appendix for additional information.* The appendix should help the reader in further understanding the details of your solution.

THE BOTTOM LINE

The appendix of the document can cover a lot of information. You want to obtain a competitive advantage through the information included in the appendix. The goal is to provide necessary details to support your capture strategy and your solution. The appendix will not win or lose the proposal for you but it can provide enough detail to help support your capture strategy and convince the client that you should be awarded the contract.

This book has free materials available for download from the Web Added Value™ Resource Center at www.jrosspub.com.

PART III: PRESENTING THE PROPOSAL

18

PRESENTING A WINNING PROPOSAL

Stand and deliver.
—Adam Ant

INTRODUCTION

A straightforward, dynamic, client-centered sales presentation wins e-learning business. A lackluster, boring, or arrogant presentation loses business. Most e-learning business is not won simply because of a well-written proposal; it takes a dynamic sales presentation to close the deal. A polished, well-organized presentation is often the difference between winning the e-learning business and going home empty-handed.

One of the final steps in the E-BAP is the demonstration and presentation of the proposed solution. Clients want to see what they are buying and expect the vendor to provide an exciting, informative overview of the e-learning project. Clients also expect to see a prototype or a demonstration of the proposed software.

This part of the E-BAP requires great skill and expertise on the part of the vendor. The vendor firm must not only summarize the essence of its proposal into a short, effective presentation, but it must also address any client concerns, instill confidence in its ability to get the job done, overcome objections, and provide a sense of what the finished, implemented e-learning product will look like. This process of presenting the solution to the client typically involves an electronic slide show with information about your firm's history, similar projects you have undertaken, a timeline for the project, an estimated budget, and assurances of quality. It also involves a demonstration of past projects or a prototype or, in the case of LMS or LCMS, a step-by-step demonstration of how the product works.

THE SHOOTOUT

When vendors compete for the same e-learning business by giving presentations in a short period of time, it is called a "shootout." This presentation is usually your first opportunity to speak face-to-face with the entire client selection team. During the bidder's conference typically only one or two representatives from the client organization are present. You might have had a phone call or two with some client representatives or exchanged e-mails. The shootout is the time for you to gain an understanding of all of the players who will be involved in making the final "buy" decision.

Not all vendors are afforded the opportunity to present to the client selection team. Only vendors that make the "final cut" are given the privilege of presenting. The number of vendors invited to present is usually less than the number that were initially asked to respond to the RFP. The number of vendors presenting their solutions can range from two to six. Usually several vendors are scheduled over a one- or two-day period so that the selection team may see all the vendors and make comparisons of the various solutions within a short period of time.

These events are called shootouts because these presentations are the last opportunity you have to impress the client. After all the vendors present, the client makes a final decision. The vendor presentations provide the client with an opportunity to ask specific questions about each proposal and to get an idea of the e-learning capabilities of the vendor. It also provides the client with a chance to meet the people who will be working on the project. The goal for the client is to determine, from the quality of the presentation, which vendor is most capable of delivering the desired solution on time and within budget.

Clients want a vendor that is easy to work with and with whom they feel comfortable. Most e-learning deals are signed because of the comfort level of the client and not because of the specific technical details of the solution.

While clients do a lot of research and narrow down vendors based on pricing, functionality, technical capabilities, and other considerations, the final choice is usually made on a personnel level. The client's selection team chooses the vendor with whom they feel most comfortable and confident. Clients need to feel that they can trust and communicate with their e-learning vendor easily and with few misunderstandings. They gauge the level of trust and comfort in the sales presentations and through other interactions they have had with the vendor.

If you present yourself as arrogant or condescending during the shootout or E-BAP process, you will have a difficult time winning the business no matter how practical, cost effective, or elegant your solution.

A straightforward, dynamic, client-centered presentation highlighting the firm's ability to work with the client is what leads to victory. When selling e-learning, concentrate on what your solution will do for the client. Highlight how you will help the client overcome any challenges they are facing.

■ ■ ■

A PRACTICAL GUIDE TO SELLING E-LEARNING

Robert P. Delamontagne, Chairman and Founder, EduNeering, Inc.

Let us assume that your RFP has been prepared and submitted. You now learn that you have been elevated to the short list, meaning you are in final competition for the account. A meeting has been scheduled where you are to present your case for winning the business. This is a "make-or-break" opportunity with the final award going to the company with the best presentation. You are now challenged. How do you make the most persuasive and compelling presentation that will win the business? Let me introduce you to a very powerful sales concept called *authentic selling*. This approach relies on three basic components: (1) factual analysis, (2) sales strategy, and (3) a deeply ingrained reliance on the truth.

Factual analysis is developed by carefully researching the prospect's current situation. During this phase of preparation, you need to determine answers to questions such as: What problem is this company trying to solve with this project? What hard-core value does e-learning bring to this prospect? What are the business or economic reasons this project has been initiated? What person or department is going to fund this project? What obstacles are present that must be overcome? Once answers to these types of questions are developed, they must be transformed into a *business scenario* into which you will sell. This business scenario will describe the major points of leverage that must be addressed, which will have meaning and resonate with the prospect.

I have learned over the years that failure to win business is mostly due to lack of adequate preparation. Faulty analysis of the prospect's situation will put you at a major disadvantage against a competitor that performs this necessary research and uses it effectively in developing its sales presentation. This is very important because a sales decision is ultimately a human decision. Managers want to work with people who understand their situation and help them achieve their goals.

The second component of authentic selling, developing an effective sales strategy, is built by linking the information gained from research on the prospect to your company's greatest strengths. In other words, an effective strategy will clearly articulate why your firm represents the optimum choice to meet the prospect's needs. It could be your approach to instructional design, your previous successful experience serving companies in the same industry, or the unique features of your technology. You must make certain that this linkage is tied directly and specifically to the requirements of the prospect. You must build a conceptual bridge from the needs of the prospect to the unique advantages that you bring to the project. This could be enhanced with the use of charts, graphs, diagrams, and illustrations. Your goal for this stage is to make it clear to the prospect why selecting your organization for this assignment is in his or her best interest.

The last component of authentic selling, truth-telling, is based on honest and forthright communication with the prospect. Managers typically want to deal with people they can trust. Authenticity creates a powerful psychological presence because truth is interpreted both intellectually and subconsciously. If you have thoroughly researched the prospect's situation and clearly understand the benefits you bring to the project, you can be forceful and assertive in your demeanor during the sales presentation. Your comments, however, must be based on truth for this to be effective. That is why this approach is called *authentic selling*, for its foundation is based on clear and factual communication and not on hype or coercive selling techniques.

There is another important reason why telling the truth is essential during your sales presentations. Truth is inevitably experienced by the prospect after the sale is made. In fact, you could say that the customer must live with the truth once the sale is concluded. You do not want the prospect to have one set of expectations before the sale and then experience another reality after the sale is concluded. If this were to occur, your long-term relationship with this customer would be damaged beyond repair.

Since founding EduNeering 22 years ago, I have participated in the sale of e-learning and CBT projects in excess of $30 million. There has never been one instance where these principles did not enhance the power and effectiveness of the sales process.

■ ■ ■

PRESENTING YOUR SOLUTION

The most important part of presenting your solution and demonstrating your product is to center on your client while emphasizing your capture strategy. You should have spent a great deal of time carefully developing a well-crafted capture strategy. If nothing has happened to cause a change to that strategy, you must use that strategy when presenting your solution. It is important to maintain a consistent theme and strategy from the written proposal to the presentation and product demonstration.

Once you make it into the shootout, your focus must be on driving home your strengths and convincing the client that you are the best vendor for the e-learning project. One of the best ways of convincing the client that you are a capable vendor is to develop a well-crafted presentation.

A well-crafted presentation starts with an agenda. In some shootout situations, the client will provide an agenda. This agenda will contain information on what you should discuss, questions you should answer, and the order in which you should present information. Some clients want a controlled presentation so that each vendor is presenting similar information in a similar order. Typically this is done so that the client can easily keep a score for each vendor on an evaluation sheet keyed to the agenda.

In the case of an LCMS or an LMS, the client may even have a "script" of information they want entered into your system. In this case, your sales presentation and product demonstration will be evaluated on how well the client information flows through your LMS or LCMS. Other times, you will be provided with instructor-led content and asked to use your e-learning software to place the content online. The client will then evaluate how your designers presented the content within the e-learning product.

Whether or not you follow a client script or your own, make sure your demonstration functions smoothly. You do not want a technology failure during an e-learning presentation. You are a technology firm with a technology product. If your technology does not work during the demonstration, your potential client will have little faith that your technology will work on a day-to-day basis in their environment.

Have multiple redundant backup systems in place. If you cannot get to the Internet, have an electronic slide show version of your product handy. In case your laptop crashes right before the demonstration, have a CD burned with all of the files for viewing on any available computer. Think of possible disasters and then plan for those potential pitfalls. Having a backup plan will impress the client. If a technical failure occurs and you can continue the demonstration because you are prepared with a backup, you just might win points with the client for thinking ahead.

PRESENTATION AGENDA

If you are not given a script or an agenda, you will need to develop your own. Make sure you design an agenda to keep the presentation running smoothly and within the allotted time. One of the first things you want to determine is how long you have for your presentation and demonstration. If the client does not provide that information in the invitation to present in the shootout, contact the client. Whether or not you have one hour or four hours will impact how much information you present.

Regardless of the amount of time you have available, some basic elements should be covered in your presentation and demonstration. The longer your allotted time, the more detail you can go into for each element.

The agenda elements below are presented in an order that makes sense and is effective; however, the order of the agenda elements is not an absolute. You may want to change the order depending upon the needs of the client and your capture strategy. The basic agenda elements are:

- Agenda/overview of the presentation
- Statement of the problem
- Overview of the solution (technical and instructional)
- Prototype/sample/demonstration
- Discussion of the budget/ROI
- Presentation of the project timeline
- How you ensure quality and mitigate risk within the project
- Your corporate capabilities
- Ask for the business

Agenda/overview of the presentation — Start the presentation with the agenda and an overview of what you are going to be discussing and presenting. Sometimes the person who has organized the demonstrations has not properly informed his or her fellow selection team members of the content of the sales presentations. Some of the people attending the demonstrations may not be familiar with the entire process or may not be informed of what the client company is trying to achieve. Also, with a long presentation, some people may want to come and go. The IT person may only want to sit in on the technical portion of your presentation (not a good strategy but it happens). Know the order in which you will be presenting your information and describe it to the client group before you present. You must take some time to set the agenda and provide an overview. At this point, you must also reestablish your allotted presentation time.

In some cases, you may be surprised by a "change in plans." You may have thought that you had four hours to speak when, in fact, you now have only one hour or vice versa. You need to double check your time allotment with the entire group when you start speaking. It is better to know that you must lengthen or shorten your presentation at the beginning rather than to be cut off halfway through your demonstration or be told when you finish that you have three hours to go. Recheck your time allotment.

Statement of the problem — This section of the presentation is where you frame the client's problem in terms of your capture strategy. Describe the problem in a manner favorable to your solution. Highlight the main aspects of the problem and preview how your firm's e-learning solution is going to solve the client's problem. It is best to keep the problem simple and straightforward. Boil the problem down to three or four bullet points and then present those points to the client. For example:

- Need to reach 5000 employees in a short period of time.
- Scores are to be tracked and recorded.
- If minimum competency is not reached by an employee, test is retaken.

These three simple points highlight the client's problem and identify issues that you will address during your presentation. These points should be taken from your written proposal. Although the written proposal may have more details or even more points to discuss, you need to keep the sales presentation simple in order to keep the client's interest.

The goal of presenting the client's problem is to provide the client with a level of comfort concerning your ability to recognize the problem. During the presentation walk the fine line between letting the client know that you have dealt with similar problems in the past and demonstrating that you understand the unique qualities of this client's particular e-learning challenge.

Overview of the solution (technical and instructional) — In this section of the presentation, highlight the fact that the technical and instructional solutions are intertwined and that they work together to positively impact the client's organization. Clearly explain how you are going to ensure that the instructional solution is high quality. Explain how you use the ADDIE model to design the instruction and how you carefully develop objectives, storyboards, and prototypes to ensure success.

Also explain any software tools and procedures you use for the development process. You can also describe the infrastructure of your LMS or LCMS as well as any technical problems such as security or browser compatibility that will be addressed by your particular e-learning solution.

You must keep the instructional and technical explanations simple. You will most likely have trainers and technology specialists in the audience as well as managers and staff. Make sure everyone can understand your explanations.

The main thing you want to highlight in the *Overview of the Solution* section is the benefits the client will receive. It is a good idea to describe the ADDIE model and the type of server that will house the solution but, more importantly, you need to describe why the ADDIE model or the server you chose is good for the client. Do not simply give information from the proposal; provide a compelling reason why your solution is *the solution* for the client. Describe how you will save the client time, money, and effort.

Describe the benefits not only from an organizational view but from a personnel view as well. What will your solution do for the team sitting in the seats evaluating three or four vendors? You must answer the question "What's in it for me?" Client team members are usually looking for an individual win as well as a corporate win. You must point out the benefits of your solution to the client even if the benefits seem obvious. The more benefits you can list for your proposal, the better off you will be when the client decides to make the final decision.

Prototype/sample/demonstration — While presentations are good for conveying a certain amount of information to potential clients, nothing speaks as loud as a flashy demonstration of the proposed software solution. No matter how much time you have allotted for your presentation, save some time for a demonstration of your solution. Build a small prototype of a solution for the client using the client's materials, jargon, and information. A prototype that is pleasing to view and that uses the client's information will receive high praise from the client team. An example of the software solution functioning properly is key to an effective e-learning presentation.

If you do not have time to develop a prototype or you choose not to develop one, then you need to show a variety of samples of your work in line with what you are proposing to the client. Allow the client to see a number of different solutions that will help him or her to visualize the proposed solution.

If you are selling an LMS or LCMS, take the time to get some client titles to place into the system. If possible, gain access to a client course and place it within your LMS to show how easily your system works with the client's existing courses. Find out what information the client wants to track and then, before the demonstration, run those sample reports with client information (or information similar to what the client would see).

It is amazing that even sophisticated clients can have trouble seeing through unfamiliar content to the functionality of the system. You do not want the prospective client caught up in the content while ignoring the functionality of the system. If you can remove unfamiliar content as an obstacle, you can help to eliminate a potential snag in your effort to win the e-learning business.

You also want to keep in mind that your prototype will, most likely, be projected in front of a large audience. What might look good on a small screen may project horribly when shown in a dimly lit conference room. Always project your presentation and prototype in an environment similar to the one in which you will be presenting. You need to know and understand what the client will see. Viewing the presentation from the perspective of the client will help you present it to the client. Be aware that not all colors project well and not all shades and color combinations visible on a personal computer screen will be visible when projected in front of a large room. Avoid yellow and light blue at all cost.

Discussion of the budget/ROI — Do not try to hide the budget from the client during the presentation. Present the budget and stand behind the numbers. Clients will try all kinds of techniques to get you to lower your price. While there is always room for negotiation, you do not want to appear as if you picked a number out of thin air that can easily go up or down depending on who is the stronger negotiator. You need to carefully explain how you developed the price and what goes into your price. If you are presenting several options to the client, make sure you do not confuse the client with the different prices. The client may inadvertently start mixing features in one solution with features in another.

You may even want to explain only one pricing solution (your preferred one) to the client and refer the client to the proposal for other pricing options. This will help to minimize the confusion clients sometimes encounter when they are confronted with too many options.

Another effective technique is to emphasize the ROI to the client. Remember that the return to a company can be in the form of a Net Benefit, Benefit Cost Ratio, or the ROI. Most clients will need something to help "sell" the idea to themselves and upper management, and a good solid ROI can make a big difference in winning the business. You need to emphasize the value of your solution over the current situation. Stressing value will help the client to understand the need for action and the reasonableness of your solution.

■ ■ ■

GUIDELINES FOR EFFECTIVE USE OF ELECTRONIC SLIDES

Timothy L. Phillips, Director, Institute for Interactive Technologies, Bloomsburg University

1. Use a light background with dark letters. Too many times the creator of the slides develops a multicolored background with multicolored words and expects the prospective client in the back of the room to read the dark text on the dark background. It doesn't work. The tried and true method is white background, dark text.
2. Do not walk in front of the projector light. Stand to one side when using a projector. Too many presenters want to stand in the light; it is distracting.
3. Use a 24-point font or larger. Remember that when you are creating the visual you are right there and you can see it up close. In a conference room, the prospective clients are sitting farther away from the screen, they do not all have 20/20 vision, and they are not all interested in straining to see the small print. The guideline of 24-point font accommodates most rooms and most people.
4. Follow the rule of 6 × 6. This means a slide should have no more than 6 lines of text and no more than 6 words per line. The slide should not be your notes. It should contain key words that prompt you to recall the information you are presenting.
5. Avoid fancy text attributes. Do not underline text, add italics, or use all capital letters. Each of these additions to the text on the screen will make it more difficult for the clients to read the screen. Avoid making the slides too busy and too dense; the text should speak for itself.
6. The graphic images you put on your slides should have a direct link to the information on the slide. "I put this picture here because I like it" is not a good reason to add a visual. At the least the graphic should be neutral,

neither adding meaning nor distracting. Ideally, the graphic should add meaning and make an impact.

7. Not all projectors project in the same color. Be careful when using colors to convey meaning because a projected image is not as clear as one on a computer screen. An image that looked clear on your laptop may become blurred on the screen because the two shades of green you used were too close and blended when projected.
8. When you display a visual, explain the visual. Some clients will understand the visual immediately. Other clients will want you to explain it. Take some time to explain the visual to the clients.
9. Do not talk to the screen. When presenting software, most people tend to look to the screen for keywords to remind them of what to say and then they say those words to the screen. Look at the screen and then turn to the clients and explain your point. Clients cannot hear or understand you when you talk to the screen. Look at your audience when you speak.
10. Every once in a while, turn off the projector. Your entire presentation to the client should not be a contest to see how many slides you can put up in the allotted time. If you have the projector on during the sales demonstration, you are not engaging the client in meaningful conversation. Find opportunities to have discussions with clients with the lights on, looking them in the eye. Turn off the projector at least once during the presentation.

■ ■ ■

Presentation of the project timeline — One thing clients want to avoid is an unfinished project or a project that drags on while consuming valuable time and resources. Clients want to know that you can manage a project and bring it in on time. They also want to know how long it will take to complete the project.

In this part of the presentation you need to carefully describe the major milestones of the project and the estimated time frame required to complete each milestone. You can also take this opportunity to gently remind the client that completing the project on time requires a quick turnaround of reviews and revisions in accordance with the timeline you have presented. This needs to be presented gently; do not put the client on the defensive.

How you ensure quality and mitigate risk within the project — Clients want to know that you have processes and procedures in place to avoid or mitigate any problems that may be encountered. The most effective way of assuring the client that you can handle a large-scale e-learning project is for you to discuss safeguards that you use to ensure a high-quality product completed on time and within budget.

To help persuade the client, you may want to briefly discuss your change order practices, what you do to avoid scope creep, and how you deal with client requests once the project has begun. You need to convey the message that you are flexible, but will draw the line when necessary. You want to convince the client of your ability to ensure quality and mitigate risk.

Your corporate capabilities — Clients want to know with whom they are dealing. It is important that you spend time discussing your firm, what it has done in the past, and what it can do in the future. You do not want to spend a lot of time on this area because you want to focus more on your client's problem, but you do need to establish some level of credibility. This can be done by discussing the number of years your firm has been conducting e-learning, the philosophy of your firm, your client list, and work you have completed for other clients. When you discuss your firm's capabilities, make sure that you describe them in such a way that they have value to the client. Throughout this part of the presentation make sure the focus is on the solution for the client and not on your firm. This can be tricky when presenting your firm's history. Remember, clients want to hear how you are going to solve their problem, not the "life and times" of your firm.

You may want to save this section for the end of your presentation because, if you run out of time, it can be cut. It is much better to shorten the presentation in terms of your firm's history and general corporate capabilities than to shorten the presentation in the area of solving the client's problem.

Ask for the business — This is the most critical aspect of the presentation. You want to let the client know that you value their business and would like to have them as a client. You need to ask about the next steps. Ask "What do we need to do to close the deal?" or "What are the next steps toward finalizing our agreement?" or "How do we formalize an agreement between our two companies?" Sell during your close; let clients know you want to work with them and that you are ready to take the next step.

USE A TEAM APPROACH

For e-learning proposals, a team approach is often used for the presentation. Sometimes the team members are the same individuals who wrote the proposal and sometimes the team consists of only one salesperson and a technical expert. The size of the team will depend on the size of the client and the size of the proposal as well as the size of the client's selection team.

Since an e-learning project requires many areas of expertise (hardware, software, instructional design, Web design, etc.) many individuals may be needed for an effective presentation. On some occasions when a large client is involved, the number of presentation team members may be as high as five or six.

A presentation team for an important client may include the president of your firm or some other high-level executive. Having your firm's president at the presentation shows the commitment and interest of your firm in this particular e-learning project. Other members of the team may include the project manager slated to run the project, the project's lead instructional designer, a representative from the graphics department, a quality control representative, a technical specialist who understands networking and computer architecture, an interface designer, and a Web designer. Not all of these individuals travel to every shootout. However, when the stakes are high and you want to impress the client, a well-rounded team shows commitment to the project and helps to answer all of the client's questions.

One note of caution: your team should not be larger than the client's team. If you have too many people, you will overwhelm the client and appear desperate. Keep the number of your representatives to one or two less than the client's.

Regardless of the number of team members you have present, they must all be enthusiastic, confident, and knowledgeable. A client who is purchasing an e-learning solution is looking to the vendor for experience and expertise. The client also wants to deal with people who are enthusiastic about the potential of e-learning without the hype.

Effective presentations include enthusiastic vendors confidently discussing the merits and demerits of a proposed e-learning solution. You can appear thoughtful and incisive by being up-to-date on statistics and trends in the industry and by knowing when an e-learning solution makes sense and when a more traditional approach is appropriate.

Each member of the team should speak clearly, confidently, and convincingly. You want your team to instill confidence in the client each time an individual speaks. A lot of verbal interrupts or pauses makes it appear that a person does not know what he or she is talking about. If one or two team members are looking off into the distance and not paying attention, the client will notice. Excessive pacing or doodling while other team members are speaking can be distracting to the client. Before sending an e-learning team member to a client site for a shootout, provide training in the art of presentation.

The members of your team need to understand how to present themselves and the proposed solution in the best light. You want to keep each section of the presentation running smoothly and quickly. You do not want the presentation to be rushed, but you do not want it to be long and drawn out either. Pick a comfortable pace and make sure each presenter can work at that pace. This may be difficult for some of the more technical people who may not want to spend much time in front of the client; however, it never fails to impress a client when a technical person presents effectively. You also want to make sure that the presentation team practices together at least once to gain some understanding of who is handing off to whom. Even if you are all individually great presenters, you need some practice presenting together.

It is a good idea to always have your best speaker lead and close. As with any situation in which an audience listens to a speaker, the first and last things said are the most memorable. This is also the reason you want to include your budget as an item covered in the middle of your presentation and not at the end. You do not want the last item ringing in the client's head to be the large six-figure number you presented as your budget. It would be far better to have the client selection team remember your best speaker's elegant close and request for the sale.

Each speaker, regardless of his or her position in the presentation effort, should reference outside or third-party sources and statistics whenever possible. It is one thing for your firm to make claims about the effectiveness of e-learning; it is another for those claims to be backed by a third party. It is usually a good idea to use information from a source such as the American Society for Training and Development (ASTD) to back your claims of cost and time savings due to e-learning initiatives. It is one thing to discuss the value of SCORM compliance; it is another to have an industry expert discuss the value of compliance. On the other hand, if your entire presentation seems to be referenced from somewhere else, the clients will think they are sitting in on a book review. Reference outside information only when it makes sense.

Throughout the entire presentation and interaction with the client, all team members must behave professionally. This means team members do not bad-mouth the competition (it makes you look unprofessional). It also means that they do not bicker or fight among themselves. Also, team members should not tell inappropriate jokes or make offensive remarks. You never know what might offend a potential client so the best rule is to play it down the middle. Avoid the topics of religion, politics, and sex during small talk with the client. The weather and local sports are safe topics. Pick up a local newspaper before going to the shootout and remember the saying "discretion is the better part of valor."

The presentation team should also know when to keep quiet. Often the client team will begin to discuss your proposal. If this seems to be moving in a positive direction, do not interrupt. If you can get one or two members of the client team to support your solution, then they are selling for you. When clients chat, sit back and listen for a while and use what you learn to help you make the sale.

The presentation team also needs to agree to be flexible given certain client requests. If the potential client suggests reasonable alterations to the proposed solution or wants to approach the development process differently, be flexible. Do not be afraid to pose variations to your original solution if it looks like the client would prefer another path. Do not radically scrap what you have planned and develop an entirely new approach on the fly, but rather be flexible within the parameters of your current solution. If you radically change your solution, clients will get suspicious that you are just telling them what they want to hear or that you really did not think through your first solution.

The presentation team has a delicate task. It must present a dynamic, exciting presentation while simultaneously conveying a sense of confidence and trust. The team must carefully prepare its agenda but be flexible enough to rearrange it if the client leads it in a different direction. The team must address the needs of the client while highlighting its capture strategy. The team needs to know when to talk and when to remain quiet. The team must keep the conversation friendly but always professional and be careful not to offend the client by bad-mouthing a competitor or making an inappropriate remark.

■ ■ ■

POLISHED PRESENTATIONS: FIVE QUESTIONS TO BETTER PREPARE YOUR SALES PRESENTATION

W. Scott Wein, Director of Learning Support,
Century 21 Real Estate Corporation

Sales presentations are an important part of how business gets done. Your written proposal will be scrutinized and, if you provide a good solution, you may be invited to give a presentation. This is where the decision will be made. How you present your solution is key to your firm being selected. To prepare for a sales presentation you need to know the answer to five seemingly simple questions. Here is a list of questions to ask before all sales presentations:

1. **Who is your audience?** Knowing your audience is the first key part of a presentation. This will dictate what type of presentation you can give. If this is a company with which you have previously worked, your delivery can be more relaxed. You know who is there and you have a common goal. If you do not know your audience, you need to use common language. Every industry, company, and group has jargon. When you present, avoid using it. You can confuse your audience. Your audience will also dictate what style you use for your materials. Test how your presentation will look when projected. If you have a black background and a blue hyperlink, some people may not be able to see it. Create a style and use it consistently. Do not use ten different colors and fonts. Keep it simple. Use no more than two fonts and four text colors.
2. **What are they looking for from you?** Are you the answer? Are you just the next vendor? Sure, they want to hear your solution. What else are they looking for? They want to see how you and your company look and act. A formal presentation is different from a casual discussion. If this is a formal presentation, have the tools you will need to do your best presentation. Make sure that you test your laptop, your prototype, your projector, your prototype (again), your laser pointer, and finally your prototype (again). You want to know that you have control over your part in the presentation. The client is not waiting for you to make a mistake. When a mistake happens, do not draw undue attention to it. This is one of the most difficult

skills to control in presentations. You have to acknowledge the problem. Do not gloss over it or say that the QA person was fired. It is a point in your favor if you can recover with a great answer and continue on.

3. **Do you know your topic?** If we sat down at a restaurant would you be able to talk to me for 20 minutes on your solution? If you said yes, you can do your presentation. That is all you have to be able to do. You have been working on this project for a while, you know your solution, all of the financial figures, and you even know your proposal's flaws. You do not need to concentrate on your facts; they should be a part of you. Concentrate on your audience. Make eye contact with your audience. Think about your body language. Have you ever been to the zoo? Did you see the tigers? They just walk back and forth in their cage. I have seen many presentations where the speaker paced during the entire presentation. I was watching the speaker, but I did not hear a word he or she said. You need to balance your movement. I move when I am changing to the next major point. If I am just explaining, I have my feet planted and I look at the audience.

   If you know your topic, you do not need to memorize. Memorization is a dangerous trap for speaking. We remember things in blocks. If you forget your place, you usually have to start at the top of that memorization block. It is painful for both speaker and audience when this happens. You are sweating, trying to find your words, and the audience is happy to be in their seats and not in your shoes. Use your slide presentation to guide you. You should have a couple of points on each slide and then fill in the details. You should not have all of the detail on the slides. It does not look professional when the presenter turns away from the audience and then just reads the slide.

4. **How much time do you have?** You need to be respectful of the time that you have been allotted. If you have been given 1 hour, plan your presentation for 40 minutes to allow time for questions. It is good to arrive a few minutes early and set up your equipment. If you are a fast talker when you present, there is a simple solution. Breathe. If you take a bunch of short shallow breaths, you will get or appear nervous. You need to take full breaths. It will be a calming influence and make you appear more confident. If you breathe regularly you will have more consistent timing.

5. **What are the questions that the audience will ask you?** It is always better to have an answer ready and not have to use it than to have to give an answer that is not prepared. You know there are questions that are asked every time you present your solution. Have these answers in your back pocket. You also know every mistake in your proposal. Have your answers ready. If you are going to be presenting as a group, sit around and ask each other the tough questions. Ask questions that are different from the

stock "Can you please explain your ROI estimation?" (You should already know the answer.) Have people who are not part of the industry ask you questions. In your audience, inevitably you will have someone who is not part of the e-learning industry, and he or she will ask some weird questions.

If you know the answers to these questions, you will be better prepared for your presentation. If I had to sum it up in a few words it would be this:

- Think about your audience
- Don't memorize
- Breathe

That is what the focus should be. If you are focused on your audience you will engage, educate, and entice them. If you use your slides as a guide, you will not lose your place. If you breathe, you will not pass out. It would be difficult to seal the deal while the paramedics are giving you oxygen.

■ ■ ■

HANDLING OBJECTIONS AND DIFFICULT QUESTIONS

During the sales presentation, the job of the client is to ask tough questions and to raise concerns about your solution. At times client representatives may seem adversarial or even nasty. Regardless of the style in which the difficult questions are asked, you must be able to handle the situation with grace and poise. Here are some guidelines that may help when you are confronted with that situation.

The first rule is to stay calm. When a person becomes upset, he or she becomes irrational, reacts without thinking, and generally is not at his or her best. If you are upset with a question or comment, take a deep breath and compose yourself before you answer. Or ask a colleague to handle that particular question. If you have worked with a client for a while and you know you do not like a particular person on the client team, make arrangements for someone else on your team to address issues with that person. You need to remain calm.

One way to remain calm when confronted with an adversarial prospect is to look at the confrontation as a request for more information. Sometimes a client will try to challenge your assumptions or find fault with your solution. This is not the time to prove that you are "smarter" than the client or that the client "doesn't know what he or she is talking about." Instead, view the line of questioning as an opportunity for you to further inform the prospective client of the merits of your proposal.

There is one thing that can help with difficult questions and can serve as an effective reference is your written proposal. Always have your written proposal available for quick reference. Do not get caught without a copy of your proposal. It will make you nervous and give the potential client the upper hand because you will not have your own proposal to reference.

At least one person on the client's team will have studied the proposal and will refer to a specific page and paragraph when asking a question. You need to have the proposal at your fingertips to answer the question. If you arrive at the client site without the proposal, you will look bad. It is not enough to have an electronic copy; you must have a hard copy of your proposal as well.

Another effective technique for addressing client concerns is to use analogies or metaphors to mitigate objections. Remember, the e-learning business is about making information more understandable and memorable. If you cannot do that in the presentation, clients may reason that you cannot do that to their content. For example, you can explain that learning how to create e-learning courses is the same as learning how to ride a bike; it is awkward at first and a little scary, but once you get the hang of it, you have the freedom to go places you never could before. Or you could state that learning objects created in your LCMS are like building blocks that snap together regardless of their color or size. When creating an analogy, make sure the image is something with which everyone is familiar and that it can be visualized easily. If you use an obscure or little known analogy, you risk confusing the client.

Another point to keep in mind is that it is not productive to get defensive or put the client in a defensive position. In fact, a member of the client team may be asking certain questions for a variety of reasons that have nothing to do with you or your solution. Sometimes a member of the client team thinks the e-learning solution should have been built internally and so is looking to torpedo your off-the-shelf solution, or a client team member wants to show colleagues how much he or she knows about e-learning or may have an allegiance with another vendor.

Whatever the reason, do not enter into a bickering match with the client. If you find yourself getting upset with a client or with the situation, take a deep breath, take a drink of water, and consider the fact that you are selling to the client and must be on your most professional behavior. You can also take comfort in the fact that if you remain calm and handle the individual professionally, most of the other members of the client team will recognize your tact and your professionalism will work in your favor.

Sometimes clients will find a mistake in your proposal or in your presentation and then call you on the mistake. How you handle this situation is crucial for building credibility and trust with the client. If you make a mistake or accidentally misstate something during the presentation, admit it. You want to avoid getting backed into a corner by trying to talk your way out of something you have said. If you are evasive and vague, the client will recognize it and you will come across as untrustworthy. Oftentimes, instead of getting out of the awkward situation you just dig yourself a deeper hole. Simply admit a mistake and move on.

A frequent mistake is a typographical error within the presentation or proposal. The first rule of thumb is to proofread, proofread, proofread. However, we have all been in the situation where we have proofed something a thousand times and missed a typo in the first sentence. This leads to the inevitable question, "If you make typos in your proposal, what makes you so sure you won't make mistakes in our e-learning courses?"

If you get caught with a typo, admit that you do make mistakes (you are, after all, human) in spite of your best efforts and due diligence and that if you make a mistake, you will fix it at no cost to the client.

While typos are embarrassing, they are usually not "showstoppers." There are other kinds of questions that can be more difficult to answer. These include multipart questions, direct comparison questions, and technical questions.

MULTIPART QUESTIONS

The first type of difficult question you will probably encounter is the multipart question. For some reason, potential clients seem to enjoy asking as many things as they can in a single question. It can sometimes seem like a contest; whomever asks the most questions in a single statement wins.

When confronted with a multipart question, the first step is to take your time to listen to the entire question. Then you need to paraphrase the question to make sure you understand it and to gain more time to think about the question. If you are really confused, ask the questioner to restate the question or a specific part of it. Then answer the question one part at a time. After you have answered a segment of the question, check with the questioner to make sure you have answered that part of the question. At this point, you may even ask the questioner for the second or third part of the question. Then address the next segment of the question. Also, do not be afraid to clarify the question or ask for more details when confronted with a multipart question.

DIRECT COMPARISON QUESTIONS

Direct comparison questions are when the prospective client asks you to compare your solution to the solution of your competitor. This is usually in the form of a question such as "Your price seems really high while your competitor's is more reasonable. Why is that?" or "You offer to complete the entire project in eight months but the competitor says they can complete it in six. Can you explain the time difference?" or "Your competitor's hourly price is well below your hourly price. Why the difference?"

When clients want you to compare your services to that of a competitor they are testing you to see if you will "bash" the competition and to see if you will come down in price. They are really asking, "Did you inflate your price and can I get you to deflate your price by applying pressure?"

You must respond on two fronts. The first is that you must not bad-mouth or bash your competition. You simply respond by saying something like "I have not seen the competitor's proposal so it would be difficult for me to comment on its time frame, development process, or work plan" or "Without all the facts, it is difficult for me to make an apples to apples comparison." This will usually satisfy the questioner but does not address the underlying issue, which involves price. The client wants you to view your e-learning service as a commodity and, therefore, price it accordingly [1]. A competitor's lower price allows the client to open that dialogue.

In response, you must indirectly defend your price. Instead of justifying your price, turn around and ask the client: "I am not sure of the reasons for the price difference. Why do you suppose they value their services at that price?" Ask the question carefully and in a matter-of-fact manner. Now the client will be questioning the reason for the price difference. You can even force the issue a little by saying "Do you have any competitors that are lower priced than you? Do they offer the same value as your products? What do they sacrifice to offer a similar product at a lower price?" If the client thinks seriously about your response, he or she will realize that typically a higher price equals higher quality [1]. You can even use an analogy to bring home your point. Say something like "You can get a hotel room for $40 a night or $240 a night and both have a bed and a bathroom. Which one would you rather stay in for a week?"

When clients ask for a lower price, what they really want is for you to reassure them that they are getting a tremendous value for their investment [1]. Clients want to know that you are not ripping them off and charging extraordinarily high prices. This is especially true in the e-learning industry where most clients have no idea what it takes to build quality e-learning products.

TECHNICAL QUESTIONS

Another type of difficult question that you may encounter is the technical question. Usually there is someone from IT sitting in on your sales presentation. This person will want to know all of the technical ins and outs of your solution. Unless you have your technical expert with you, some of the questions will be out of your reach. With these questions, you need to answer as much as you can but you should not be afraid to respond as follows: "That is a good question. Unfortunately, my technical expertise is not as proficient in that area as our technical expert. Let me have her get in touch with you to answer that question." Once you have made that statement, ask for the person's e-mail and have your technical person contact that prospective client. Many salespeople say they will get back to a client but never do. If you get back to the client, your firm will look good when compared to others.

FINAL WORD ON QUESTIONS

With any type of question, make sure you satisfy the questioner, then stop. Often, a salesperson will be too anxious to add information and will drone on and on answering a simple client question. Usually a client has a specific question or concern that needs to be addressed. Answer that question and then move on. If you try to embellish the answer or add more information you risk confusing the client or, worse, exposing an area of concern for the client. For example, you may answer a question about SCORM compliance by stating, "Yes, we are SCORM compliant," or you could answer, "Yes, we are SCORM compliant in two areas that we deem to be of most importance."

In the second case, the client may immediately say something like "What about the other areas? We need all-around SCORM compliance or no deal; you just said only two." Now you must explain yourself and try to pacify the upset client. You gave too much information. Answer the question that is being asked and then stop. If clients need more information, they will ask.

THE BOTTOM LINE

Exciting, enthusiastic presentations win e-learning business. The written proposal is your foot in the door; the presentation separates winners from losers. In some cases, clients start with presentations and then narrow the field of vendors from there. You need to concentrate on having a solid presentation that focuses on the needs of the client. All the presentation team members must be excellent presenters and must focus on meeting the client needs while sticking to the agreed upon capture strategy. Remember, good presentations win e-learning business.

This book has free materials available for download from the Web Added Value™ Resource Center at www.jrosspub.com.

ENDNOTES

CHAPTER 1

[1] This widely cited quote is from an article appearing in the November 17, 1999 *New York Times* titled "Next, It's E-ducation" by Thomas Friedman. This quote has been taken somewhat out of context by myself and many others. What Chambers was really talking about was that the amount of Internet *capacity* consumed for the delivery of online education would make the Internet *capacity* needed for e-mail look like a rounding error. Of course this is true because e-mail takes so little bandwidth compared to sending graphics, videos, animations, and other training-related media over the Internet.

However, everyone seems to have left off the *capacity* part of the statement and focused only on the part about how e-learning will dwarf e-mail usage. This quote, taken out of context, contributed to the e-learning hype of the late 1990s and early 2000s. The entire original quote from the article is:

> "Education," said Mr. Chambers. "The next big killer application for the Internet is going to be education. Education over the Internet is going to be so big it is going to make e-mail usage look like a rounding error in terms of the Internet capacity it will consume."

[2] Galvin, T. "2002 Industry Report," *Training Magazine*, October 2002, pp. 24–73.

[3] Founded in 1944, ASTD is a professional association and leading resource on workplace learning and performance issues. According to its Web site, "ASTD provides information, research, analysis and practical information derived from its own research, the knowledge and experience of its members, its conferences, expositions, seminars, publications and the coalitions and partnerships it has built

through research and policy work. ASTD's membership includes more than 70,000 people, working in the field of workplace performance in 100 countries worldwide." For more information see www.astd.org.

[4] Aldrich, C. "Industry Watch: Don't Look Down," *Online Learning Magazine*, Summer 2002, p. 53.

[5] The term "client" will refer to both a prospective client as well as an actual client throughout the book because we always hope that a prospective client will eventually turn into an actual client.

[6] Although you can contact the client to determine why your proposal was rejected and use that information to strengthen your next proposal. Sometimes you can even work your way into the "shootout" but it is not likely, and if you do get invited, it may only be as a courtesy and you really don't have a chance of winning.

CHAPTER 2

[1] A note of caution: With these types of Web markets, your product runs the risk of becoming a commodity. When you begin to market your services to the lowest bidder, through the Web exchange, you could turn your product into a commodity. The nature of a commodity is that it is sold on price alone. Be careful to keep your e-learning services or software as a value-added service or your margins will begin to erode.

CHAPTER 3

[1] A note of caution: Do not send files via Microsoft Word if you have used the *Reviewing* function. In one instance, a client received the MS Word document and turned on the Reviewing feature and was able to see all the changes the vendor firm had made to the budget while creating the proposal. Needless to say, this was an extremely embarrassing situation. Adobe Acrobat is recommended to avoid any possible problems.

CHAPTER 5

[1] Kern, H., Johnson, R., Galup, S., and Horgan, D., with Cappel, M. (1998). *Building the New Enterprise: People, Processes, and Technology*, Palo Alto, CA: Sun Microsystems Press, p. xiii.

[2] Peters, T. (1997). *The Circle of Innovation: You Can't Shrink Your Way to Greatness,* New York: Alfred A. Knopf, pp. 309–329.

[3] Holtz, H. and Schmidt, T. (1981). *The Winning Proposal: How to Write It*, New York: McGraw-Hill, pp. 134–139.

[4] Copyright 1997 Lisa Verge. Used with permission.

CHAPTER 6

[1] *Publication Manual of the American Psychological Association*, 5th ed. (2001). Washington, DC: American Psychological Association, p. 61.

[2] Guidelines were developed based on the American Psychological Association's (APA) guidelines as set forth in the *Publication Manual of the American Psychological Association*, 5th ed., pp. 61–76.

[3] Campbell, N. J. (1998). *Writing Effective Policies and Procedures: A Step-by-Step Resource for Clear Communications*, New York: American Management Association, p. 85.

[4] Corbet, E. P. J. (1984). *The Little English Handbook*, 4th ed., Glenville, IL: Scott, Foresman and Company, pp. 73–75.

[5] Campbell, N. J. (1998). *Writing Effective Policies and Procedures: A Step-by-Step Resource for Clear Communications*, New York: American Management Association, p. 88.

[6] Guffey, M. E. (1995). *Annotated Instructor's Edition Essentials of Business Communication,* 3rd ed., Cincinnati, OH: South-Western College Publishing, p. 58.

[7] Corbet, E. P. J. (1984). *The Little English Handbook*, 4th ed., Glenville, IL: Scott, Foresman and Company, pp. 73–75.

[8] Campbell, N. J. (1998). *Writing Effective Policies and Procedures: A Step-by-Step Resource for Clear Communications*, New York: American Management Association, p. 115.

[9] Varner, I. I. (1991). *Contemporary Business Report Writing*, 2nd ed., Chicago, IL: The Dryden Press, p. 55.

[10] Guffey, M. E. (1995). *Annotated Instructor's Edition Essentials of Business Communication,* 3rd ed., Cincinnati, OH: South-Western College Publishing, p. 30.

[11] Varner, I. I. (1991). *Contemporary Business Report Writing*, 2nd ed., Chicago, IL: The Dryden Press, p. 45.

[12] Guffey, M. E. (1995). *Annotated Instructor's Edition Essentials of Business Communication,* 3rd ed., Cincinnati, OH: South-Western College Publishing, p. 63.

[13] Corbet, E. P. J. (1984). *The Little English Handbook*, 4th ed., Glenville, IL: Scott, Foresman and Company, pp. 82–86.

[14] Baker, S. (1984). *The Complete Stylist and Handbook*, 3rd ed., New York: Harper & Row, pp. 58–60.

[15] Campbell, N. J. (1998). *Writing Effective Policies and Procedures: A Step-by-Step Resource for Clear Communications*, New York: American Management Association, p. 117.

[16] Baker, S. (1984). *The Complete Stylist and Handbook*, 3rd ed., New York: Harper & Row, pp. 61–62.

CHAPTER 7

[1] Reider, L. P. (1994). *Computers, Graphics, and Learning*, Madison, WI: Brown & Benchmark Publishers, p. 3.

[2] One of the best books on the subject of using charts to enhance a message is *Say It with Charts: The Executive's Guide to Visual Communication*, 4th ed., written by Gene Zelazny and published by McGraw-Hill.

CHAPTER 8

[1] McKenna, P. J. and Maister, D. H. (2002). *First Among Equals*, New York: The Free Press, Chapt. 1.

[2] Mascitelli, R. (2002). *Building a Project-Drive Enterprise: How to Slash Waste and Boost Profits Through Lean Project Management*, Northridge, CA: Technology Perspectives, p. 128.

CHAPTER 9

[1] Stewart, R. D. and Stewart, A. L. (1992). *Proposal Preparation*, 2nd ed., New York: John Wiley & Sons, p. 210.

[2] Stewart, R. D. and Stewart, A. L. (1992). *Proposal Preparation*, 2nd ed., New York: John Wiley & Sons, p. 212.

[3] Stewart, R. D. and Stewart, A. L. (1992). *Proposal Preparation*, 2nd ed., New York: John Wiley & Sons, pp. 212–213.

[4] Holtz, H. and Schmidt, T. (1981). *The Winning Proposal: How to Write It*, New York: McGraw-Hill, pp. 178–179.

CHAPTER 10

[1] Copyright 1997 Pam Berman. Used with permission.

[2] Holtz, H. (1986). *The Consultant's Guide to Proposal Writing: How to Satisfy Your Clients and Double Your Income*, New York: John Wiley & Sons, pp. 226–236.

CHAPTER 11

[1] Holtz, H. and Schmidt, T. (1981). *The Winning Proposal: How to Write It*, New York: McGraw-Hill, pp. 159–160.

CHAPTER 12

[1] I will use the terms "instructional systems design" and "instructional design" interchangeably even though technically they are not interchangeable. However, many times in the e-learning industry, they are used interchangeably. ISD is the entire design process (analysis, design, development, implementation, and evaluation), while ID usually refers only to the design of the instruction without the concepts of analysis, development, or evaluation.

[2] The concept of the MADDIE model was first brought to my attention by my colleague Dr. Mary Nicholson. Mary is a faculty member of Bloomsburg University's Department of Instructional Technology. She is quite the instructional design expert.

[3] Gagné, R. M., Briggs, L. J., and Wager, W. W. (1992). *Principles of Instructional Design*, 4th ed., Fort Worth, TX: Holt, Rinehart and Winston, pp. 190–199.

[4] Leshin, C. B., Pollock, J., and Reigeluth, C. M. (1992). *Instructional Design Strategies and Tactics*, Englewood Cliffs, NJ: Educational Technology Publications, p. 2.

[5] E-Learning Guild, http://www.elearningguild.org, accessed December 2002.

[6] A SCORM Primer, Advanced Distributed Learning (ADL), http://www.adlnet.org, accessed October 2002.

[7] Kottler, H., Parsaons, J., Wardenburg, S., and Vornbrock, F., Knowledge Objects: Definition, Development, Initiatives, and Potential Impact, in *The 2000/2001 ASTD Distance Learning Yearbook*, Mantyla, K., Ed., New York: McGraw-Hill, p. 177.

CHAPTER 13

[1] Johnson, J. "Turning Chaos into Success," *Software Magazine,* 31 (December 1999), 30.

[2] *A Guide to the Project Management Body of Knowledge*, 2000 ed. (2000), Newton Square, PA: Project Management Institute, p. 205.

[3] Actually, the most frequently asked question is "How much does it cost?"

[4] Zenger, J. and Uehlein, C. "Why Blended Will Win," *T+D* (formerly *Training and Development Magazine*), ASTD, August 2001, p. 57.

[5] Hall, B. (1997). *Web-Based Training Cookbook*, New York: Wiley Computer Publishing, p. 108.

[6] *A Guide to the Project Management Body of Knowledge*, 2000 ed. (2000), Newton Square, PA: Project Management Institute, p. 88.

[7] *A Guide to the Project Management Body of Knowledge*, 2000 ed. (2000), Newton Square, PA: Project Management Institute, p. 204.

[8] Russell, L. (2000). *Project Management for Trainers*, Alexandria, VA: ASTD, pp. 42–45.

[9] *A Guide to the Project Management Body of Knowledge*, 2000 ed. (2000), Newton Square, PA: Project Management Institute, p. 58.

CHAPTER 14

[1] Lord, M. "They're Online and On the Job," *US News & World Report*, October 2001.

[2] Vass, L. "Cashing in on Smarts," *e-week Magazine*, February 4, 2002, p. 45.

CHAPTER 18

[1] Wax, K. "How Low Can You Go?" *VarBusiness*, April 15, 1996, p. 110.

TRUCKCO PROPOSAL

Example 9.2, Example 9.3, Example 10.2, Example 11.1, Example 12.1, Example 12.2, Example 13.5, Example 14.1, Example 16.1, Example 17.1, and Example 17.2 are from the Truckco Proposal, Copyright 2001 by Nancy Kapp, Beth Bailey, Peter You, Shannon Mausteller, and Bridget Geist. Used with permission.

INDEX

C

Q

R

S

T

U

V

W